Feathers, Horns and Guardians

A Study of Social Transition in an African Community

SHIN-ICHIRO ISHIDA

Department of Social Anthropology,
Tokyo Metropolitan University

Feathers, Horns and Guardians

A Study of Social Transition in an African Community

SHIN-ICHIRO ISHIDA

*Department of Social Anthropology,
Tokyo Metropolitan University*

Kyoto University Press

TRANS PACIFIC PRESS

Published in 2024 jointly by:

Kyoto University Press
69 Yoshida Konoe-cho
Sakyo-ku, Kyoto 606-8315, Japan
Telephone: +81-75-761-6182
Fax: +81-75-761-6190
Email: sales@kyoto-up.or.jp
Web: http://www.kyoto-up.or.jp

Trans Pacific Press Co., Ltd.
PO Box 8547
#19682
Boston, MA, 02114, United States
Telephone: +1-6178610545
Email: info@transpacificpress.com
Web: http://www.transpacificpress.com

© Shin-ichiro Ishida 2024
Copyedited by Dr Karl E Smith, Melbourne, Australia
Layout designed and set by Ryo Kuroda, Tsukuba-city, Ibaraki, Japan
Cover designed by Klassic Designs

Distributors

USA and Canada
Independent Publishers Group (IPG)
814 N. Franklin Street
Chicago, IL 60610, USA
Telephone inquiries: +1-312-337-0747
Order placement: 800-888-4741 (domestic only)
Fax: +1-312-337-5985
Email: frontdesk@ipgbook.com
Web: http://www.ipgbook.com

Europe, Oceania, Middle East and Africa
EUROSPAN
Gray's Inn House,
127 Clerkenwell Road
London, EC1R 5DB
United Kingdom
Telephone: +44-(0)20-7240-0856
Email: info@eurospan.co.uk
Web: https://www.eurospangroup.com/

Japan
For purchase orders in Japan, please contact any distributor in Japan.

China
China Publishers Services Ltd.
718, 7/F., Fortune Commercial Building,
362 Sha Tsui Road, Tsuen Wan, N.T.
Hong Kong
Telephone: +852-2491-1436
Email: edwin@cps-hk.com

Southeast Asia
Alkem Company Pte Ltd.
1, Sunview Road #01-27, Eco-Tech@Sunview
Singapore 627615
Telephone: +65 6265 6666
Email: enquiry@alkem.com.sg

Library of Congress Control Number: 2023924172

All rights reserved. No reproduction of any part of this book may take place without the written permission of Kyoto University Press or Trans Pacific Press.
ISBN 978-1-920850-31-9 (hardback)
ISBN 978-1-920850-32-6 (paperback)
ISBN 978-1-920850-33-3 (eBook)

Up at Meru I saw a young Native girl with a bracelet on, a leather strap two inches wide, and embroidered all over with very small turquoise-coloured beads which varied a little in colour and played in green, light blue, and ultramarine. It was an extraordinarily live thing; it seemed to draw breath on her arm, so that I wanted it for myself, and made Farah buy it from her. No sooner had it come upon my own arm than it gave up the ghost. It was nothing now, a small, cheap, purchased article of finery. (Dinesen 1938, 257)

Kanyîrî kainachua nî mweene. [The long tail-feathers of the *kanyîrî* can only dance with its owner, the bird itself.] (A Kîmîîrû proverb)

Njûri îtî mweene. [The Njûrincheke council of elders should not be privatised.] (A Kîmîîrû proverb)

Contents

List of Figures viii

List of Tables viii

List of Photos ix

Introduction 1

Acknowledgements 11

Chapter 1 A farming community: Circuit cultivation in transition 13

Chapter 2 The field is theirs: *Kûrûmithua ndewa*, age-class formation and the persistence of local memory 35

Chapter 3 Man who never dies: Clan revival for new generations 55

Chapter 4 The Athimba: Fifteen years of clan making in a local context 93

Chapter 5 Clanship and *îchiaro*: The individual, the depersonalised and the indeterminate 143

Chapter 6 Feathers and guardians: The perpetuation of shared personhood 169

Chapter 7 Transcending inner conflicts: Election day for the Athimba clan 199

Postscript 209

Appendix 1 Homicide compensation in Kenya 213

Appendix 2 A witchcraft accusation in Mûringene in September 2005 215

References 223

index 229

List of Figures

1.1 Map of the greater Meru region 16
1.2 Transect of agro-ecological zone, Îgembe Southeast 19
3.1 Home communities of the invited *îchiaro* men 84
4.1 Sketch map of Mûringene village, 2012 96
5.1 Distribution of compensation items among M'Ikîrîma's sons 147
6.1 Genealogy of Nkoroi's daughters and *ntaau* 188

List of Tables

1.1 Population, 1979–2009 18
1.2 Rainfall in Kîegoi, 2000–2001 18
1.3 Analysis of 57 Ridgetop farmers' land holdings, Îgembe Southeast 2003 20
1.4 Agricultural calendar in Îgembe Southeast 22
1.5 Major grain legumes cultivated in Îgembe Southeast 23
1.6 Classification of popular dry beans in Îgembe Southeast 23
2.1 Nine offenders punished during *kûrûmithua ndewa*, 1989 42
2.2 Member-recruitment years of age-classes; schematic and historical 45
2.3 Circumcision years for subordinate age-class sets 45
2.4 Chronology of events in Athîrû Gaiti 52
3.1 *Îchiaro* men invited to Mwithûne village on 11 August 2016 58
3.2 Alleged witchcraft cases in Mwithûne village 60
3.3 *Îchiaro* men invited to Anjarû on 28 May 2016 82
4.1 Athimba households in Mûringene village and its neighbourhood, 2012 97

4.2	Chronology of homicide compensation, August 2001 to August 2002 ... 100
4.3	Elders appointed as *mûkirîra* and *mûtûngûri* for homicide compensation 131
4.4	Chronology of homicide compensation, March–April 2015 131
5.1	Distribution of compensation items 146
5.2	The six *îchiaro* men summoned for group cursing 155
5.3	Timeline of the group cursing 156
6.1	Nkoroi's children 183
6.2	Kainchua's children 185
7.1	Attendance record of three agnates and *mwîchiaro* 206

List of Photos

1.1	The White Hill, seen from the upper Athîrû Gaiti, July 2006 15
1.2	A *kîoera* for zero-grazed goats 25
1.3	The Iombe crater, 2002 26
2.1	Kînoti exposed to the public in the Athîrû Gaiti open field 36
2.2	Tail skins wrapped around an antelope horn 38
2.3	The offender with a bunch of unripe bananas 39
3.1	*Îchiaro* men inspect the list of complaints 62
3.2	The prayer to bring back missing people 65
3.3	Community members throw cursing plants on the fire 67
3.4	Sacrificed sheep exposed in the dead fire 68
3.5	Community members interrogated by the *îchiaro* men 69
3.6	Community members queue to swear before the *îchiaro* men 69
3.7	Collective cursing in the *kwiita rwîî* style 74

3.8   The horn blown to summon clan members 78
3.9   A man swearing before the *îchiaro* men in Anjarû 81
3.10 The Akachiû clan meeting on 30 August 2016 87
3.11 The author gives a speech at the Akachiû clan meeting 87
4.1   Athimba clan meeting, 18 December 2001 104
4.2   Invocation to remove evil intentions, 18 December 2001 105
4.3   Fundraising party, 18 November 2001 111
4.4   Athimba clan meeting, November 2001 113
4.5   Clan house surrounded by a leather strip 116
4.6   An elder sprays honey from his mouth across the walls
      of the clan house 116
4.7   Clan house at Karatho's homestead (10 August 2015) 129
5.1   The *îchiaro* men collect cursing plants 157
5.2   'Cutting the neck' of a *mwîchiaro* 158
5.3   Participants being interrogated by *îchiaro* 159
5.4   *Îchiaro* men placing the curse while standing on one leg 161
5.5   An *îchiaro* man turns his back to the large bundle on the ground 161
5.6   Clapping of hands to conclude the group cursing 164
6.1   The *kanyîrî* 170
6.2   Athimba clan meeting, 3 September 2015 182
6.3   Mûtûma giving a speech 190
6.4   Nkoroi's namesakes and daughters wearing *leso* 191
6.5   People holding mattresses with Benditah and Mûkiri 191

Introduction

During two decades of fieldwork in the Central Highlands of Kenya – from 2001 to 2019 – I studied the lives of the Îgembe people in the community of Athîrû Gaiti. The results of my research are presented in the following pages, under three broad categories.

First, this book draws an ethnographic portrait of the Îgembe's social and cultural lives; lives marked by complexity and unpredictability. In the process of composing this ethnography, I have aimed to allow the fruits of my research to speak for themselves rather than overlaying them with anthropological theories.

Second, I examine generational changes among the Îgembe – focusing on the 2010s when, as some Îgembe seniors relinquished their leadership (or passed away), the younger generation accommodated age-old traditions while negotiating ever-changing socio-economic conditions.

Third, I consider the Îgembe's propensity to retrieve and materialise 'communal intentions' (a term discussed at the end of this introduction), in order to generate 'collective immortality' (Lienhardt 1961, 319) – and how, in so doing, the community transcends both the lives and deaths of individual members and the contradictions of lived experience.

Among the many revelations of my fieldwork, I have learned that the Îgembe appreciate the merits of *waiting* for any material conflicts of interest to subside before addressing them – or of waiting for a time in the future when they may be better resolved[1] (Chapter 5). In other words, although the community may appear to be inactive at a given moment, its people are probably 'actually *not wasting* time, but either waiting for time or in the process of "producing" time' (Mbiti 1969, 19). Turner (1957) examined the *schism* of groups and the *continuity* of society in the village life of the Ndembu people of Zambia. In contrast, this study discusses the *hiatus* in communal intentions among the Îgembe that may

---

1 Thomas (1995, 233) notes, 'Waiting responsibly for rewards brought by the passage of time thus represented an important theme in the life course' of the Amîîrû.

precede their revitalisation. Such a collective – perhaps subconscious – ethos underpins and illuminates many of the social and cultural processes I describe.

During my time in Athîrû Gaiti, I observed a cycle of abandonment and renaissance of certain indigenous institutions; specifically, the social institutions of clan and age-class. At the root of the abandonment – similar to Ortega's (1932, 74) description of 'a renunciation of the common life based on culture' – was widespread indifference. This, in turn, arose from the inertia of clanship in Athîrû Gaiti during the first decade of the 21st century (see Chapter 1). The renaissance was subsequently sparked by a new generation of leaders in the mid-2010s, with new initiatives and commitments for clan revival (Chapter 3) – proving that there had been no irreversible deterioration of traditional interests, ethics or norms. Indeed, the cycle of abandonment and renaissance had been held in the collective consciousness all along, as something that would play out in time.

In the course of generational changes of age-class and power, actors in the indigenous institutions – drawing on knowledge and experience from the past (Chapter 2) or from neighbouring villages (Chapters 3 and 4) – were able to *choose* whether to replicate the decisions and actions of their predecessors or not. The Athimba – an agnatic clan of Athîrû Gaiti – continued to meet throughout the 2000s and early 2010s while other clans did not (see Chapters 4, 5 and 7), maintaining their social institutions in a consistent but not ordained manner.

After briefly summarising the work, my concluding chapter comprises a description of a meeting of the Athimba clan, held in Athîrû Gaiti in 2014. I have highlighted this case for the following reasons. First, it is a clear and succinct example of generational change – a key component of my research. Second, it draws together many of the thematic and narrative strands described elsewhere in the book. Finally, the case demonstrates how the Athimba have transcended the inner conflicts of the past decade to successfully maintain their unity.

*

The 'feathers', 'horns' and 'guardians' of this volume's title grew both iconic and symbolic to me over the course of my research, in time coming to guide my ethnographic documentation.

The feathers – of a bird – refer to the proverb of the book's epigraph (see also Chapter 6). They represent everything precious to the Îgembe – including their rich natural environment, their way of life, their indigenous knowledge systems, their means to prosperity, and the reproduction of invaluable crops, livestock and, above all, human beings.

Horns symbolise the social institutions of age-class and clan, which retain antelope horns for ceremonial purposes (Chapters 2 and 3).

The guardians are the Îgembe themselves, who employ feathers and horns – literally and figuratively – to perpetuate their way of life, while adapting to socio-economic change (Chapters 4, 5 and 6).

Contexts of communal intention

This section presents contextual information regarding the Îgembe's social organisation, together with definitions of key terms used throughout this work. It does not reflect the complexities and contradictions that became apparent during my research, which are depicted in this book. It is rather a generalised account, intended not only to guide the reader but to reflect the Îgembe's indigenous essentialism – as discussed at the end of this introduction.

The Îgembe form one of the nine subgroups of the Amîîrû[2] – inhabiting the eastern area of the Kenyan Central Highlands' Nyambene hill region. The Tigania inhabit the western area. Both subgroups (and others, to some extent) share social practices, with some variation. The Tigania, for example, 'keep more cattle' (Peatrik 2019, 25), while the Îgembe cultivate more *mîraa* (*Catha edulis*, also known as *khat*).[3]

---

[2] Fadiman (1993, 4) writes, 'Before the colonial conquest in 1906 the name 'Meru' was used by only five of the present nine subgroups that now make up the tribe: the Igoji, Miutini, Imenti, Tigania, and Igembe.' See also Lamont (2005, 2).

[3] For the development of *mîraa* industry, see Chapter 1, Goldsmith (1995) and Carrier (2007).

All the Îgembe I encountered maintain that their people inhabit a single socio-cultural universe which, in some cases, extends to the Amîîrû as a whole. This universe is maintained by structured age-organisation, a united council of elders and an unsegmented clan system – which together inhibit inclinations towards localism and individualism.[4]

A clan (*mwîrîa*), for the Îgembe, is a strictly exogamous unit – the members of which are never permitted to intermarry. However, as Peatrik (2019, 120) notes, '*Mwîrîa* is not so much a clan as a clan category'. It is difficult to identify agnatic 'kins' which share the same clan affiliation because consanguineous ties do not necessarily constitute a local neighbourhood community. 'Branches' of each clan are widely dispersed, via sequences of minor migration, driven by natural demographic growth. These branches retain their clan names, as opposed to identifying as independent sub-clans or lineages. Members of the Athimba clan, for example, are found everywhere in the Îgembe and Tigania communities. The genealogical relationship between branches does not necessarily work in their favour, and is thus not well remembered.

The term *îchiaro* denotes a conceptual, institutionalised system in which related clans share exogamous rules and reciprocal obligations. It also sometimes denotes *îchiaro* counterparts in the plural; while *mwîchiaro* refers to a 'person of *îchiaro*' in the singular. People related by *îchiaro* are required to extend mutual loyalty and generosity, and are not permitted to marry. Any behaviour that violates these norms is thought to engender misfortune – the fear of which is often invoked to settle disputes. If an individual is insincere in either word or deed before their fellow *mwîchiaro*, the power of *îchiaro* will bring misfortune upon both them and their family.

---

4 During my fieldwork, however, I observed varying, sometimes contradictory, understandings of Kîmîîrû customs – concerning, for example, bride price claims at the official law courts (Ishida 2010) and homicide compensation payments in one village community (Chapter 4).

Introduction 5

The *îchiaro* relationship is egalitarian in two senses.[5] First, people related by *îchiaro* hold each other in mutual fear and respect. Second, the power of *îchiaro* is universally and equally distributed among the people. For example, anyone born into the Athimba clan is automatically *mwîchiaro* to the Antûambûi and Andûûne clans. From the local perspective, such biological determinism is the predominant means of identifying and understanding human relationships (see Chapter 5).

Age is central to the social organisation of the Îgembe. A group of men circumcised within a given period of around 15 years constitutes an age-class (*nthukî*) – with each age-class bearing a name mutual to the Îgembe and Tigania. Current age-classes include Mîchûbû (almost extinct), Ratanya, Lubetaa, Mîrîti, Bwantai, Gîchûnge and Kîramunya. Theoretically, each age-class is divided into three subordinate sets – Nding'ûri, Kobia and Kabeeria.

Age-classes function as 'a primary means of maintaining…social identity' (Lamont 2005, 105). Men often imagine their political and generational rivalries are based on their age-classes (see also Peatrik 2005), which 'materialise' – or are invoked – in varying social contexts (Lamont 2005, Epilogue).

The concept of women's age categories – or rather *daughters'* or *wives'* age categories, given that they are linked to their fathers' or husbands' age-classes (Peatrik 2019, 81) – remains valid in contemporary Îgembe society. However, the proper names for these categories exist only in the memories of community elders (see Chapter 2).

The Amîîrû are often represented by Njûrincheke – a united council of elders who are expert in Kîmîîrû traditions.[6] Such councils are 'well established in Igembe and Tigania, less so in Imenti, and almost nonexistent in the other Mount Kenya divisions' (Peatrik 2019, 372–373).

---

5 Peatrik (2019, 183) recognises the egalitarian nature of the Îgembe in their setting of bride prices, noting that they maintain 'it should remain low to allow everyone to marry'.

6 Kîmîîrû refers to everything indigenous to the Amîîrû, including their language, way of life and customs.

Among the Îgembe, applicants for full council membership must undergo a secret initiation ritual, and it is believed that elders keep the core parts of their knowledge hidden. The most successful elders hold persuasive oratory skills and are often invited to functions beyond their villages to speak on indigenous law.

When hearing disputes, elders do not necessarily make judgements, but rather encourage the parties involved to wait until one or the other of them recognises their responsibility for the issue at hand. This approach may appear lackadaisical, and to relate to the generalised 'African' concept of time, on which several writers have commented: '[They are] on friendly terms with time, and the plan of beguiling or killing it does not come into their heads' (Dinesen 1938, 244; see also Kapuściński 2002, 17; and Stasik, Hänsch, and Mains 2020 for an integrative review of existing literature on the temporality of waiting). As noted above, for the Îgembe waiting is not *killing* or *wasting* time but rather *producing* it. Further, although elders do sometimes resort to an adversarial approach, they may sidestep any clear judgement at all – instead settling cases with the use of conditional curses or the power of *îchiaro* (Chapters 3, 4, 5 and Appendix 2), either as a step towards a solution or a kind of bluff[7] (Krueger 2016, 429–431).

*

The above outlines the contexts of the Îgembe's 'indigenous essentialism' (Hviding 1993) and is itself a generalised, ahistorical account of the terminology to be found – and the socio-cultural phenomena referred to – in this study. The case studies I present in this book, however, reveal the contradictions of lived experience and the 'historicity' of social imagination (Lamont 2005) in Athîrû Gaiti.

---

7   While both colonial administrators and anthropologists once noted African litigiousness in various contexts, the colonial report of 1919–1920 for the then Meru District stated, 'The "kiamas" in my opinion are useless and are not doing any work ... their decisions are generally arrived at by the easy way of ordering one party "Kuringa Nthenge" [trial by ordeal on a goat]' (cited in Peatrik 2019, 353).

My first assumption was that the Îgembe's essentialism was a form of strategic essentialism in Spivak's sense. However, it does not necessarily work for any purpose of 'a scrupulously visible political interest' (Spivak 1988, 13) but rather works 'as a means of dealing with the outside world by attempting to present a uniform picture of one's own world, or as a means of addressing fundamental variabilities, or indeed perceived inconsistencies' (Hviding 1993, 814). As Sylvain (2014, 253) notes, referring to Hale (2006, 114), 'not all forms of indigenous essentialism are strategic. Many essentialist expressions of identity are sincere attempts to gain "recognition" in a morally robust sense'. Dismissing their narratives from an anti-essentialist perspective is to impose an outsider's perspective (Ishida 2023).

After twenty years of research among the Îgembe, I have reached the understanding that my interviewees' generalised statements about, and descriptions of, their culture and society do not necessarily reflect social facts – but rather a truth 'arrived at and stated by a *communal* intention' (Lienhardt 1961, 247).[8] A similar phenomenon was observed by Godfrey Lienhardt in his classic ethnography of the Dinka people of Southern Sudan:

> This 'truth' is something more than the opposite of lying, though that is part of it. The truth ideally spoken by masters of the fishing-spear, and guaranteed by their ancestors, is the truth which is the opposite of error; and in Dinka thought it is this kind of truth which is arrived at and stated by a *communal* intention. (Lienhardt 1961, 247)

---

8 As an ethnographic study on the Îgembe's communal intention, this book uses Lienhardt's terminology as well as Paul Sillitoe's as discussed below. The concept of communal intention here may relate to the philosophical discussions on collective intention by John Searle (1990) and Raimo Tuomela (2013). In anthropology, Duranti (2015) is a leading work on intention and intersubjectivity. Exploring the philosophical concepts of intention and collective intention is beyond the scope of this book (see Gallagher 2017 for a critical review of Duranti 2015).

Communal intentions among the Îgembe accord with the Kîmîîrû concept of personhood, which is broad, fluid and not to be equated with individual identity or agency. During my fieldwork, I have observed community members concealing their individuality, or depersonalising themselves, as they represent their clan, village or age cohort (or any other social entity) at cursing and blessing ceremonies. Masks and skins (Peatrik 2019, 208) are sometimes used to hide the identities of dancers. Curse words are uttered by *îchiaro* men in such a way that onlookers cannot tell who they are (see Case 5.10, Chapter 5). Each of these 'actors' should be perceived not as a personalised individual, with a name and a face, but rather imagined as a 'social person' representing the communal intention.[9]

Paul Sillitoe (2016, 2), while discussing the possibility of engaged anthropology, questions 'the imposition of the concept of "society" and associated social science "theory"' by Western or outsider anthropologists. According to Sillitoe (2016, 3–4), the concept 'society' represents a 'term of second intention' in logic, 'for which we have no empirical sense derived evidence, unlike a "term of first intention" such as "human individual", which refers to someone/thing that we can see, touch, hear, smell etc.' He then questions, 'What other ways are there to conceive alternative "terms of second intention" for collective social behaviour?' (Sillitoe 2016, 5). The Îgembe have cultured their indigenous 'terms of second intention for collective social behaviour' (Sillitoe 2016, 5) or, in other words, their own terms of communal intention.

My case study of Kîmîîrû personal names (see Chapter 6) sheds further light on the Îgembe's propensity for shared identity. In the Kîmîîrû naming system, every community member has a namesake (*ntaau*), with whom he or she shares a reciprocal relationship and sometimes even personality. Children's *ntaau* are selected alternately (by order of

---

9   Beidelman (1993) notes, 'What is paradoxical about masks is that, like words, they may both reveal and conceal identities.' I have borrowed the term 'social person' from Beidelman (1986) – having been inspired by Hashimoto's (2018) discussion of Nuer prophets and prophecies.

Introduction 9

birth) from their paternal and maternal relatives – so forming a web of connections within and beyond the clan. Thus, while agnatic membership and seniority may claim more attention in politico-economic contexts (see Chapters 3 and 4), personal names may indicate more about matrimonial/affinal, inter-generational and inter-familial bonds – as well as personal friendships.

To conclude, *ntaau* names are not the exclusive property of their holders. Rather, they are shared with members of both younger and older generations – meaning a name can outlive its owner. Hence, community members are not necessarily remembered as individuals within a genealogy (see also Peatrik 2005, 295), but rather as components of a wider entity. Human individuals, however, do not fully dissipate within the society or within the terms of communal intention. The ethnography of the Kîmîîrû-speaking people, therefore, must depict the indigenous methodology of materialising both communal intentions and irreplaceable individuals.

A note on pseudonyms

The natural outcome of studying a relatively small community over a relatively short timeframe is that the same individuals repeatedly wander in and out of the narrative – in various locations and contexts (similarly to Victor Turner's writings on a Ndembu village in the 1950s).

In certain sections of this book, I have used pseudonyms for both individuals and villages to protect personal identities. Village pseudonyms include Mwithûne (Chapter 3) and Mûringene (Chapters 4, 5, 6, and 7). In Chapter 3, I have used both James' and Mwasimba's real names, with their informed consent. Chapter 6 also uses real names, with the interviewees' informed consent. Throughout this work, real names are also used for towns or markets such as Maûa, local administrative sections such as Îgembe Southeast Division and Athîrû Gaiti Location, and clans such as the Athimba.

Acknowledgements

This work was supported by JSPS Grant-in-Aid for Scientific Research (KAKENHI). Above all, I would like to thank the people of Athîrû Gaiti – my source community – for kindly sharing their time, experience and knowledge. These include the late Silvester Ntorûrû, Miriam Kathure, Gerald Mûng'ania, Jeremiah Karûtî, as well as those to whom I refer only by pseudonyms. Special thanks to Paul Kîrîmi Mûriûki, who assisted with my initial transcription and translation work, and to my editor, Matthew Singh Toor, for his thoughtful and scrupulous editing, suggestions and reworking. Thanks also to Makio Matsuzono, my advisor and mentor of more than twenty years, as well as Njũgũna Gĩchere, Stephen Mûgambi Mwithimbû and my other colleagues in research collaboration based at the National Museums of Kenya – all of whom, since 2005, have contributed invaluable suggestions and support. I am grateful to the National Museums of Kenya, the National Commission for Science, Technology and Innovation, Tokyo Metropolitan University, and the JSPS Research Station, Nairobi, for facilitating my research in Kenya. I am also indebted to those colleagues and pioneers in the study of Kîmîîrû-speaking communities who have shared their expertise via both publications and personal communication – namely James Krueger, Mark Lamont, and Anne-Marie Peatrik. For their multifarious advice and assistance, I thank Jun Baba, Stephen Christopher, Atsunori Ito, Werner Menski, Masaru Miyamoto, Satoshi Tanahashi, Takeshi Tsunoda as well as current and former colleagues from the Department of Social Anthropology, Tokyo Metropolitan University. I am also grateful to Hirokazu Ohashi, Yuko Uematsu, and Karl Smith, who have been helpful throughout the editing and publishing of this book at Trans Pacific Press and Kyoto University Press.

Parts of the Introduction were published in 2023 as 'Anthropology, indigenous methodology, and the restatement of African laws,' *Legal Pluralism and Critical Social Analysis* 55(3). Parts of Chapter 1 were previously published in 2008 as 'Contemporary agriculture in Nyambene district' in *The Indigenous Knowledge of the Ameru of Kenya*, edited by Njûgûna Gîchere and Shin-ichiro Ishida, Meru: Meru Museum. Chapter 2 appeared in 2008 as part of 'The indigenous law of the Îgembe of Kenya' in *Legal Culture in South-East Asia and East Africa*, edited by Masaru Miyamoto and Judeth John Baptist (Kota Kinabalu: Sabah Museum). Chapter 3 appeared in 2018 as 'For a man who never dies and who eats his own,' *Journal of Social Sciences and Humanities* (*Jimbun Gakuho*) 514–2. Chapter 4 appeared in 2014 as 'Egalitarian conflict management among the Îgembe of Kenya,' in *Conflict Resolution and Coexistence: Realizing African Potentials* (*African Study Monographs*, Supplementary Issue 50), edited by Itaru Ohta, Shuichi Oyama, Toru Sagawa, and Shinichiro Ichino. Chapter 5 appeared in 2017 as 'Homicide compensation in an Îgembe community in Kenya, 2001–2015,' *African Study Monographs* 38(4). Chapter 6 appreared in 2020 as 'Name-sharing among the Igembe,' in *Family Dynamics and Memories in Kenyan Villages*. edited by Njũgũna Gĩchere, S. A. Mûgambi Mwithimbû, and Shin-ichiro Ishida (Nairobi: National Museums of Kenya). I have benefitted greatly from comments made by editors and anonymous reviewers of my previous works.

Chapter 1
A farming community: Circuit cultivation in transition

The White Hill (*Kîrîma-kîerû*) is one of the most widely known historical landmarks of the Îgembe district (see Photo 1.1 and Figure 1.1); a beacon beyond which a great plain of wilderness extends to the southeast. This small, solitary volcanic peak is visible from miles around, despite being dwarfed by the southwestern slope of the greater Nyambene hills. The hill is not white in any literal sense. Rather, it is pale green during the rainy season and yellow-brown during the dry season, and covered with long grass – traditionally used by locals to thatch their huts and houses. During the 19th and early 20th centuries, besides providing bearings to the local Îgembe people, the hill probably orientated travelling pastoralists, ivory traders and white explorers (see Steinhart 1989; 2006, 34–36, 195 for colonial hunting and 'poaching' in Nyambene).

The Îgembe – a subgroup of the Kîmîîrû speakers of the Kenyan central highlands – have traditionally inhabited and farmed the agriculturally rich and perpetually verdant dissected stream valleys of the Nyambene hills. During my research, I came to think of the southwestern slope as the Black Hill; in Kîmîîrû aesthetic and dualistic terminology, something black is considered deep-rooted and authentic, and is therefore highly prized, while something white is considered shallow, exotic and, in some contexts, less auspicious.[1]

The fertile volcanic soils, mild climate and abundant rainfall (which follows a regular seasonal cycle) render the Îgembe's homeland particu-

---

1   According to local classification, for example, the best quality *mîraa* (known outside of Kenya as *khat*) is called *mîraa-î-mîîrû* (black *mîraa*) – in contrast to *mîraa-î-mîerû* (white *mîraa*). Bernardi (1959, 92) notes that 'the idea of the sacred character of black' was shared only by the Amîîrû and the Masai. Further, Mahner (1975, 403) writes that the black uniforms given by the first British colonial administrator to local

larly rich for agriculture. Indeed, by comparison with neighbouring ethnic communities, such as the Thaichû and Kamba, the Îgembe were little affected by the widespread famines that occurred in the 20th century – from 1918 to 1919, and from 1983 to 1984 (Goldsmith 1995, 78 & 114) – during which refugees actually fled to the Nyambene hills for survival (Ambler 1988; Fadiman 1993, 185). The Îgembe themselves have historically benefited from symbiotic interactions arising from migration,[2] which cross ecological zones and ethno-linguistic families (Bernard 1979, 267; Goldsmith 1995, 42).

The geographer Frank Bernard observed that, from the 1950s onwards, both government-initiated land tenure reform and the introduction of new varieties of food and cash crops brought about radical change in Kîmîîrû speaking communities – together with the expansion of communication networks. Prior to this reform, the Amîîrû would 'exploit several environments, spreading out risks inherent in this highly variable setting over three or four ecological zones' (Bernard 1972, 141). This exploitation of scattered agricultural holdings required farmers to walk from location to location in their work – a practice I term 'circuit cultivation'. With the new system of land tenure, writes Bernard, 'no longer is it possible for each farmer to spread his risk over the entire mountain slope'. Thus, traditional social organisation and a belief system rooted in agricultural activities were gradually undermined and replaced by 'a new whole' (Bernard 1972, 143).

Bernard's generalisation about the enormous impact of government land reform on the traditional land holding system – subsequent to which commercial crops were planted to the exclusion of subsistence crops (see also Dolan 2001) – explains the agricultural development

---

leaders as a sign of distinction were 'not a traditional feature of Meru or Tigania life but a recent development'; assuming that 'the colour black should be reserved for the *Mugwe* only' (See also Needham 1960, 23). Since 2001, I have observed that the Mugwe – once the paramount leader/dignitary in Kîmîîrû speaking communities – no longer exists.

2   Also see Parsons (2012) for another rather colonial context of the tribal geography of Kenya and the Amîîrû's absorption of Agîkûyû and other outsiders.

A farming community

Photo 1.1 The White Hill, seen from the upper Athîrû Gaiti, July 2006
(All photos by Shin-ichiro Ishida, unless otherwise noted)

of some high-potential areas of land. It does not, however, account for developments in the Îgembe Southeast Division and some other areas (Figure 1.1) – simply because reforms there were revised in the late 1960s, as this chapter expounds. Agricultural development in localised Îgembe communities cannot thus be characterised merely as a linear change from the old to the new. Carrier (2005, 216) notes, 'Regarding *miraa*, its crucial economic importance for the people of the Nyambenes strengthens the value attached to it culturally, and vice versa.' Îgembe farmers simultaneously exploit indigenous resources to the maximum *and* participate in the interregional market economy.

Given the correction of Bernard's thesis, this chapter further progresses the academic record by detailing how the people of the Îgembe Southeast also experienced socio-economic changes in the late 1980s and mid-2010s, while maintaining circuit cultivation. In 1989, land

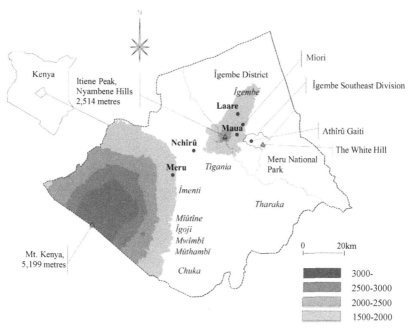

Figure 1.1 Map of the greater Meru region

adjudication commenced in the Îgembe Southeast and farmers – dependent on cash income – began to cultivate *mîraa* (a stimulant, traditionally chewed by local people) instead of coffee. In the mid-2010s, those farmers began to receive official title deeds to their land but, concurrently, the Netherlands and the UK banned *mîraa* imports from Kenya, destroying their European market. During my research, I observed that these abrupt turns in the local economy coincided with a generational shift in traditional age-class organisation. This phenomenon is the focus of Chapter 2. Those turns also affected clan identity in local communities, as discussed in Chapters 3 and 4.

Circuit cultivation

Athîrû Gaiti Location is one of three administrative sections within the Îgembe Southeast Division of Meru County; with each section administered by a government-appointed chief. Its headquarters have been developed as a trade depot and community hub, which houses public and private schools, churches of several denominations, shops, restaurants, medical clinics and barbershops. They are also the meeting point for the Njûrincheke council of elders.

Historically, Athîrû Gaiti referred to an area loosely corresponding with the contemporary upper half of Îgembe Southeast Division (covering the present Athîrû Gaiti and Kîrîmampio Locations), which is the definition followed in this book. Athîrû Gaiti was a 'territorial section' (Peatrik 2019, 121–122), where inhabitants of various villages and members of different clans shared communal events such as mass circumcision. The lower part of the division was inhabited by the Thaichû community, with whom the Îgembe proper have developed a symbiotic relationship over many decades.

The Îgembe Southeast covers a wide range of altitudes, sloping down from the northwest. Its hilly highlands, between 1,000 and 1,500 metres above sea level, are densely populated, while the sparsely populated lower areas – known as *rwaanda* – are less than 1,000 metres above sea level. Small-scale farmers on the ridgetop rely heavily on the lower slope and plain for food; arable resources adjacent to their own homes are limited due to demographic pressure and intensive *mîraa* cultivation. These farmers walk on an almost weekly basis between one and seven kilometres from their homesteads to the lower slope and plain, to plant, weed and harvest maize and grain legumes. Electricity has been supplied since 2010, and parts of the area have been covered by mobile phone networks since 2003. The Îgembe Southeast also has several enduring water sources, which provide a secure everyday supply.

The whole Nyambene region has two annual rainy seasons, although annual rainfall varies by ecological zone (see Table 1.2 for monthly figures, as recorded at Kîegoi, near Maûa). The first rainy season (*ûthima*) runs from March to May, and the second (*uruûra*) begins in mid-October, continuing until December. In the local communities of the Îgembe Southeast, *ûthima* is said to be shorter than *uruûra*, although

Table 1.1 Population, 1979–2009

Year	Îgembe (total)	Persons/sq. km	Îgembe S. East	Persons/sq. km
1979	171,307	88.4	7,367	117.5
1989	256,461	132.3	14,375	229.3
1999	364,286	187.9	18,700	298.2
2009	482,466	248.9	26,731	426.3

Notes: Calculations of population density are mine, based on government statistics (Kenya 1981, 76; 1997, 13; 2001a, 84–88; 2010, 74–75). The area of Îgembe district, excluding Meru National Park, is 1,938.7 km²; that of Îgembe Southeast Division is 62.7 km². In 1979, Îgembe Southeast Division was officially known as Thaichû Sublocation.

Table 1.2 Rainfall in Kîegoi, 2000–2001 (mm)

Year	Jan	Feb	Mar	Apr	May	Jun	Jul	Aug	Sep	Oct	Nov	Dec
2002	63.2	21.8	376.9	306.1	211.4	19.4	20.0	39.1	24.5	49.5	410.3	302.1
2001	82.7	12.5	233.3	510.9	77.6	36.4	22.8	6.3	7.4	110.2	534.5	90.1
2000	16	0	23.5	149.2	77.7	13.7	41.3	26.9	35.9	57.4	493.5	99.2

(DALEO 2001, 2002, 2003)

some publications describe the latter as shorter (Bernard 1972, 22–23; Giorgis 1964, 179). It seems the total rainfall of the first rainy season is heavier, but not sufficiently reliable to produce necessary crop yields.[3]

Figure 1.2 provides a schematic transect of agro-ecological zones in the Îgembe Southeast. My definitions of 'ridgetop,'[4] 'lower slope' and 'plain' coincide, respectively, with the common agro-ecological zone classifications[5] of Upper Medium 3 (marginal coffee zone), Lower Me-

---

3   The District Agriculture and Livestock Extension Office reported in 2001: 'The first season was unfavourable for crop production… Since the onset, the rain remained of low intensity and was poorly distributed… The second season was favourable for crop production in most areas' (DALEO 2001). The same office reported in 2003: 'During the first season, the early onset caught farmers unaware. Harvesting of annuals of the previous season and land preparation were incomplete… Yields of the season were equally negatively affected since the rain intensity increased beyond normal within a very short span, causing considerable leaching and erosion… The second season (October/November) was fair for production of most crops. The only crops that might be somewhat negatively affected might be beans due to extended rains in December' (DALEO 2003).

4   See Fadiman (1993, 70) for the terminology of 'ridgetop'.

5   While the government considers the lower slope and plain to be potential areas for cotton cultivation (LM 3 and 4 zones), local people are mostly yet to exploit this.

A farming community

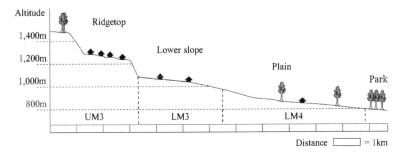

Figure 1.2 Transect of agro-ecological zone, Îgembe Southeast

dium 3 (cotton zone) and Lower Medium 4 (marginal cotton zone). Most of the area is covered with fertile loam soil and hence has great potential for crop cultivation.

The Îgembe people practise the intercropping of various plants and trees, which Goldsmith (1995, 130) recognises as the principle and beneficial 'distinctive feature of the Nyambene farming system' (1995, 131).[6] Legumes, maize and bananas are widely cultivated as staple food crops. Neither millet nor sorghum is currently common, although both constituted staple food crops before the introduction of maize.[7] Sweet potato, cassava, mango, papaya and avocado are cultivated as subsidiary crops in all areas, while banana, Napier grass, arrowroot, yam and kale are commonly found on the ridgetop. The steep slopes within the UM 3 zone are blanketed with tea shrubs.

Besides perennial crops, such as banana and yam, the cultivation of major food crops is subject to seasonal cycles.

In 2003, I interviewed fifty-seven ridgetop farmers about their land use.[8] Four were commercial farmers with large holdings of more than

---

6 Goldsmith (1995, 122) also mentions 'the progression of a plot from field crops to mixed holding to a mainly tree-dominated holding.'
7 Bernard (1972, 132) notes, 'Millet and sorghum would have been dominant staples in both highland and lowland agricultural systems, [and] today, throughout the most accessible parts of the highlands, maize has become a co-staple, usually with beans, almost completely replacing millet, sorghum, and traditional pulses.'
8 I originally interviewed sixty farmers, but a follow-up study found that I had made methodological errors with three of the samples. I have thus excluded these from my analysis.

Table 1.3 Analysis of 57 ridgetop farmers' land holdings, Îgembe Southeast 2003

	Total	Ridgetop	Lower slope	Plain
Total Acreage	240.0	84.0	48.5	107.5
Average (acres)	4.21	1.47	0.85	1.89
Percentage	100%	34.9%	20.2%	44.9%

ten acres; the rest were engaged in subsistence crop production. The then average size of land holdings owned by a single farming family was 4.21 acres, compared with the average of 3.22 acres belonging to small-scale or subsistence farmers.[9] The average farming family thus held plots of.1.47, 0.85, and 1.89 acres, on the ridgetop, lower slope and plain respectively (Table 1.3).

The designation of land use in the Îgembe Southeast has evolved throughout the history of circuit cultivation. According to oral accounts by elders of the Mîchûbû and Ratanya age-classes (see Chapter 2 for Îgembe age-organisation), most of the ridgetop inhabitants did not exploit the plain for permanent cultivation until the late 1970s,[10] although several ridgetop clans did hold claims in the vast forest territory, which is demarcated by natural boundaries. However, local interests in land resources have gradually transformed through a sequence of historical events: natural demographic growth on the ridgetop; rapid expansion of the *mîraa* industry since the 1980s; and land adjudication, which began in 1989.[11]

Some parts of the lower slope and plain have been inhabited and cultivated by the Thaichû people for decades. Until 1992, the present

---

9 Goldsmith (1995, 77) notes, 'The average land holding in Igembe Division is three acres. In the high zones, where average holdings are usually smaller, even a developed farm of less than an acre can support a family.'

10 Goldsmith (1995, 10) also notes, 'During the 1960s the upward movement of the population slowed as the last belt of agriculturally viable forest reserve – the tea zone – was cleared and settled.' Then, 'during the 1970s the flow reversed as people migrated down to establish farms in areas formerly used for grazing and temporary cultivation.'

11 An influx of Agikûyû immigrants from the early 1980s, and the Îgembe-Tharaka armed land conflict of the 1990s may be other contributing factors.

Îgembe Southeast Division was officially known as either the Athîrû Gaiti or Thaichû Sublocation. The Thaichû people's pronunciation of Kîmîîrû and its vocabulary differs slightly from that of the Îgembe proper. The two communities also have different agricultural spheres. A white hunter who travelled in the area during the 1890s wrote that, 'Laiju was one of the most deadly places in Africa for domestic animals' (Neumann 1898, 28) – because the Laiju (now known as Thaichû) people were unable to keep livestock on the plain due to the presence of tsetse flies.

Mîchûbû elders in the ridgetop village remember that their ancestors kept more livestock than the Thaichû, and that the ridgetop boasted an abundance of banana plants, while the Thaichû produced a great quantity of traditional pulses.

The two communities used to barter with one another.[12] Parties from the *gaiti* (lowland) would visit the ridgetop while singing a type of traditional song known as *kîbûcha*. Inhabitants of the ridgetop village remember that *kîbûcha* was often sung by millet cultivators from below, while guarding and harvesting crops. Although there is no single interpretation of the songs' meanings, they are said to have signified a challenge (not necessarily antagonistic) to privileged highlanders (*arûrû*; singular *mûrûrû*), who enjoyed abundant food resources without the need to engage in laborious millet production.

Since the discovery that the plain area also had high potential for the cultivation of introduced crops (maize and some varieties of beans), assumed contrasts between the ridgetop and plain communities have become less significant. Both highlanders and lowlanders regularly cultivate the plain to produce maize and grain legumes as staples. Consequently, such crops are no longer bartered between the two communities, nor is *kîbûcha* sung.

Table 1.4 shows a typical agricultural calendar for grain legumes and maize. Land preparation starts a month before the onset of the rainy

---

12 One of Goldsmith's (1995) key findings is that such a symbiotic exchange across different ecological zones has oriented and sustained the agricultural and social development of the Îgembe community.

Table 1.4 Agricultural calendar in Îgembe Southeast

	Jan	Feb	Mar	Apr	May	Jun	Jul	Aug	Sep	Oct	Nov	Dec
Rainy seasons					■	■				■	■	■
Ploughing			■	■					■	■		
Planting				■						■		
Weeding					■	■	■	■			■	
Harvest (grain legumes)	■						■					
Harvest (maize)		■	■									

season and weeding continues throughout it, with farmers at their busiest in October. Most small-scale farmers use a *jembe* (hoe) and *panga* (long-bladed slashing knife) for ploughing and planting. Animal labour is not commonly used.

A wide variety of grain legumes (*nthoroko*) are planted as co-staple crops in the Îgembe Southeast. These are grown mostly on a small scale, with intercropping.[13] The most common varieties are dry bean (*mûng'aû*), pigeon pea (*nchûgû*), hyacinth bean (*nchaabî*), green gram (*ndeengû*) and cowpea (*nthoroko chia nyoni*). These crops are locally named and classified according to their physical characteristics, habitation and modes of consumption. In everyday life, all dry beans are classified as *mûng'aû*, although some people divide them into five or more subcategories. Tables 1.5 and 1.6 outline a popular classification system that is widely shared in the Îgembe Southeast. They do not, however, provide a complete botanical survey.

Dry beans are the most common of the Îgembe Southeast's grain legumes. Pigeon pea and cowpea are planted as subsidiary crops in all agro-ecological zones, while hyacinth bean and green gram are mostly found on the plain (LM 4 zone). A typical legume crop takes around ninety days to mature. However, legume grains are consumed at various stages of development – as both immature and mature pods, and as fresh

---

13 Grain legumes play an important role in nitrogen fixation during soil fertilisation (Kokwaro 1979, 63) and are suitable for intercropping (Kenya 2002, 1).

Table 1.5 Major grain legumes cultivated in Îgembe Southeast

Common name	Scientific name	Kîmîîrû name	Distribution
Dry bean	*Phaseolus vulgaris*	Mûng'aû	UM3, LM3, LM4
Pigeon pea	*Cajanus cajun*	Nchûgû	LM4 (UM3, LM3)
Hyacinth bean	*Dolichos lablab*	Nchaabî	LM4
Green gram	*Vigna radiata*	Ndeengû	LM4
Cow pea	*Vigna uginculata*	Nthoroko chia Nyoni	UM3, LM3, LM4

Table 1.6 Classification of popular dry beans in Îgembe Southeast

Kîmîîrû name	Seed characteristics
Kabutulu	White with dark purple spots
Kachûû	Light ochre; small oval beans
Kasumongo	Dark purple; kidney-shaped beans
Kînasarî	White with large wine-red spots; kidney-shaped beans
Mûtukû	Light ochre with dark ochre spots; Mwîtemania type

and dry beans. Leaves of some species are also harvested as supplemental greens. Dry beans can be harvested from premature pods during the early stages of their life cycle. Farmers also harvest some of the green pods containing ripe beans – although they normally wait for the final harvest of dry pods. After uprooting a plant or picking dehydrated pods during a dry spell, the pods are threshed with a long pole, causing them to dehisce (burst open) and so release their beans. Threshed grains are then dressed with ash, or chemical or botanical insect repellents, before storage.

The second co-staple food crop of the Îgembe Southeast – maize (*mpeempe*) – is often intercropped with grain legumes and planted two to three weeks before the onset of the rainy season. Maize is not indigenous to the region and the number of available varieties is much smaller than that of dry beans. Hybrid seeds (especially H512 and H513) are favoured over composite seeds (Katumani) because the former are higher yielding. They do, however, require a higher density of soil nutrients. Hybrids are obtained by crossing two varieties. Hence, 'the subsequent crops using saved seed will not have the same characteristics and yields will be much lower' (Kenya 2002, 1). Composite varieties are genetically stabilised during the reproduction process. H512 takes four to five months to mature, while H622 takes six to eight months (Kenya 2002, 1–2). Consequently, maize plants are still immature when intercropped dry beans are harvested.

There are also many banana groves in the Îgembe Southeast. Common varieties include *mûtaato, mûrwaru, wainaina, kîgaanda* and *kiisraîli*. People in the Îgembe Southeast remember that a plant disease during the 1990s destroyed a large quantity of bananas, especially on the lower slope. Bananas are planted for local consumption, while any surplus provides a minor source of cash income. Ripe fruits are eaten raw as snacks, and unripe fruits peeled and pounded into a thick mush, which is used in the preparation of *irio,* or *kîthanda* – a common dish. Stems, peels and leaves are fed to livestock, with leaves also used as wrapping materials in the *mîraa* industry. Dried banana leaves, sheaths and petioles are used as tying materials, thatch, screens for plant pods, and circular pads for carrying head loads.

Livestock are widely reared in the region. Domestic farm animals include cattle, goats, sheep and poultry, with pigs and rabbits found in smaller numbers. All are kept as a source of income – farmers engage in dairy production but rarely slaughter their livestock for consumption (rather, buying meat from local butchers). Cattle and goats are fed on grass and tree leaves in their natural state on the homestead. Common fodder prepared by farmers includes *thaarra* (Napier grass), *nthangari* (couch grass), *mîtindi* (banana stems), *mariû* (banana leaves), *nyaki* (comprising many varieties of wild grass), *machakwe* (maize cobs), *mabua* (maize stalks) and *makoolo* (the remains of legume plants).

The grazing of cattle on grassland is uncommon, due to the scarcity of public pasture. Goats are said to prefer browsing tree leaves,[14] the most common of many varieties being *machikichiki* (tithonia), *mîraa,* and indigenous trees leaves such as *mûtûngûû, mûthatha* and *mwenjela.*

---

14 See Kokwaro's definition of a 'grazer' as feeding on grass and a 'browser' as eating forbs or shrubs (Kokwaro 1979, 61).

A farming community

Photo 1.2 A *kîoera* for zero-grazed goats

Grasses, including Napier grass, are also sometimes fed to goats. However, the people of the Îgembe Southeast have a firm grasp of their livestock's natural habits; classifying goats as browsers and cattle as grazers. Thus, when goats are fed picked leaves, they are bundled together with a wooden post (an arrangement known as *kîoera)* to resemble a natural shrub (Photo 1.2). According to Goldsmith (1995, 135–136), the 'zero grazing' of goats is 'a wholly indigenous practice the Igembe have raised to a very high form,' which elevates the price of those animals to 'over twice the price of range goats'.

Minerals habitually fed to domestic animals, especially dairy cows, include natron (*mûonyo*) – a naturally occurring compound consisting mainly of soda and salt (Sutton 1994, 164), coloured dark grey by impurities. According to the Kîmîîrû taxonomy, natron falls into three categories – *mûonyo*, *îgati* and *îthûi*. Elders of the Mîchûbû age-class vividly remember travelling on foot to the Iombe crater (Photo 1.3) to collect natron. Nowadays, the people of the Îgembe Southeast refrain

Photo 1.3 The Iombe crater, 2002

from this journey; instead obtaining *mûonyo* either from peddlers or the natural source of Kîng'enyonne – an open pasture on the plain where cattle are led to graze. Additionally, refined salt can be purchased from local shops, to provide cattle with saline water.

The people of the Îgembe Southeast sometimes keep dogs, cats and doves as pets. They also collect honey – on a small scale – from traditional log beehives set on trees. Fishing is of marginal interest.

The *mîraa* industry

As noted by Bernard (1972, 121–123), the people of the Nyambene hill region began to expand coffee production in the 1950s and, although by the late 1960s the resulting income remained lower in Nyambene communities than in other Kîmîîrû-speaking communities, coffee farms continued to develop in the 1970s and 1980s. By the late 1980s *mîraa* (more widely known as *khat* outside Kenya) had begun to replace coffee as the primary source of cash income, due to a major decline in coffee prices (see Goldsmith 1995, 117–118). *Mîraa* farming then underwent 'major expansion during the 1980s as the export of small quantities of *miraa* to western Europe began' (Goldsmith 1995, 106). Between the late 1980s and early 1990s, the people of the Îgembe Southeast made the final shift from coffee cultivation to the commercial farming of *mîraa*, which was, in fact, not a newly introduced plant – having been consumed and traded even before British colonial rule.[15] When I first visited and stayed in Athîrû Gaiti in 2001, people did however still pick coffee from remaining, albeit neglected, plants.

The *mîraa* tree is propagated mainly by means of suckers, as opposed to from seed. With appropriate management, most trees do not reach more than six metres tall, because farmers trim the upper branches – to both encourage lateral growth and facilitate harvesting. Weeding, mulching, fertilisation and pest control are all a necessity. Well-managed crops can be harvested four to five years after planting, with mainly the young twigs – the quality of which decrease as fibre content increases – being harvested.

The farming and processing of *mîraa* is relatively simple and provides a significant source of income in the Îgembe Southeast. Only modest capital outlay and no advanced technology are required. Further, the processing sector is completely open to the public. Yet, there is a contrast between the 'haves' and 'have-nots' in their access to the industry. Generally speaking, the economically weak, who do not own arable land, are involved in the processing sector, while the relatively wealthy dominate production. Thus, school dropouts, unmarried young men and

---

15 A white explorer who visited the area in the late 19th century wrote that 'They are much addicted to a habit of chewing the leaves of a certain shrub, indigenous to the country, but which they also cultivate for convenience. Some of the old men are never without their mouths full of this green stuff' (Neumann 1898, 32–33). Goldsmith (1995, 79, 100–101) notes that the former Mîrîti age-class 'presided over the initial commercialization of *miraa*', and the former Bwantai was the first age-class 'to actively trade *miraa* dating to before the turn of the century'. According to Carrier (2007, 57), 'In the early 1970s, *miraa* was already giving farmers a better return than coffee'.

single mothers characteristically staff the processing workshops. It is, however, frowned upon for school students, unmarried young women or any married person to partake in such work – since fraternising, gossiping and earning money in such an environment are thought to engender moral decadence. By way of contrast, the production sector is apparently free from such infamy, with *mîraa* farming considered indispensable to financial security and the means to, for example, pay for children's education and hospital bills.[16]

Mîraa circulates as a cash crop both within and beyond Kenya. In some countries however – including the United States, Canada, Saudi Arabia and Tanzania – it has long been classified as a narcotic and its importation is banned. In 2013, the Netherlands also outlawed the stimulant and, on 3 July 2013, the British Home Office announced similar plans. The Îgembe people immediately responded to Britain's policy change. On 22 July and 23 August 2013, large-scale protests were held at a sports ground in the Maûa suburb of Maili Tatu (known as 'Three Miles' because of its distance from Maûa). Songs were performed extolling *mîraa*'s virtues, and local consumer groups, members of parliament and assembly representatives delivered speeches. Citizens from diverse backgrounds explained that *mîraa* formed a part of traditional culture and was the foundation of the local economy, maintaining livelihoods and enabling the improvement of educational resources. William Ruto, deputy president of Kenya, attended the rally and gave a speech, during which he promised to protect the *mîraa* industry – employing the Swahili proverb: 'A promise is a debt'. Local producers responded with rapturous applause[17] and, the following day, the press published photographs of Ruto and a local member of parliament standing side by side chewing

---

16 Lamont (2010) depicts other pro-*mîraa* counternarratives by Amîîrû gospel singers in the 1990s and 2000s.

17 Deputy President Ruto formally promised to use the planned Isiolo Airport as an air transport base for *mîraa* and to issue land title deeds to local residents who requested them. President Uhuru Kenyatta, who was elected during the March 2013 election, made similar promises when he visited the area.

mîraa. Despite the protests, however, Britain's ban was implemented at the end of June 2014 and Europe lost its legal distribution hub for *mîraa*. The effect on the Îgembe region's *mîraa* producers was devastating.

Land adjudication

The Îgembe Southeast Division – then Athîrû Gaiti (Thaichû) Sublocation – was declared an adjudication section in 1966, under the Land Consolidation Act. The area was considered to be of high agricultural potential and the Kenyan government accordingly planned land tenure reform to facilitate development. The programme consisted of 'replanning the proprietary land units within a given area and redistributing them in units of economic size and shape' (Kenya 1966, 7) – a process known as 'fragment gathering'. Small holdings, scattered over a wide area, were merged to form single farms with straightened boundaries. This entailed *songasonga* – the relocation of farm families from within a neighbourhood, with landowners sometimes required to give up their ancestral holdings and cultivate a consolidated farm in another area. Fragment gathering was launched within the Îgembe divisions in 1966 – shortly after the creation of the adjudication section – in Kîegoi, Kangeta and Ntunene.

Undoubtedly, the new land ownership system caused an overall change in local agronomy, replacing traditional circuit cultivation with the farming of single consolidated plots. This generalisation, however, applied only to areas where fragment gathering was conducted in the 1950s and 1960s. The government actually reversed its land administration policy soon after the publication of the *Report of the Mission on Land Consolidation and Registration* (Kenya 1966). An official announcement issued on 28 June 1967 stated: 'Adjudication work will not be started in a new area until the problem of fragmentation in that area has been studied and a decision taken as to the need, if any, for consolidation.'[18]

---

18 Ministry of Lands and Settlement (Nairobi), *Lawrance report on land consolidation and registration: Consequential changes in government policy* (28 June 1967), Kenya National Archives, DC/MRU/2/4/19/76.

Despite being programmed in 1966, land tenure reform remained uninitiated (due to staff shortages) in Îgembe Southeast until 1989, when the area was again declared an adjudication section under the Land Adjudication Act (Cap 284). It was then divided into the Upper and Lower Athîrû Gaiti adjudication sections. Shortly before this, public hearings were held to decide whether to accept Cap 284, to sustain circuit cultivation, or Cap 283, to facilitate fragment gathering. Eventually, Cap 284 was applied and, consequently, the present system of land tenure in Îgembe Southeast differs greatly from areas where Cap 283 was implemented.

It was reported that fragment gathering in Kîegoi was completed as early as March 1967.[19] However, the adjudication office and committees continued to hear objections lodged against the register well beyond that time, and the registration process proceeded at a painfully slow pace – a fact considered by local people to have severely impeded economic development in the region. The District Consultations Forum, for example, which was held as late as February 2001,[20] placed the issue at the top of the agenda. According to its consultation report, 'The people of Meru have expressed great frustration in the way the land adjudication has dragged on for a whole generation' (Kenya 2001b, 25). The report proposed that the land adjudication process should be accelerated and landowners given title deeds – the absence of which prevented them from securing bank loans (See also Buruchara 1986). Land tenure reform

---

19 Ministry of Lands and Settlement (Meru), *Land consolidation monthly report, March 1967*, Kenya National Archives, DC/MRU/2/4/19/61.

20 'In an effort to solicit views and opinions of people at the grass roots level, the Government facilitated forums in all the 70 districts in Kenya to discuss poverty in their respective districts, identify the problems that contribute to their poverty and recommend measures that should be taken to reduce poverty in the district. Meru North was selected as one of the 25 districts to hold comprehensive consultations, during the process of developing the Poverty Reduction Strategy Paper (PRSP). This paper is comprised of views presented by the people of Meru North during divisional consultations, which were held in all fifteen divisions in the district as well as those of the various stakeholders in the district who met in the District Consultations Forums (DCF) held on 20th and 27th February 2001' (Kenya 2001b, v).

was, and remains, a challenging proposition – even under Cap 284. When adjudication started in the Îgembe Southeast in 1989, demarcation officers were stationed in each adjudication section, to register all plots and inscribe land boundary maps. Thereafter, each plot was allocated a reference number, to be shared by its owner and the office, so legitimising land ownership until title deeds or other legal documents were issued. It was not until 2015 that the people of the Upper Athîrû Gaiti adjudication section began to receive deeds to their land properties.

Cultivated forest areas on the plain were first demarcated by clan representatives between the early 1980s and 2000s and were subsequently allocated to highlanders – with decisions informed by the applicants' clan affiliations. However, in the Îgembe Southeast non-agnatic members were not entirely excluded from receiving a share of land, with other conditions endowing eligibility to outsiders. This kind of property alienation may be described as a gift, and differentiated from inheritance or purchase. In the Îgembe Southeast, the agnatic clans of Athimba, Amwari, Amunjû, among a few others, claimed *mbûrago* (ancestral land) on the plain, and were thus allowed to distribute properties both to their agnatic members and their *îchiaro* clans. From the initiation of land reform in 1989 until the end of the 1990s, land boundary disputes intensified between the various clans and were settled using the indigenous method of *kûringa nthenge*.[21] However, the boundary disputes I have observed since the

---

21 *Kûringa nthenge* (to strike a he-goat) is used only to settle large-scale land disputes between clans. When the plaintiff (X), claims a piece of land that is being cultivated by the defendant (Y), he is responsible for bringing a he-goat for the oath administration. Initially, all of the goat's orifices – its mouth, eyes, ears and anus – are stitched up. X then walks along the boundaries of the disputed land with the suffocated goat shouldered on his back and asks Y to repeatedly cut various parts of the animal's body with a knife, while uttering curse words. Y swears that if X unjustly takes the land under dispute, he should die in suffering, like the ritual goat. After X has completed his walk along the boundaries, the body of the mutilated goat is burnt to ashes and its remains put into a small pot and secretly hidden. Y is then permitted to occupy the land permanently. However, if Y and his family suffer a series of subsequent misfortunes, his occupation of the plot is declared unlawful. X is then required to hand over the hidden pot for the cleansing and blessing of the otherwise dangerous *nthenge* – after which he is recognised as the rightful owner of

early 2000s have been between individuals; a factor in the waxing and waning of clan identity in local communities.

A farming community in transition

Bernard (1972) observed that, in some Kîmîîrû-speaking communities, the land reform programme under Cap 283 (Land Consolidation Act) replaced circuit cultivation with single-plot cultivation. This was not the case in areas such as the Îgembe Southeast, where circuit cultivation continues to date – not because the Îgembe Southeast is trapped in a timeless, unchanging tradition, but rather because circuit cultivation in the region is a historical phenomenon; fashioned by context and conditioned by official land laws and international cash crop markets.

Most ridgetop inhabitants only began to exploit the plain for permanent cultivation in the late 1970s, although some did previously farm there on a small scale; a symbiotic barter system of food crops and livestock existed between the Îgembe proper and the Thaichû. With gradual demographic growth, both communities extended their economic activity zones on the plain. Land registration, beginning in 1989 under Cap 284 (Land Adjudication Act), eventually gave both parties a concrete form of land ownership, under which they began permanent cultivation of maize, legumes and *mîraa* on the plain area. Consequently, the assumed differences in socio-economic activities between highlanders and lowlanders have become less significant.

Today, the Îgembe people's primary source of monetary income is *mîraa*, which is farmed on both the ridgetop and the plain. *Mîraa* farming has not, however, replaced sustenance farming. The Îgembe have learnt lessons from the decline of the coffee industry in the late 1980s and the *mîraa* crisis of the mid-2010s – realising it is too risky to rely solely on

---

the land (see also Rimita 1988, 74). It is believed that intra-clan claims should not be settled by this method because not only the perjurer and his family, but all of his clan, will be affected (Lambert 1956, 127).

a cash crop. *Mîraa* farming is by no means a failsafe source of income because, due to international import restrictions and bans, there is no true market stability. Thus, the people of the Îgembe Southeast have maintained food crop cultivation as a protective measure. Commercial production of *mîraa* undoubtedly commands a large quantity of resources, but is not necessarily a major threat to subsistence farming, so long as farmers manage their agricultural holdings in a rational way.

*

This chapter has outlined socio-economic turns in the late 1980s and mid-2010s, as they have affected one Îgembe farming community. Chapter 2 concerns age-class formation; illustrating how the Îgembe's experience of socio-economic change coincided – during the late 1980s and mid-2010s – with generational change in traditional age-organisation. As I will show, this is exemplified by the first circumcision of the Bwantai age-class in 1989, and the handing over of ruling elderhood to the Mîrîti age-class in 2014.

Goldsmith notes that age-classes provide 'a convenient scale against which to measure historical developments, and Igembe elders uniformly fall back on the cycle of generations to describe the development of *miraa* trade'. The initiation of the Bwantai and the expansion of the international *mîraa* market are somehow conflated in local understanding (Goldsmith 1995, 100–101, see also 78–79). This does not necessarily mean that socio-economic turns *determine* generational developments, but it does suggest that age-categories 'materialise' when populations consolidate socio-economic turns with generational changes (Lamont 2005, 341). Those turns also influence clan identity in local communities, as demonstrated in Chapters 3 and 4.

Chapter 2
The field is theirs: Kûrûmithua ndewa, age-class formation and the persistence of local memory

On the morning of 19 July 2006, a group of men in Athîrû Gaiti assembled to exact punishment on a man named Kînoti, who had raped his two daughters, both primary school pupils. Kînoti had also assaulted his wife when she challenged and condemned him for this.

Later the same day, at around 1pm, a group of approximately 50 men gathered in the community's largest open field and surrounded the captive Kînoti, whose hands were tied with sisal rope. They then formed a procession and, in an act of public shaming, sang, 'Kînoti, he is crying! See the one is made to cry. That's our festivity!' (Photo 2.1). Kînoti belonged to the Mîrîti age-class, whereas the men who rebuked him and claimed all of the Mîrîti's daughters to be their 'wives'[1] were Bwantai, the Mîrîti's junior adjacent cohort.

This incident exemplifies how *kûrûmithua ndewa* (a local form of collective sanction) has, relatively recently, been organised by the Îgembe to address sexual violence, immorality and circumcision-related offences, among others.

According to an elder I interviewed on 24 August 2006, *kûrûmithua ndewa* was first performed in Athîrû Gaiti in 1977, following the establishment of the Lubetaa age-class. A second such incident transpired in 1989, after the establishment of the Mîrîti. These cases, together with Kînoti's in 2006, may be understood not only as *ex post facto* responses

---

1 Peatrik (2019, 78) notes, 'Among the Igembe, the rule of matrimonial prohibition is accompanied by a positive rule by virtue of which the girls of specific sets are destined to become the wives of certain other sets of men. It is said, for example, that the daughters of Ithalie are forbidden to the Ithalie and destined to marry the Michubu and Ratanya.'

Photo 2.1 Kînoti exposed to the public in the Athîrû Gaiti open field

to crimes but also as neo-traditional events, informed by local memories of age-class formation.

Among the Îgembe, an age-class, or *nthukî*, constitutes a group of men who are circumcised within an approximately fifteen-year timespan. At the end of each given period, the age-class is sealed and its members ascend to a higher life stage, or age-grade. During my research, I observed that *kûrûmithua ndewa* provides an opportunity for members of a new age-class to fulfil their potential for self-organisation (which would remain otherwise latent) by punishing social offenders, including those from senior age-classes.[2]

This chapter describes Kînoti's case, as well as the two previous incidences of *kûrûmithua ndewa*, in detail. It goes on to provide an overview of the age-class system. Finally, it postulates an association between

---

2 *Kûrûmithua ndewa* is distinct from the now defunct *ntuîko* ceremony, which was formerly performed during age-class formation and is discussed towards the end of this chapter.

kûrûmithua ndewa and age-class formation in the local historical context; an association not previously made in ethnographical literature concerning the Amîîrû.

Kînoti and *kûrûmithua ndewa*, July 2006

Kînoti was born in the Îgembe Central Division in the 1960s. In 1989, when land adjudication began in the Southeast Division, he migrated to Athîrû Gaiti and was allocated a parcel of farmland, or *shamba*. He then married a woman of the Imenti – another Kîmîîrû speaking subgroup – and the couple had four children: two sons and two daughters. In time, Kînoti began to sexually abuse both of his daughters.

A few weeks before his arrest on 19 July 2006, Kînoti seriously assaulted his wife, as she tried to protect her second daughter from harm. At around midnight, the family's neighbours surmised the situation from Kînoti's wife's screaming, and she was taken to hospital. Finally, Kînoti's crimes were exposed.

The men of Athîrû Gaiti called for punitive action and, on 19 July (as described above) Kînoti was shamed by a group of Bwantai men who conducted *kûrûmithua ndewa* – and argued that, as a fine, Kînoti should contribute a large bull to the community. According to an elder I interviewed on 20 July 2006, when a bull is slaughtered during *kûrûmithua ndewa*, the offender should receive no share of the meat, and the animal's tail skin should be wrapped around a *rûgoi* (antelope horn) as a reminder of the incident.[3]

Kînoti's case may be interpreted as a straightforward criminal one. However, my research revealed the incident to have deeper significance;

---

3   The same elder also told me that *kûrûmithua ndewa* is the imposition of the fine, and is more important than the shaming process. Further, in a personal communication, Stephen A Mûgambi Mwithimbû (a local historian from Îmenti, and a Kîmîîrû expert, with whom I have collaborated since 2005 on research based at the National Museums of Kenya) argues that *kûrûmithua ndewa* is actually the process of re-admitting an errant, excommunicated (*kûingua/kwiingua*) age-class member. In other words, excommunication comes first and *kûrûmithua ndewa* follows. However, in

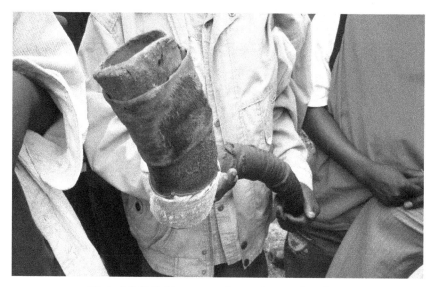

Photo 2.2 Tail skins wrapped around an antelope horn

specifically, the administration of justice as a social performance, rooted in local memory of age-class formation. Indeed, during Kînoti's punishment, I recognised old tail skins wrapped around the *rûgoi,* in evocation of the 1977 and 1989 cases (Photo 2.2).

Kînoti becomes an outcast

In Kîmîîrû, *kûrûmithua ndewa* literally means 'to be incited to bite a bull'; with 'bite' denoting 'steal'. During the operation, while being beaten, the offender is incited – or driven by distress – to find a large, fit bull within the community, 'steal' it and jump over it, in a symbolic gesture of acceptance of his responsibility to compensate the owner. Only then will the community avengers call his physical punishment to a halt.

Kînoti's case, I observed that excommunication *was not* followed by re-admittance. During this chapter, contradictions sometimes arise between mine and Mwithimbû's interpretation of *kûrûmithua ndewa*. Besides the possibility of this being attributable to regional differences between our subjects of study – the Îgembe and Imenti – these contradictions might also indicate differences in perception within local communities, a subject for possible further research.

The field is theirs

Photo 2.3 The offender with a bunch of unripe bananas

On 19 July 2006, after being publicly humiliated by the Bwantai age-class, Kînoti was released – simply because it was growing dark. On 20 July, he was rearrested and forced to carry a bunch of unripe bananas (*nchoodi*) on his back (Photo 2.3);[4] if bananas are too young to be harvested, it is said to be shameful for a mature man to bear them. So, Kînoti was once again paraded before the crowd, to a chorus of insults.

Eventually, Kînoti found a bull that was returning home after grazing with other cows on pastureland. Its owner, Maore, was not notified that his property would be 'stolen' as part of *kûrûmithua ndewa* and, during an interview conducted on 27 July 2006, expressed his surprise to me:

> Kînoti stole my bull. At first, the reason was not known to me. The report was brought by my houseboy. Then I found my bull kept at the gate of our community dispensary. I asked, 'Who brought my bull here?' Nobody but Kînoti answered, 'Mr Maore, I am the one.' I told him to bring it to my homestead. He refused and said, 'Let me call my father and brother.

---

4 Peatrik (2019, 208–209) describes a similar method of punishment involving the use of a cluster of unripe bananas, observed in the Tigania region in April 1989.

Then we talk.' He told me that he was required by *nthukî* to find a bull. He continued, 'It is a fine since I slept with my own daughter and also beat my wife. Let me take your bull and I will refund you ten thousand shillings.' I found our chief and came with him. The chief said that the bull should stay at the chief's camp until the next day. The following morning, we arrived at the chief's office at around eleven o'clock in the morning. The chief told his subordinates to take Kînoti to the Maûa Police Station together with the bull.

During *kûrûmithua ndewa*, it is required that the offender provide full compensation for the 'stolen' bull; with the owner entitled to name his own price. In this case, Kînoti offered 10,000 shillings but Maore demanded at least 12,000.

The Bwantai vindicators, however, refused to accept this bull (in reality a small calf) and argued that Kînoti should present a larger one. So, Kînoti's burden was doubled. First, he was required to compensate Maore with 12,000 shillings (which would have been enough to purchase a larger bull). Second, he was instructed to purchase another larger bull, at a cost of more than 12,000 shillings. The outcome: to meet his obligations, Kînoti was forced to raise more than 24,000 shillings.[5]

As reported by Maore, the chief of Athîrû Gaiti Location took Kînoti to Maûa Police Station, as a criminal before the law. En route, however, Kînoti's father appeared and pleaded to be allowed to mediate in the case. His request was accepted and Kînoti's crimes remained unreported.

Despite his escape from formal prosecution, Kînoti lost everything. His wife and daughters left him and he had to sell his small piece of land to raise Maore's 12,000 shillings' compensation. Finally, in order to buy the second bull demanded by the Bwantai, he had to cancel his farm-leasing contracts in order to claim back the deposit held on them. This final blow was fatal to Kînoti's livelihood, since the cultivation of *mîraa*

---

5   At the time, 24,000 shillings was almost equivalent to the annual fee of a typical secondary school in Kenya.

on leased land was his only source of monetary income. Further, having lost his neighbours' trust, he became an outcast and only the small bull he 'stole' during *kûrûmithua ndewa* remained in his compound.[6]

As several locals explained to me, the people of Athîrû Gaiti assumed that, following Kînoti's punishment, the Bwantai men would arrest and punish other evildoers – to procure more livestock for a grand feast the following December. This supposition was based on their experience of the 1989 *kûrûmithua ndewa*, after which nine bulls were killed. Their expectations, however, remained unmet – no further performances of *kûrûmithua ndewa* were enacted; neither was there any feast.

Kûrûmithua ndewa in 1977 and 1989

In 1976, according to local sources, just as the first circumcision of the Mîrîti age-class was being organised in Athîrû Gaiti, a man named M'Mauta arranged for a group of dancers to perform an unauthorised circumcision celebration. The following year, a group of young men of the Lubetaa age-class rebuked M'Mauta and ordered him to present a bull, which was the first *kûrûmithua ndewa* performed in Athîrû Gaiti.

The second *kûrûmithua ndewa* was performed in December 1989, with the punishment of nine offenders and subsequent slaughtering of nine bulls in Athîrû Gaiti's open field (see Table 2.1). Five of these cases were circumcision related;[7] the other four concerned sexual immorality or domestic violence. Crimes such as theft, homicide, bodily injury, arson and sorcery were not included.[8]

---

6 According to Stephen A. Mûgambi Mwithimbû, in a personal communication, 'This is very unusual. This man must have been a criminal who should have been executed by the Njûrincheke council of elders with capital punishment. The result described here does not comply with the customary law of the Amîîrû.'

7 Forced male circumcisions sometimes occur in the local community. However, as Lamont (2018) notes, it is not seen as a human rights violation or criminalised but tolerated by the local population and the state.

8 Although the case of 'F' (see Table 2.1) might be categorised as theft, it actually occurred in the course of a circumcision ceremony.

Table 2.1 Nine offenders punished during *kûrûmithua ndewa*, 1989

	Age-class	Nature and details of offences	
A	Mîrîti	Sexual affair (incest)	A man married a woman of his mother's age and slept with his daughter, to whom the woman had given birth.
B	Bwantai	Circumcision (abetment)	A man tempted uncircumcised boys to enter the seclusion of newly circumcised youth without their parents' permission. This led to the boys being circumcised.
C	Mîrîti	Circumcision (insult)	A man took a woman into the seclusion of newly circumcised youth, wherein they became inebriated and made jokes.
D	Lubetaa	Violence (domestic)	A man beat his mother several times.
E	Ratanya	Circumcision (negligence)	A man took care of the newly circumcised sons of his age-mate. According to the Kîmîîrû custom, nobody is allowed to enter the seclusion of the newly circumcised son of his age-mate. When the man was ordered to present a bull, the age-mate contributed to its purchase.
F	Mîrîti	Circumcision (theft)	A man stole a circumciser's cash allowance, together with *îraa* (white ochre for body painting) – leaving these possessions unavailable for several circumcised youth's homecoming, which was thus delayed.
G	Lubetaa	Circumcision (negligence)	A man neglected his responsibility during a circumcision ceremony and was responsible for holding the money stolen by F.
H	Lubetaa	Sexual affair (quasi-incest)	A man married a woman of his mother's age, with whom his father had shared intimate relations.
I	Mîrîti	Sexual affair (incest)	A man married his sister's daughter.

From another perspective, the majority of the cases – seven out of nine – related to the violation of social boundaries, such as wife/mother, wife/daughter, father/son, man/woman and uncircumcised/circumcised. Such boundaries infer sexual prohibitions: no man is permitted to seek a lover or wife of his mother's age; or to look after the sons of his age-mate in circumcision; or to have sexual intercourse with his daughter or any daughter of his age-mates. Further, neither women nor uncircumcised boys are permitted to enter the seclusion of newly circumcised youth. Any behaviour contrary to this local role theory constitutes an offence.

There are rumours of incidents of incest in the community prior to the aforementioned cases, although details are seldom disclosed.[9] Some have historically led to punishments; others have not – and the punishments I am aware of were not necessarily *kûrûmithua ndewa*. In 1999, for example, a man of the Mîchûbû age-class was rumoured to have slept with his daughter – resulting in the birth of a baby girl – and to have killed his son by sorcery. When the Njûrincheke elders interrogated him, the defendant explained, 'Even dogs eat their offspring.' He was subsequently charged and fined (*mîrongo îthatû*)[10] a bull, a cow, a ram, a *kiempe* (drum of honey) and 1,000 shillings.

Circumcision and age-class formation

As noted above, rather than being organised by chronological age, Îgembe age-classes (*nthukî*) consist of groups of men who have been circumcised within a given interval of around fifteen years. In recent times, initiates have generally been circumcised during their teens; in the past, circumcision was more common during the early twenties.[11]

A particular name is allocated to each age-class; taken from a repository of eight consecutive, and cyclical, titles. As shown in Table 2.2, seven age-classes were extant in the Athîrû Gaiti community between the 2000s and the 2010s: Mîchûbû; Ratanya; Lubetaa; Mîrîti; Bwantai; Gîchûnge; Kîramunya. The Mîchûbû men were nearly all deceased by

---

9   I came across these rumors during my fieldwork but was unable to confirm their veracity.

10 *Mîrongo îthatû* literally means 'thirty'. However, when it stands for a traditional fine charged by the Njûrincheke council of elders, it is completely unrelated to that number.

11 Parents often arrange for their sons to be circumcised after eight years of primary education (around the age of 14), especially when they want their sons to join secondary school (see Lamont 2005, Chapter 6). However, some boys are circumcised before reaching their tenth year.

the end of the 2010s, while the Kîramunya began to recruit new initiates in 2013.

In theory, each age-class emanates every 120 years – the Gîchûnge, for example, were previously instated in the late 19th century, and again at the end of the 20th century. In actuality, historical contingencies and local eventualities can affect the inception of each age-class – including famine and other natural catastrophes, socio-political and colonial predicaments, and intergenerational negotiations (see Peatrik 2019, 85–92). Data on this is lacking and would be an apt subject for archival and oral historical research.

Age-classes are divided into two categories: Mbaine (Kîruka) and Ntangî (Ntîba)[12] (Bernardi 1959, 21; Lamont 2005, 108; Peatrik 2019, 71). During my fieldwork, locals explained that paternal lines fall within single categories. Within the Mbaine category, for example, the Mîchûbû are fathers to the Lubetaa, and the Lubetaa are fathers to the Bwantai.

Furthermore, each age-class consists of three subsidiary sets – Nding'ûri, Kobia, and Kabeeria – which are formed during circumcision ceremonies. In the past, these rites were held every four to five years (as opposed to annually, as is now the case).[13] For example, when circumcision of the Mîchûbû age-class began in Athîrû Gaiti in 1933, the Mîchûbû Nding'ûri subset was formed (Table 2.3). Four years later, in 1937, the Mîchûbû Kobia subset was instated; followed in 1942 by the youngest subordinate set – the Mîchûbû Kabeeria. Fifteen years later, in 1948, the whole age-class cycle continued with the inception of the Ratanya.

*

---

[12] 'Mbaine' and 'Ntangî' are commonly used terms in Îgembe and Tigania communities, while 'Kîruka' and 'Ntîba' are employed by the Imenti (Lamont 2005, 175). However, it has also been reported that the Tigania use all of these terms (cf. Peatrik 2019, 71), and that the Îgembe at least understand the terms 'Kîruka' and 'Ntîba'.

[13] 'During the closed period no circumcision was to take place, all attention being given to the training of the newly initiated. An open period could last one year or more (two or three seasons), according to the number of candidates.' (Bernardi 1959, 21).

Table 2.2 Member-recruitment years of age-classes; schematic and historical

Age-class	Affiliation	Year of first circumcision		
		Schematic	Historical (Athîrû Gaiti, Îgembe)*	Historical (Tigania)**
Gîchûnge	Ntangî	1885		
Kîramunya	Mbaine	1900		
Îthaliî	Ntangî	1915		1918
Mîchûbû	Mbaine	1930	1933	1933
Ratanya	Ntangî	1945	1948	1946
Lubetaa	Mbaine	1960	1959	1959
Mîrîti	Ntangî	1975	1976	1973
Bwantai	Mbaine	1990	1989	1983
Gîchûnge	Ntangî	2005	1998	1996
Kîramunya	Mbaine	2020	2013	

*As per my fieldwork. **As per Lamont (2005, 108 & 205).

Table 2.3 Circumcision years for subordinate age-class sets

Age-class	Subset	Year of circumcision	
		Athîrû Gaiti, Îgembe*	Tigania**
Mîchûbû	Nding'ûri	1933	1933
	Kobia	1937	1936
	Kabeeria	1942	1940
Ratanya	Nding'ûri	1948	1946
	Kobia	1954	1952
	Kabeeria	1957	1956

*As per my fieldwork. **As per Lamont (2005, 108) for Mîchûbû, and Rimita (1988, 58) for Ratanya.

Male circumcision ceremonies, performed by local practitioners, used to be central to the formation of age-based Îgembe society. Nowadays, however, traditional (Kîmîîrû) methods are being replaced by modern (Kiswahili) practices (see Lamont 2005, 87–88; Peatrik 2005, 31) – with (according to my estimate) the clinical administration of circumcision by trained surgeons having been introduced in Athîrû Gaiti during the 1980s. Further, although traditional circumcision is still practised to

This change of circumstances has contributed to the growth of discrete parental initiatives in circumcision and a decline in the significance of age-based social formation in Îgembe communities. In contemporary Athîrû Gaiti, circumcisions take place biannually – usually during the August and December school vacations. It is thus now difficult to differentiate the three subordinate sets of Nding'ûri, Kobia and Kabeeria by their circumcision years. Further, there is disagreement among locals over the year in which the current Gîchûnge and Kîramunya age-classes began to recruit initiates; although, from my interviews, I estimate the former began in 1998 and the latter in 2013 (Table 2.2).

Generation change, age-classes and the decline of councils

Generation change – the alternation of political domination between the Mbaine and Ntangî – is known as *ntuîko* or *ntwîîko* in Imenti language (M'Imanyara 1992, 113; Nyaga 1997, 45; Rimita 1988, 60), and *kwîîra mîthega* (Rimita 1988, 59) or *nkûra aarû* (Mahner 1975) in Tigania. In 1955, Bernardi (1959, 22) wrote:

> The ceremony of the *ntuiko* (a word which means break) was, and still is, the occasion for the handing over, or breaking, the authority of an age-class, generally called the ruling age-class, to the next following age-class. The latter is thus formally and first recognized as an age-class.

In former times, following their formation, age-classes were organised into three councils: Kîama Lamare or Ramare (junior council of warriors/circumcised men); Kîama Kînene or Kîama kîa Nkomango (senior council of retired warriors/married men); and Njûrincheke (paramount council of ruling elders). The members of a specific age-class would occupy a single council for around fifteen years, before vacating it in favour of their junior adjacent age-class. In the early 1930s, for example, when, following their first circumcision, the Mîchûbû age-class were recruited to the Kîama Lamare, its senior age-class – the Îthaliî – moved up to the office of Kîama Kînene. In turn, the Kîramunya ascended to the ruling elderhood (see also Fadiman 1993, 74; Mwithimbû 2014, 72–73).

> Foremost among these was the council of ruling elders, composed of men whose sons had reached warrior age. In theory fathers and sons formed a partnership in which the ruling group could call upon its warrior sons to enforce communal decisions (Fadiman 1993, 25).

However, subsequent researchers (Lamont 2005; Peatrik 2005, 2009), including myself, have observed a less clear-cut and more disputed process; and Fadiman's theory that, within the same alternative (Mbaine or Ntangî), fathers occupied the ruling elderhood simultaneously with their sons being in their warriorhood has not held true over time. During the *kûrûmithua ndewa* in July 2006, for example, although the Gîchûnge age-class of the Ntangî alternative was in its warriorhood, their fathers – of the Mîrîti age-class – had not yet ascended to ruling elderhood. Indeed, during my observations in Athîrû Gaiti, I observed that the Mîrîti's senior adjacent cohort, the Lubetaa, had not established their ruling elderhood until the early 2000s.

Peatrik notes that the Lubetaa claimed their ruling elderhood in the late 1980s and the early 1990s:

> During the national election in 1988, with the introduction of the 'queueing system' in the KANU (Kenya African National Union), and in 1992 when multi-partyism was introduced for the first time in Kenya, candidates used the *nthukî* idiom in a joking and boasting way, claiming that the time of Ratanya as Ruling Father was over and that it was the time of Lubetaa in the running of the country. It is a fact that in 1992 all the newly elected members of the Parliament from Tigania-Igembe belonged to the Lubetaa generation. (Peatrik 2005, 294; see also Peatrik 2019, 383–384).

Lamont (2005, 162) contradicts this in his observation that the Ratanya (the Lubetaa's adjacent seniors) remained the 'fathers of the country' until the early 2000s. However, fifteen years later – during the 2002 to 2003 general election campaign – Lamont witnessed a situation similar to the one reported by Peatrik, albeit in a rather different form: in an incident of rivalry between two age-classes, some participants perceived that the Ratanya were attempting to bypass the Lubetaa by handing power directly to the Mîrîti (the Ratanya's son) (Lamont 2005, 43–44 & 164).

A question therefore emerges: by the time of the *kûrûmithua ndewa* in July 2006, which age-class – Ratanya, Lubetaa or Mîrîti – comprised the ruling elderhood? My understanding is that the Mîrîti had already begun to claim their status of ruling elder at that time, but the Lubetaa, who had established it sometime earlier, refused their demands. The Ratanya, on the other hand, had then maintained their superior authority over the Lubetaa.

I witnessed (or, rather, overheard) an incident I consider relevant to Peatrik's and Lamont's observations when, on 9 August 2014, the Njûrincheke elders of the entire Îgembe community held a general meeting at their headquarters; a school ground in Mîori. As an outsider, I was refused entry at the school gate and, unable to either participate or observe, could only hear that the meeting had something to do with the official transfer of power (*kwamûrwa*) from the Lubetaa to the junior adjacent age-class of Mîrîti. I surmised that the Mîrîti were entering into the life-stage of ruling elderhood with the Lubetaa assuming the status of superior authority from the Ratanya, and that the circumcisions of the new Kîramunya (the Bwantai's sons') age-class had already begun. This episode indicates to me another divergence from Fadiman's theory of the transfer of power.

Traditional councils have become less significant in contemporary Îgembe communities, with Kîama Lamare and Kîama Kînene no longer organised to admit local and retired warriors. The only exception to this is the neo-traditional Njûrincheke council, which has retained its political and judicial power over the course of negotiations with colonial and post-colonial administrations (Fadiman 1993; Lamont 2005, Chapter 4; Peatrik 2019, Chapter 10). This body may initiate and accommodate members, regardless of their age-class affiliations; with the allocation of roles such as chairmanship conducted *within* the council, and dependent upon individuals' ages. The ruling elderhood, in other words, is succeeded internally, with power transferred approximately every fifteen years.

Generation change and *kûrûmithua ndewa*

According to some of the Îgembe elders I encountered in Athîrû Gaiti, a local saying asserts, 'The field is theirs (*kîaani ni kîao*)' – meaning the open space that serves (or, rather, historically served) as both the location for mass circumcision and the warriors' dormitory (*aarû*) subsequently becomes the property of, or is reserved for, the circumcised warriors themselves. Since the ban imposed by the administrative chief and assistant chiefs in 1998, two of Athîrû Gaiti's open fields (one large, one small) have no longer been used for mass circumcision, with the final ceremony held in 1997. Further, the fields are no longer open spaces: in 2012, several stone buildings, with iron sheet roofs, were constructed in the large field, to shelter the community's open-air market, while the small field has been fenced in to house the assistant chief's office. Nevertheless, the local saying holds true, in as much as 'the field' remains a dedicated arena for the community's youth – ranging from their late teens to their twenties – to hold everyday meetings and perform business activities.

Given that generation change among the Îgembe has persisted despite 1998's prohibition of mass circumcision, merit may be found in Lamont's suggestion that such change is best understood not simply in the context of age-class formation and councils, but as part of a longer process:

> By the time I moved to Mikinduri in January 2002, a small marketing and administrative centre for central and eastern Tigania, I was hoping to observe and perhaps participate in a 'planned' inauguration of a new

age-class, that of the young cohort of adolescents touted to be called the Gîcûngî. More exciting, however, was the chance to witness the ritual contexts of an anticipated generational succession between two senior adjacent age-classes in the Nyambene hills. I had expected the advancement of the 'junior elders' of the Lubeeta and the retirement of the 'fathers of the country' of the Ratanya. By the end of fourteen months living in the Nyambene Range, I came to the conclusion that such an 'event' had either occurred and I missed it, or that it was not an 'event' as such, but a process, occurring over a much longer time frame than thirty months of fieldwork would allow. (Lamont 2005, 26)

Indeed, the marking of generation change in Îgembe communities *has* become indistinct – as a result of the discontinuation of *ntuîko* by newly elevated age-class members, the decline of traditional councils and the annualisation of circumcision. This leads me to hypothesise that there may be greater fluidity of tradition and its social function among the Îgembe than previous academic research has recognised.

Daniel Nyaga's explanation of the transfer of power during *ntuîko*, below, resonates with my observations of *kûrûmithua ndewa*, in as much as both are characterised by the accusation of offenders against morality, together with the accusation of seniors by juniors:

This [*ntuîko*] was an occasion when everything was revealed: defects, faults and secret misbehaviour were brought to light. The young husbands were sarcastically ordered out of the dormitories: unpleasant incidents between husbands and wives were revealed: a statesman who had spoken badly was mocked: a child born out of wedlock was revealed: a mono-eyed fellow or anyone with an amusing defect was teased, and so forth. And throughout the singing, the victims were humiliated and taunted with unpleasant words. (Nyaga 1997, 46)

Nyaga's commentary suggests that, for newly initiated warriors, *kûrûmithua ndewa* (as last performed in 2006) may have taken on at

Table 2.4 Chronology of events in Athîrû Gaiti

1976	The first Mîrîti circumcision
1977	*Kûrûmithua ndewa*
1983–1984	Famine*
1989	The first Bwantai circumcision *Kûrûmithua ndewa* Beginning of land adjudication*
1997	The last mass circumcision
1998	The first Gîchûnge circumcision
2006	*Kûrûmithua ndewa*
2013	The first Kîramunya circumcision Netherlands' ban on *mîraa* importation*
2014	The Njûrincheke meeting in Mîori on the transfer of power UK's ban on *mîraa* importation*

*See Chapter 1

least some of the functions formerly served by the *ntuîko* ceremony. Further, the inception of new age-classes and *kûrûmithua ndewa* shared some chronological proximity, suggesting a possible association. This is evident in Table 2.4, which presents a timeline of modern historical events from 1976 onwards. The table shows that a *kûrûmithua ndewa* was reported in 1977 – one year after the first circumcision of the Mîrîti age-class; and that both the first circumcision of the Bwantai and a *kûrûmithua ndewa* took place in 1989.

This association may also be inferred from the fact that, during the performances of *kûrûmithua ndewa* in 1977, 1989 and 2006, age-class affiliation was taken into consideration at the moment of collective punishment – with the senior age-classes of Lubetaa and Mîrîti organising 1977 and 1989's ceremonies, respectively, and the Bwantai organising that of 2006. In other words, these events were influenced by the Îgembe community's structural history.

Ntuîko and *kûrûmithua ndewa* (the latter being a relatively modern phenomenon) have both served a traditional social function as conduits for the expression of power by younger generations. Whichever age categories might be involved, it seems this social function always finds a means to manifest itself.[17]

*

As described above, the process of creating age-classes via circumcision has been eroded over time, transforming in 1959 (at the time of the first Lubetaa circumcision) from an approximately four to five-yearly to an annual event. Nevertheless, despite the decline of *ntuîko*, the Lubetaa, Mîrîti and Bwantai *did* demonstrate their agency in law enforcement, via *kûrûmithua ndewa*, in 1977, 1989 and 2006, respectively; suggesting that age-classes continued to wield traditional power, even though the process by which they originally inherited it had now disappeared.

In 1998, also as previously described, mass circumcisions were banned outright and, since the 2010s, the open field where they were once conducted has been repurposed. Further, to my knowledge, since the Kîramunya's first initiation in 2013 (by my estimate), no *kûrûmithua ndewa* has been organised by their Gîchûnge seniors (see Postscript for the Gîchûnge rebellion in the late 2010s and the early 2020s).

Although the transfer of power from the Lubetaa to the Mîrîti was evidently marked in 2014 by the Njûrincheke council, there is no consensus about the time of the Kîramunya's inception. However, it is clear age-class does always find a means to assert itself – albeit it in different forms, congruent with era and social context (Lamont 2005, 341).

---

17 In his critical personal communication concerning my interpretation, Stephen A. Mûgambi Mwithimbû counters, '*Kûrûmithua ndewa* and *ntuîko* are *not* related at all,' and, even though they have historically borne similarities in appearance, 'this was purely coincidental; *kûrûmithua ndewa* occurred as a deterrent of anti-social activities among members of an age-class'. However, Mwithimbû's statement does not disprove my theory that, underlying the overt differences in form and function between and *ntuîko* and *kûrûmithua ndewa*, the collective sanction associated with the latter has come to provide an alternative means for a newly established age-class to assert its (otherwise latent) power in contemporary Îgembe society.

Further, the notion of ownership of Athîrû Gaiti's larger open field by circumcised warriors persists – alongside the associated communal memory of it being the site of *kûrûmithua ndewa*. In that sense, at least, the people of Athîrû Gaiti's understanding that 'The field is theirs' prevails; even though traditional, formalised processes of justice, retribution and age-class formation are apparently fading into history.

Chapter 3
Man who never dies: Clan revival for new generations

On 11 August 2016, I observed a collective cursing ceremony (Case 3.1) in Mwithûne village, at the northwestern end of Îgembe Southeast Division. The event was organised by the Antûambui clan[1] and attended by its members, their neighbours, their male *îchiaro* (inter-clan partners) and local administrative officers. The Antûambui community had experienced a series of misfortunes, which they attributed to unknown ill-wishers or sorcerers who were thought to be hiding in the neighbourhood. The aim of the ceremony was to remove such agents of harm from the village.

The ritual, known in Kîmîîrû as *ûtaara ngeere*, involved the sacrificial slaughter and burning of a sheep of a single colour (*mwîîrî yûmwe*) – in this case a small nulliparous ewe (*kamwati*).[2] The animal, whose orifices (*tûkutho*) had been stitched up,[3] was wrapped in dried banana leaves (*ndaara*), tied with grass fibre ropes (*mîrii*) and placed on a fire. Some participants stood and cursed the ewe's body as it burnt, while others sang and danced in groups. Meanwhile, the *îchiaro* men interrogated each attendee as to whether they practised witchcraft and, upon receiving a reply of 'no', required them to jump over the sheep's ashes to prove their innocence.

---

1 The Antûambui clan is distinct from the Antûambûi clan, which is an *îchiaro* counterpart to the Athimba clan (see Chapter 4).
2 During my research, local opinion differed on the requisite sex of the sheep, with some elders of the Îgembe Southeast noting that it could either be a ram or ewe. Most of my interviewees agreed that the sheep must be of a single colour, with no blemishes.
3 This type of operation is also performed during *kûringa nthenge*, to settle inter-clan land disputes (see Chapter 1, footnote 21). Some experts in the Îgembe Southeast, however, report that stitching methods vary between subgroups of Kîmîîrû speakers.

Prior to the ceremony, the clan elders had informed the whole neighbourhood that, excepting pregnant women and young children, all were obliged to attend, and that any absentees might be considered as implicated in the community's misfortunes. Before jumping over the sheep's remains, participants were also required to surrender or report any suspicious items held either in their or someone else's possession or known to be present in the locality. In the event, some people did bring items, including inexpensive jewellery, accessories and animal horns, that might be regarded as harmful either to themselves or their neighbours.[4]

*

This chapter illustrates the strong leadership necessary to organise and perform *ûtaara ngeere*. It also shows how the ceremony can either engender an entire clan renaissance, or simply provide temporary relief from local woes. For example, in the wake of the case described above (and in further detail below), the Antûambui underwent a complete revival, whereas the *ûtaara ngeere* organised by the Anjarû and Antûambeti clans in upper Îgembe Southeast[5] – in May 2016 (Case 3.2) and September 2015 (Case 3.3) respectively – served remedial purposes only.

The inhabitants of the Îgembe Southeast became generally less conscious of their clanship from the early 2000s onwards, after the demarcation of clan boundaries in the lower Îgembe Southeast (see

---

4 During my research, I interviewed a carpenter of the Gîchûnge age-class – a man in his thirties – who had surrendered a personal charm during an earlier performance of *ûtaara ngeere*, in May 2016 (Case 3.2). The carpenter had been working in Athîrû Gaiti for years when, one day, a trader in Maûa town sold him a necklace, with the promise that it would bring his business good luck and prosperity. The charm cost 700 shillings (approximately seven US dollars) and the carpenter used it for around a year; his business thriving. However, he eventually concluded that his success might be at his competitors' expense. Thus, when he heard about the upcoming *ûtaara ngeere*, the carpenter relinquished the necklace – fearing that his safety might be compromised if he participated with it still in his possession. This decision was well received by the local elders, and the carpenter was spared blame for his previous use of the charm.

5 Also known as the Athîrû Gaiti community – see Chapter 1.

Chapter 1). The revival of the Antûambui clan in Mwithûne village was consonant with a community policing programme initiated by the government, which aimed to enhance security at grassroots level while also fostering political autonomy in local communities. In popular parlance, the Antûambui were reaffirmed as 'a man who never dies' and 'a man who eats his own' – common greetings by which all members of a clan community are addressed as a single entity.[6]

Another clan of the Athîrû Gaiti also began to enhance their governance in the changing socio-political environment that developed under the new leadership of the Mîrîti age-class (see Chapter 2). This chapter details a second clan revival, among the Akachiû in the upper Îgembe Southeast (Case 3.4). Chapter 4 later expounds how, over the fifteen years of my research, the agnatic Athimba of Mûringene village proved exceptional in consistently developing their own clanship system.

Case 3.1: *Ûtaara ngeere* and clan revival in Mwithûne village

Prior to the Antûambui clan's *ûtaara ngeere* in August 2016, the elders of Mwithûne village were consulted on the biological status of each villager, to determine who should be invited from beyond the community to serve as '*îchiaro* men'. Each guest was then selected to match an *îchiaro* counterpart, or counterparts, from within the village. In the event, sixteen *îchiaro* men were chosen, as listed in Table 3.1: two from the Akinying'a clan, to match the village's Antûambui clan agnates, and fourteen others to match their wives and migrants from other clans.[7]

---

6 This kind of greeting is particular to clan meetings: 'Greetings, clan. Greetings, a person who doesn't die. Greetings, a person who eats his own' (*Mweni, mwîrîa. Mweni, muntû ûtîkuya. Mweni, mûrîa biawe*). While *mweni* is used as a general, everyday greeting, *muntû ûtîkuya* literally denotes 'a *single* person who doesn't die'. This may be interpreted as both a greeting to all assembled members and a celebration of the wellbeing of one's clan as a single entity, or socio-legal personage.

7 In another case of group cursing, observed in Mûringene village on 7 September 2012 (see Chapter 5, Case 5.10), the host invited only six *îchiaro* men. Their task was to

Table 3.1 *Îchiaro* men invited to Mwithûne village on 11 August 2016

No.	Invited *îchiaro* men (age-class)	Clan (village)	*Îchiaro* counterparts in Mwithûne village
1	Kîlaku (Lubetaa)	Akinying'a (Gîtûra)	Antûambui
2	Kîanîra (Ratanya)	Akinying'a (Kîrîmene)	Antûambui
3	Ntuala (Lubetaa)	Anjarû (Anjarû)	Akachiû
4	Mûroki (Lubetaa)	Naathû (KK)	Akachiû
5	Francis (Mîrîti)	Antûamboa (Anchenge)	Akinying'a
6	Ntonjîra (Lubetaa)	Antûamboa (Anchenge)	Akinying'a
7	M'Mauta (Ratanya)	Akachiû (Nthare)	Anjarû, Aîri [Antûanthama]
8	M'Kîarao (Ratanya)	Akachiû (Nthare)	Anjarû, Aîri
9	Mûturi (Lubetaa)	Ankûrani (Kîthetu)	Antûborii
10	M'Ikîara (Mîchûbû)	Antûamauna (Antûbochiû)	Aîri
11	Kînyiinga (Lubetaa)	Andûûne (Gîtûra)	Athimba
12	Kabeeria (Ratanya)	Antûamûtî (Antûbakîîru)	Antûambeti
13	Nchûngi (Mîchûbû)	Andaarû (Amung'enti)	Antûamûtî
14	Kobia (Mîrîti)	Antûbakîthoro (Amung'enti)	Amwari, Antûambeti
15	Kairui (Mîchûbû)	Aîri (Amung'enti)	Bwethaa, Atunebaarûû, Anjarû
16	Mûkumu (Ratanya)	Antûamwaî (Antûbochiû)	Amwaa

Table 3.1 reveals the Antûambui clan's hybrid nature. James – the clan secretary – explained this to me, saying that during the 1950s, a migrant man of Antûborii origin had succeeded James' father as assistant chief of Thaichû Sublocation (the present Îgembe Southeast Division), under the colonial administration of the late 1950s. The migrant's family were then initiated and accommodated by the community and, under the Antûambui name, the two-clan federation evolved to form the political leadership of Mwithûne village and its surrounding area.

---

restore peace within a single family, whereas, in Mwithûne, the entire village – which had a larger population – required pacification. In both cases, however, the *îchiaro* men were selected according to the biological status of each member of the host village. For example, every woman who had married into Mwithûne's Antûambui clan should ideally have been questioned about the possession of harmful charms by her natal clan's *îchiaro* man, rather than by her husband's *îchiaro* counterpart. This local theory of biological determinism (see Chapter 5) was also applied to the community's migrant population.

Of the sixteen *ichiaro* men invited to the Antûambui's *ûtaara ngeere* on 11 August 2016, three assumed leading roles: Kîanîra [2] from the Akinying'a clan; Francis [5] from the Antûamboa clan, and Mûturi [9] from the Ankûrani clan. At 10.40 am – one hour before the opening ceremony – Kîanîra, together with other members of the Njûrincheke council, began to stitch up the orifices of the sacrificial sheep. Meanwhile, away from public view, Francis and various other *ichiaro* men reviewed the list of villagers' reported troubles, which had been compiled in advance by clan officials. Their task was to identify which problems had been caused by witchcraft and which had not – since only the former were to be resolved by collective cursing on that day. The committee established that, of 155 complaints, 127 were witchcraft related – as detailed in Table 3.2.

Of the 27 cases of family members' deaths, 25 were identified as involving witchcraft; the other two being attributed to alcoholism and suicide. Of five alleged instances of family breakdown due to alcoholism, four were dismissed – alcoholism being considered a matter of personal responsibility. Most cases of theft were also disallowed, under the rationale that theft of *mîraa*, livestock, utensils and other items of daily use most likely occurred within the same neighbourhood – and that, because family members or close relatives may have simply 'borrowed' the missing items, they should not be put at risk of an inadvertent curse.

The opening ceremony began at 11.40 am with the clan chairman's greetings, followed by remarks from administrative officers, including the chief and assistant chiefs. Mûturi [9] began speaking as an *ichiaro* representative at 12.10 pm. During his address, which lasted around fifteen minutes, he explained his understanding of the meeting from his point of view as a Christian Methodist minister; also stating that he would not participate in the cursing ceremony. The following excerpt from his greeting and speech takes the form of an ongoing dialogue; the audience punctuating each comment with either a verbal response or applause.

Table 3.2 Alleged witchcraft cases in Mwithûne village

Client No	1	2	3	4	5	6	7	8	9	10	11	13	14	15	16	17	18	19	20	21	22	23	24	25	26	27	28	29	30	31	32
Sex (F=42, M=21)	F	F	F	F	F	F	F	M	F	F	F	F	F	F	F	F	F	F	M	M	M	M	F	F	M	F	F	M	F	M	M
Death																															
Family member			1	1	1		1		1		1		1		5											1		1	2		1
Livestock							1													1											
Sickness																															
General		1											1							1			1								
Stomach	1		1									1																			
Mental	1				1	1													1	1		1									
Swelling																				1											
Epilepsy					1										2																
Tumour																													2		
Missing	1		1					1					1	1	1		1														
Family breakdown																															
Alcoholism		1	1																												1
School dropout						1			1																						
Uselessness					1			1												1	1	1									
Others																											1	1			
Assault																															
Physical																1		1										1			
Love potion																															
Damage																															
Property				1														1										1			
Business activity																				1		1									
Theft																															
Livestock				1	1		1									1															
Utensils					1																										
Others																															
Others																															
Excrement			1																												
Night patrol		1				1													1												
Fetish												1															1			1	
Others																			1		1		1								
Total	1	2	2	4	5	3	2	1	3	3	2	2	2	1	2	8	1	1	3	1	3	3	1	2	3	3	1	4	6	2	3

Man who never dies

33	34	35	36	37	39	40	41	42	43	44	45	46	47	48	49	50	51	52	53	54	55	56	57	58	59	60	61	62	63	64	65	Total	Approved
M	F	F	F	F	M	F	F	M	M	F	M	F	F	F	F	F	M	F	F	F	F	M	F	M	F	M	F	M	M	F	F	M	F	M		
			2	2								1	2						2				1								27	25
																										1					3	2
				1			1		1			1	1		1										2	1			13	13
											1																	4	4
					1									1				1	1								10	10
													1		1	1											4	4
																					1						4	4
					1																						3	3
1																												8	8
													1					1									5	1
			1				1																				4	4
1																										1	7	6
		1	1					1																	5	3
									1										1						5	3
									1																1	1
																									3	2
		1								1			1			1									6	6
															1										5	0
															1										2	0
	1				1						1							1					4	1
				1																			2	0
	1					1		1										1					7	7
	1	1										1				1	1				8	8
	1	1		1				1	1		1	1	1			1	1		1				15	11
1	1	3	4	3	2	4	1	1	2	1	2	4	4	4	2	3	1	4	2	2	1	4	3	2	1	1	4	2	4	1	1	155	126

Photo 3.1 *Îchiaro* men inspect the list of complaints

Dialogue 3.1 Mûturi's opening remarks, with audience responses in square brackets

Mûturi [9]: Greetings, all our chiefs and all the members of this clan. We are in a place for sacrifice (*tûrî kiongwanene*), and we are blessed. [Yes!] Praise the Lord! [Amen!] We want to praise God because he's the one who makes us to be alive. So, we are supposed to be praising God when we go for sacrifice (*kîongwana*).

Now I have come, but there was something I told my brothers (*atanoba*) who called me. I told them this. I won't jump over the sheep, because I am a Christian and I do preach. I told them this. I won't hold any cursing plants (*maroo*) before going back to the dais to preach.

But all other things like witchcraft and the one who will be left within the bush, let him stay with it. We shall stay because we don't want people to die, children to refuse school, or their works to become bad. If you build a house that becomes smart, then the sorcerer comes at the night and he goes around the house, and it becomes dormant and then rats (*mbîa*) start staying there. Would you like it? [No!]

Now children of our people want to be educated more. Look like our leaders here. If they didn't go to school as they were destroyed by sorcerers, who shall be with us to teach us a good thing like this? [Nobody!] If you are taken to an office, a computer is kept there, you are told to operate it, and you're thought to be the one who knows about it, but you don't know, can you do it? [You can't!]

Now sorcerers are doing a very dirty job (*ngûî îmbîî*). Let's get united today! If you're a sorcerer, even if you throw out witchcraft today, you will get it back again. All those we shall curse. [Applause.] You have come today, but if you have hidden something, and later you do the same kind of work, we shall curse, even if you are not here. We shall curse that useless work (*ngûî chia ûtheri*). [Applause.]

Because God is not seen, Balaam used to curse witches, and he didn't do any other kind of work. Balak saw the people of Israel being blessed very much and he was left jealous of them, and he told Balaam to come and curse the Israelites without no course, and they have done nothing.

Now the sorcerer feels jealous of someone's child, feels jealous of leaders, jealous of those blessed with business. He is always a servant of the devil (*mûraîka wa nkoma*). [Applause.]

Now we could do this kind of work. God is helping us. The children shall go to school and God will open their job because God gives every person his presents, but the devil of witchcraft is always interrupting people.

Now my name is Joseph Mûturi. Now respect has got a good reputation, but sorcerers don't have respect. They have good talks and very clean mouth. [It's true!] [Applause.] Sorcerers look like prostitutes, because they don't hate any person, but in their hearts, there is a total darkness (*nkorone nî kiundu*). [Applause.] They will come at night for you. [Applause.] ... At three o'clock there are two types of people. The ones who wake up with a drum (*ndarama*) is to fight against those who wake up naked, who are devil. Devil walks naked without clothes. [Laughter and applause.] For sorcerers, there are magic medicines for people, which they usually have within their pockets. Now for young men, there's a thing they are familiar with.[8] There's a competition in business, but don't go and look for that to protect you with. It's only God who protects you. Let you be protected by God from today. [Applause.] I am saying this. I won't jump over the sheep or hold cursing plants…

After Mûturi's speech, the clan officials assembled the *îchiaro* men – except for those responsible for the sacrificial sheep – into a line. They then asked the community to face the sacred mountain of Nyambene and pray for the return of those who had departed Mwithûne and the surrounding area. During the prayer – led by Mûturi at 12.26 pm and lasting around ten minutes – all of the followers raised their hands; beckoning and imploring each absent community member to, 'Just come!' (Photo 3.2). Each of the *îchiaro* men stood on one leg throughout.[9]

Dialogue 3.2 An *îchiaro* man leading the audience in prayer, with audience responses in square brackets

Mûturi [9]:   The God (*Ngai*) of Israel. The God of Isaac. The God of Jacob. We are praying on this day today. The one who

---

8 This refers to a charm considered to bring good luck and prosperity to one's business (see footnote 4).

9 Photo 5.4 shows *îchiaro* men standing on one leg during another collective cursing in Mûringene village, September 2012.

Man who never dies

Photo 3.2 The prayer to bring back missing people

did great things and sent his son and he was crucified on the cross because of us. [God!] This is a clan, those who have gathered here. [God!] Because of the people who are making others mad, [God!] witchcraft, [God!] and they make children of other people mad so that they can't be able to get education. [God!] Now God, as for us here we don't have strength (*inya*). [God!] God, you are there from the beginning. [God!] You are the one who created this clan. [God!] You're the one who created *ichiaro*. [God!] But for witches you fight with them from heaven. [God!] Even if you sent devil down here, [God!] but you sent a winner down here. [God!] He was Jesus Christ, who fought for us. [God!] We don't have any debt. [God!] That's why we have gathered here as clan to curse this act. [God!] Give us strength. [God!] Some of our people have gone. [God!] That's why we are gathering here and felt mercy.

Now we know it's you alone, you have strength. [God!] Now we are calling them back to come to the clan. [God!] Strong people can be seen in this clan. [God!] Let them not get lost far and even the offspring of the clan not get lost far. [God!]

Now, Kathure, we shall call her twice. Ooh, Kathure… [Ooh, Kathure, ooh, Kathure!] Kathure, you are being called by the clan. Just come, even if it is for your richness (*ûnoru*).[10] Just come, even if you're in a shop. Just come, even if you were kidnapped. Just come. Don't lose your way. Just come. Now come by the strength of God. The clan is waiting for you. Just come. Now, Kathure is coming. [Ululation (*nkemi*).]

As members of the Njûrincheke council of elders, Kîanîra and Francis concluded the day's events by leading collective cursing in the *kwiita rwîi* style, as described below. Mûturi declined to participate in this – having already cited his Christian faith and profession as a Methodist preacher. He thus left the village at 12.37 pm, after which the other *îchiaro* men placed the sheep on the fire, which had been lit in the middle of the road.

The participants then threw cursing plants on the burning animal's body, sang together in groups and, one by one, uttered maledictions against unknown sorcerers: 'Let him/her die like that!'; 'Let him/her burst like the sheep!'; 'Let him/her be burnt like the sheep!' When the flames began to ebb, paraffin was poured on to the fire to keep it going; with some participants arguing that it was sorcerers who were trying to kill it.

Song 1: *Yîi mûroi arîbwaa ngeere akaûra yîi, mûroi arîbwaa ngeere…*

Translation: When the sorcerer hears of a sheep, he becomes lost. When the sorcerer hears of a sheep…

---

10 The term *ûnoru* refers to fertility and richness in a socio-economic sense. Mûturi's meaning is that the missing woman should return to her natal village even if she has been seeking, or has already achieved, material wealth elsewhere.

Man who never dies

Photo 3.3
Community members throw cursing plants on the fire

Song 2: *Yîi mûroi tî weetû nî mpangaa eteerwe. Tûmwîtîra lûrûngû arîîwee mûthûmba jwa maûrû. Yîi, oo îîî, yîi îooî...*

Translation: Yes, the sorcerer is not ours, is a bad omen, which was thrown away. We have judged and cursed him to be loitering with his own legs.

Song 3: *Aroi nîi beerwe bakauna rûûi ntîrûkunda. Nî beerwe naa ngeere. Mûroi nî eerwe akauna rûûi ntîrûkunda. Nî eerwe na ngeere. Nî eerwe na Baibû.*

Translation: Let the sorcerers be told if they cross a river, I won't take the water. Let them be told by use of sheep. Let the sorcerer be told if he crosses a river, I won't take the water. Let him be told by use of sheep. Let him be told by use of Bible.

At 1.30 pm the crowd was instructed to end its cursing and singing, and form a queue. The *îchiaro* men then asked each participant in turn to hold a piece of a cursing plant, as they conducted their interrogation (see Dialogues 3.3 and 3.4 below). After swearing that he or she had never possessed any harmful items or items related to witchcraft, each member of the community was allowed to step over the remains of the sheep.

Photo 3.4
Sacrificed sheep exposed in the dead fire

Dialogue 3.3 Interrogation by Mwîchiaro (an *îchiaro* man): Example 1

Mwîchiaro:	Bring the witchcraft. Have you seen love potion? Bring the strong witchcraft (*ithiitû*[11]). Don't you have something to say? Even your eyes have not seen it?
Examinee:	No.
Mwîchiaro:	Throw your cursing plant and pass.

Dialogue 3.4 Interrogation by Mwîchiaro: Example 2

Mwîchiaro:	Bring charms, even your love potion. Have you seen it? Even the one for your business?
Examinee:	No.
Mwîchiaro:	Are you fearing God?
Examinee:	Yes.
Mwîchiaro:	Just pass over here.

---

11 The term *ithiitû* – in this context meaning 'strong witchcraft' – is thought to originate from Akamba; a neighbouring Bantu-speaking community.

Man who never dies

Photo 3.5 Community members interrogated by the *îchiaro* men

Photo 3.6 Community members queue to swear before the *îchiaro* men

Theoretically, community members should only be interrogated by their biological *îchiaro* counterparts (see Table 3.1). In the event, there were not enough *îchiaro* interrogators present at this *ûtaara ngeere* to match their subjects according to biological status. For example, Mûturi [9], the clan representative from Ankûrani, should have interrogated the Antûborii community members but, as he had already left the village, other *îchiaro* men stood in his place. This reveals that, in practice, the notion of biological determinism is not strictly adhered to. Further, during the interrogations, the *îchiaro* men did not establish the clan affiliation of each subject, instead assuming a more general role.

The questioning process took around one and a half hours, ending at 2.48 pm. At 2.50 pm, all the *îchiaro* men assembled near the ashen remains of the sheep and the surrounding throng of community members. Francis – as representative of all the *îchiaro* men – proceeded to lead a collective cursing session against all unidentified perpetrators, concluding in *kwiita rwîî* style.[12] James, the clan secretary, then recited the list of witchcraft victims, as previously approved by Francis. Finally, three *îchiaro* men – Kobia [14], Kîanîra [2], and Francis [5] – uttered joint curses (see Table 3.1).

---

12 *Kwiita rwîî* literally means 'to cut something with palms'; referring to the single clap given each time the participants finish rubbing their palms together and uttering curses.

Dialogue 3.5 Collective cursing in *kwiita rwîi* style, with audience responses and annotations in square brackets.

James:	Greetings, clan. Greetings, a person who never dies. Greetings, a person who eats his own. Greetings, a person who shoots without causing any harms.[13] Now listen. I believe, as we wrote down [in the list of villagers' troubles], we can't leave them behind. Now what we are going to do is this. We won't read each and every person's name, because we would not sleep (i.e. spend the night) here. It is because we know the issues of our people like our people who were killed, and because we don't know the cause of death. As our advisors have heard everything from us, we shall follow what they say. Then, for those who go round our homestead with wicked ways, we shall leave them here. Those who plant harmful items in our *shamba* (farmlands), we shall curse them. That's the way we should go and those who throw witches into our homestead also shall be cursed. The first thing we want to start with... Where are the elders we were with?
Elder A:	Where are our brothers, please?
Îchiaro men:	We are here.
Elder A:	Let them come in front here.
Elder B:	Please give space for them.
Francis [5]:	Greetings, clan. Greetings again. Now we shall lead you like this. We are your *gîchumi*[14] who have come to kill those who

---

13 The expression, 'a person who shoots without causing any harms' (*muntû ûû ûrathaa itii kaimbe*), or 'a person who knows how to take blood from livestock by using an arrow without hurting its body', implies that the clan can find solutions without hurting its members.

14 *Gîchumi* is often used as a polite term for those *îchiaro* men who are called to visit their counterparts. *Mûtanoba* – literally, 'son from the same father' – is another term

Man who never dies

kill you. Do you see us? Do you know us? [No!] Have you ever seen us in your place again? [No!] Now we are coming for [cursing] the one who kills a person with a stolen club (*nchuuma ya wamba*)[15] and witches, or the one who hides oneself in darkness. Now it's the person we have come to kill. Now for ourselves, we shall start with those ones who are killed completely then you meet a person already dead. We shall start cursing the secrecy of killing others in the darkness. Now, Mr James, start telling us!

James: Let's start with the ones who were killed... [James methodically recites the list of victims.] The one who killed husband to A, the one who killed husband to B, the one who killed C, the one who knows what killed D, the one killed children of E, and the one who killed two children of F.[16]

Elder C: My two children were killed in the year 2013. One was known as G and the other killed in July was known as H. The one who killed eight people of I's family and also others, we don't know. Now we should put them together and curse them. We also curse the one who killed children of J, K, L and M.

Kobia [14]: Don't I see nobody rubbing palms? [Kobia and all participants begin to rub their palms together.] I will know you belong to that team, the ones who finish the clan. Yes, let him go round with the sun, the one who doesn't want to see the prosperity of this clan and who hides himself at night. [Yes!] Yes, his seeds of boys and girls, let them finish there.

---

for an *ichiaro* man (*mwichiaro*). Further, both biological brothers and close friends are addressed and referred to as *mûtanochia* – literally 'son from the same mother'.

15 In this context, 'a stolen club' refers to a harmful item that lies in the hands of the wrong owner or user, and that is also invisible to the community because it has been purloined.

16 I have not added pseudonyms here.

[All clap once in *kwiita rwîî.*] Now step him on the ground. [Uuii!] Now we finished that.

James: Greetings, clan. Greetings again. Now we have come for the one who goes round other people's homesteads at night with witchcraft or what? [With witchcraft!] Now rub your palms. [All rub palms.] Now the one who goes round other people's homesteads at night, or plants witches at other people's homesteads at night, or plants witches at other people's *shamba*, or hides himself at night to cause harm or hides himself at night to harm advisor, his seeds, his cows, boys and girls, his beehives, his millet, let it be cut like this! [*Kwiita rwîî.*]

Kîanîra [2]: Greetings, clan. Greetings again. Where we are going now is the one who makes other people mad. [Yes!] Now I want everyone to rub his palms. [All rub palms.] Now let someone else say. The one who goes round other people's homesteads at night, and the one who confuses children of other people when being at school, his seeds of boys and girls should perish here! [*Kwiita rwîî.*]

Francis [5]: There are some people who make other people to live in hospital because of sickness. Now listen, here we are going, we are going with two things. The one who feels jealous of someone's cow, he goes and meets it on the road grazing, or he sees where the grasses are cut, and he goes and plants something bad so that cow can die, or the one who looks for some witches and hides, so that he takes back because we have left here, so that he can make people sick and always on the hospital way because of sickness. He is fearing to die and we want to finish him here. Let us finish him. Rub your palms. [All rub palms.]

The one who finishes people and makes them live in hospital and making them get lost, and the one who feels jealous of

Man who never dies 73

the neighbour's cow, and the cow doesn't talk, or he cuts the rope of a cow, so that it can go to the neighbour's *shamba* so that they can have cases, his seeds, his cows, his girls and boys, his beehives, let them finish here. [*Kwiita rwîi.*] Is there anything? Those who do business with witches so that they destroy other people's business. Do you want the person set with the sun and this animal which is here? The one who gives the children cannabis so that they can destroy the school instead of the child getting education and the father goes hungry. Now I say, let him take his item alone.

I want us to rub our palms for anyone with his witchcraft to be put down and we should kick him. When we finish rubbing our palms and clap, we shall step on him twice the way we do against the devil with our legs. [*Kwiita rwîi* while stamping on the ground twice.]

Now, Mr Chairman, you know why we are called. We don't leave a person with a problem. The reason why we came here is to unify the clan and we want the clan to stay with peace. Chairman, there's something which has come and I don't want to be disturbed again. Every child is here or even thieves are here. The one whom we shall leave in the bush is the thief without eyes. No members of the clan shall guard *mîraa shamba*. Do you hear me, *gîchumi*?

Îchiaro men: Yes, we shall guard!

Francis [5]: You have seen this with your eyes. If there's a feeling (*mwithûa*)[17] you feel, don't feel it for seven days from today. I want us to clap the last clap. The last clap and that's the end. Now let me show you I want all the *gîchumi* to come

---

17 The term *mwithua* denotes itching or discomfort of the skin as well as, in this context, an itching sexual desire. Participants in the collective cursing were required to refrain from sexual practices for seven days after the event, under the threat of personal misfortune.

Photo 3.7 Collective cursing in the *kwiita rwîî* style

forward here. Now the clan wants to clap against the one who might go back and get witches when we leave here. [Yes!] Now rub your palms. The one who has refused to give us witchcraft, and if he get it back, his seeds of boys and girls, his cow, his millet, his sorghum, let it be like this! [*Kwiita rwîî.*]

The collective cursing concluded at 3.20 pm, with each of the invited *îchiaro* men identifying himself by name, clan affiliation and village of residence. I was also asked to introduce myself and explain why I was observing the ceremony. Some attendees proposed a closing prayer but were informed that cursing (*kûruma*) and prayer were not compatible, as the function of prayer was to give blessings (*kûtharima*), and that would dilute the potency of the curses.

*

Prior to the *ûtaara ngeere* described above, the Antûambui clan held its inaugural general meeting on 1 July 2016, at the homestead of one of its members. Fifty-five people attended for three hours, and an election was held to appoint clan officials, including the chairman, vice-chairman, secretary and treasurer. Participants then discussed enhancements to the role of local security committees (as appointed by administrative chiefs) to prevent *mîraa* theft, terrorism, drug abuse, the production of illicit brew[18] and child abuse. Plans to organise further *ûtaara ngeere* were also considered – to improve community cohesion and heal the psychological wounds of victims of witchcraft. Finally, the committee decided that every male member of the community must contribute 200 shillings towards the organisation of the next ceremony; and every female 100 shillings.

Since the clan's first gathering, committee meetings have usually been held every Thursday, and general meetings on the last Friday of each month. These have adjudicated land boundaries, family and neighbourhood disputes, as well as cases of *mîraa* theft, property damage, assault and incrimination. The meetings follow an agenda and include the sharing of local knowledge. Consistent administrative competence on the part of clan officials is essential, with the huge task of recording minutes – a role assumed by James, the secretary – a prerequisite to the registration and ongoing recognition of the clan as a welfare organisation by the relevant government office. James records the proceedings in English, including statements from complainants, defendants and witnesses, together with the committee's rulings. The format is standardised, and James follows it with much devotion and efficiency.

The second general meeting, which also lasted around three hours, was held on 15 July 2016. One-hundred and sixty-seven members attended. First, the treasurer reported that 25,290 shillings had so far been collected from clan members. Second, the election of ten committee members was held to strengthen the executive body: three women; two

---

18 Both locally brewed millet beer and its distillate are subject to strict controls but are still sold in secret. Mead, on the other hand, may be openly produced, but only with the chief's permission.

men of the Bwantai age-class; five men of the Mîrîti age-class; and two men of the Lubetaa age-class. Next, the committee decided to punish those community members not present and, finally, two invited advisors from the Anjarû clan described their experiences of an *ûtaara ngeere* held on 28 May 2016 (Case 3.2). One reported that the ceremony was well attended while the other advised that the Antûambui should work with the government administration in organising their next *ûtaara ngeere*. After receiving this advice, the clan chairman stated that anybody who had used items related to witchcraft, or any other harmful items, could surrender them on the night before the following ceremony. A committee meeting was then scheduled for 22 July 2016 – subsequently amended to 21 July – and the next general meeting was set for 29 July 2016.

Three invited elders – M'Mauta [7] of the Akachiû clan (see Table 3.1), M'Imaana [17] of the Akachiû (see Table 3.3) and Nchebere of the Akinying'a – attended the 21 July meeting; serving as advisors on indigenous law pertaining to the next *ûtaara ngeere*. The first item on the agenda was to compile a list of *îchiaro* clans for invitation to the ceremony. The visitors advised that Mwithûne village was home to people of thirteen clan origins, and that all residents' biological affiliations should be taken into consideration. The list was completed on this basis. The clan treasurer then reported that 31,090 shillings had so far been collected for the ceremony, and a budget for the event was formulated as follows:

Item	Expenditure (Kenyan shillings)
One he-goat	10,000
One sheep for sacrifice	4,000
Allowance per advisor	200 x 3 (600 total)
Allowance for messengers	500 x 11 (5,500 total)
Committee allowance per member	200 x 15 (3,000 total)
Total expenditure	**23,100**

The he-goat listed was to be slaughtered for a feast for clan members and invited *îchiaro* men the day before the collective cursing. Messenger allowances were for clan members employed to convey formal invitations to *îchiaro* men from outside Mwithûne.

An additional committee meeting, attended by fourteen members, was held on 28 July 2016. There it was agreed that every invited *îchiaro* man should be paid 700 shillings, to include transport costs. One elder reported that the sheep he had been instructed to purchase for sacrifice had cost 500 shillings more than the 4,000 shillings budgeted. Further, the messengers reported that, upon visiting their homesteads, they had paid honorariums to *îchiaro* men, and were duly reimbursed.

The committee decreed that not only local clan members, but also members from outlying villages, should contribute to the ceremony – 200 shillings per male member and 100 shillings per female. They also stipulated that daughters from the village who had married men from neighbouring clans should contribute. Finally, the treasurer suggested their clan should pay 1,000 shillings to obtain a horn to call clan members to the *ûtaara ngeere*.[19]

The final agenda item concerned clan members who had gone missing for unknown reasons. The committee agreed to compile a list of such persons for the *îchiaro* men, who would call them back on the day of the *ûtaara ngeere* (See Dialogue 3.2). Two members reported that they had previously witnessed the return of missing persons after being called home in such a manner.

The third general meeting went ahead on 29 July 2016 and once more lasted three hours. It was attended by 364 clan members: 172 male; 192 female. As the first agenda item, officials were asked: how many days the *îchiaro* men would stay in the village; when clan members should surrender any harmful charms; and what other arrangements had been made for the *ûtaara ngeere*. One clan official answered that a sheep

---

19 Although it is said that every clan should possess its own horn, for this event the Antûambui borrowed one from a neighbouring clan.

Photo 3.8 The horn blown to summon clan members

had been readied for sacrifice and that the *îchiaro* men would stay no more than two days, given that a longer stay would be costly, and that prolonged and close interaction with them – including the sharing of food and water – would diminish their power. Further, the chairman explained that the *îchiaro* men would arrive on the day before the ceremony, and that any witchcraft items should be surrendered on the day they arrived. He then announced that the ceremony had been fixed for 11 August 2016.

Next, the meeting was opened to the floor. One of the elders requested that, now that their clan had been reinvigorated, all members should strive to keep it active. Another elder advised that only those designated Njûrincheke elders who were to attend the *ûtaara ngeere* as *îchiaro* should receive surrendered charms, since ordinary people never knew how to handle harmful items correctly. The chairman then instructed all clan members to bring forward the alleged witchcraft-related cases they wished to be the subject of cursing, and the secretary duly prepared a list of 155 complaints (see Table 3.2). The chairman also announced that all missing persons should be named in advance

*

The Antûambui clan performed *ûtaara ngeere* on 11 August 2016, as planned. The collective cursing did not address all the cases presented because some were unrelated to witchcraft; concerning rather the production and consumption of illicit brew, drug abuse, *mîraa* theft and gambling (see Table 3.2).

A detailed analysis of all the case hearings would require a separate paper, so only one is presented here – with the aim of demonstrating the significance of clan revival in the local social context. This case concerned a dispute between two women – X and Y – both of whom lived in Mwithûne village. X (the complainant) stated that Y (the defendant) had unreasonably prophesied the death of one of her children. X brought the matter to the clan, which summoned Y for questioning, but she failed to appear.

X later read in a public notice that the Njûrincheke council of elders had accepted Y's application for *kîthiri*[20] against anyone who incriminated her as a sorcerer. The clan immediately issued a letter to the council asking them to dismiss this request, as it had been filed without proper process and on unreasonable grounds. The clan also explained that they had already performed *ûtaara ngeere* to curse all ill-wishers in the community, and that Y was one of those irresponsible persons who had refused to attend and jump over the sheep. Y's case for *kîthiri* was subsequently dismissed.

After an *ex parte* hearing of X's case, Y finally accepted the clan's ruling that she must take an oath before her own *îchiaro* and pay a fine (*thiira/mukongoro*) of around 12,000 shillings for repeatedly dishonouring the clan's summons and for filing an unlawful application for *kîthiri*.

---

20 *Kîthiri* is a type of oath (*muuma*), the implementation of which is a secret of the Njûrincheke council. It should not be practised by *nkûrûmbû* (non-Njûrincheke members).

Prior to this case, rumours had already circulated in the neighbourhood associating Y with witchcraft. It was said, for example, that one day a suspicious woman was found prowling the village. When people from the neighbourhood asked where she was from, she replied she came from Kîegoi but, when questioned further, could not properly name the area's chief. The woman had no documents to confirm her identity, and it was decided to escort her to the main road to her destination. However, en route, just in front of Y's residence, the woman suddenly disappeared. The villagers assumed she was a ghost associated with Y, and that Y, in turn, was a witch. To make matters worse, as noted above, on the day of *ûtaara ngeere* Y had not jumped over the sheep – and another rumour was born that she refused to do so because she was in secret possession of witchcraft items.

Both this and Case 3.1, as described above, demonstrate how clan revival has led to the instruction of community members on how to develop claims. Resultantly, the clan as a social group can now mobilise its knowledge and communication network to make organised approaches to both the Njûrincheke council of elders and *îchiaro* men of other clan origins. This development is consonant with the state government's mandate for local, grass-roots administration – as discussed at the end of this chapter.

Cases 3.2 and 3.3: Sharing knowledge of *ûtaara ngeere* with neighbouring communities

This section details how, within the Îgembe region, clans of different origins share their experience and knowledge of *ûtaara ngeere*, and how this contributes to the development of the Îgembe's common law. After the *ûtaara ngeere* in Mwithûne, for example, another village in Gîtûra (from where Kînyiinga [11] originated) organised its own cursing ceremony, and officials from the Antûambui clan – together with chief advisors such as Kîanîra [2] – were invited to attend, to share their learning.

Photo 3.9 A man swearing before the *îchiaro* men in Anjarû (Photo courtesy of M Kobia)

Several other clans had organised *ûtaara ngeere* over the preceding ten years. These include Case 3.3, when, in September 2015, the Antûambeti clan organised a cursing ceremony in a village in Antûbakîîrû, and Case 3.2 when, on 28 May 2016, the Anjarû clan organised a ceremony in Anjarû village. On 18 August 2017, I interviewed Karea, chairman of the Anjarû clan, who organised both the latter *ûtaara ngeere* and a previous one in the late 2000s (the date of which is not clearly remembered) and who has also been called upon to share his experience.

Karea is the pastor of a Christian Methodist church and a member of the Lubetaa age-class. He is highly knowledgeable of his clan's history. In September 2015 (Case 3.3, cited above), he was invited to stitch up the orifices of a sacrificial sheep at the Antûambeti's *ûtaara ngeere* – their clan having been affected by more than twenty deaths from various diseases within one year. As noted earlier, the Antûambui also invited Karea as an advisor to their second clan meeting on 15 July 2016.

Table 3.3 *Îchiaro* men invited to Anjarû on 28 May 2016 (Nos. continued from Table 3.1)

No.	Invited *îchiaro* men (age-class)	Clan (village)	*Îchiaro* counterparts in Anjarû village
17	M'Imaana (Mîchûbû)	Akachiû (Nthare)	Anjarû, Aîri
18	Kamundî (Ratanya)	Antûbalînkî (Kîraone)	Anjarû
19	Kabeeria (Lubetaa)	Aîri (Amung'enti)	Anjarû, Bwethaa
20	Kîrere (Lubetaa)	Antûambeti (Antûbakîîrû)	Antûamûtî
21	M'Mûkaria (Mîchûbû)	Antûambui (Kîrîmampio)	Akinying'a
22	Kûbai (Lubetaa)	Athimba (Nkaria)	Andûûne
23	Mbiti (Mîrîti)	Andûûne (Gîtûra)	Athimba
24	Reuben (Mîrîti)	Antûbakîthoro (Kîrîmene)	Amwari
25	Ntaamû (Ratanya)	Îrotia (Kîrîmene)	Akîthîî
26	Ntorûrû (Lubetaa)	Ncheme (Gîteretu)	Amunjû
27	Kîrîambûri (Ratanya)	Amunjû (Ntheuka)	Ncheme
28	Ndatû (Ratanya)	Bwethaa (Ntheuka)	Aîri

Karea told me he had counselled the Antûambeti that there was no conflict between Kîmîîrû customs and Christianity. He also informed the clan that many of his community's members had failed to give up charms at the meeting held prior to their *ûtaara ngeere*, but that one man was said to have surrendered a harmful item for which he had paid around 300,000 shillings.[21]

In compiling the list of *îchiaro* men for invitation to the 28 May 2016 *ûtaara ngeere* in Anjarû (see Table 3.3), Karea and other officials had considered the biological status of all village members – clarifying clan affiliations, including those of agnatic members and their wives, as well

---

21 It was rumoured that the man bought the item, the nature of which remained undisclosed, from someone outside Kenya. One of his children was then born with a congenital illness and it was assumed that the item had harmful power. The man decided to surrender the item to the elders but, it was said, his prayers went unanswered, and the child died in 2016.

as migrants of other clan origins. Karea recalled for me the names and clan affiliations of those on the list.

Tables 3.1 and 3.3 reveal further instances of repeat invitations for experienced *îchiaro* men to attend this *ûtaara ngeere*.

Kîanîra [2] and Mûturi [9] were invited by the Anjarû clan to participate in the May 2016 *ûtaara ngeere*, and again by the Antûambui in August 2016. Mbiti [23] of the Andûûne clan and Reuben [24] of the Antûbakîthoro (both pseudonyms, as these two men appear later in more sensitive contexts) were among six *îchiaro* men invited to attend another cursing ceremony in September 2012, to solve problems observed within a Mûringene village family (Case 5.10, Chapter 5).

The following are additional examples of repeat invitations for *îchiaro* men to attend *ûtaara ngeere*.

When the Akachiû clan in Nthare organised their ceremony in the late 1990s, both M'Imaana and M'Mauta served as clan officials. They were subsequently invited, in May 2016 (Case 3.2), as *îchiaro* men to the Anjarû's *ûtaara ngeere*, and then as chief advisors to the Antûambui, as they prepared for their ceremony in August 2016 (Case 3.1).

In Case 3.2, Kîanîra [2] and Mûturi [9] were invited as *îchiaro* men, and later assumed key roles in Case 3.1; while Francis from the Antûamboa clan attended as an *îchiaro* man at four *ûtaara ngeere* before being invited by the Antûambui in Case 3.1.

The repeat invitations indicate that some individuals – often elders – are regarded as more powerful *mwîchiaro* than others (see Chapter 5), and thus suitable to share their experiences of *ûtaara ngeere* with clans from other administrative locations and divisions. During this process, they are also able to share their knowledge of indigenous law throughout the Îgembe region, and so nurture both certainty and flexibility in its application.

As discussed in Chapter 5, no given *mwîchiaro* should either imagine that he has been invited to an *ûtaara ngeere* in a private capacity, or

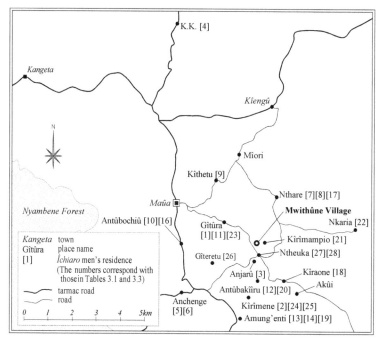

Figure 3.1 Home communities of the invited *îchiaro* men

that he can use his power for personal interest – rather, the power of the *îchiaro* men is attributed only to their biological status.[22]

Further, having provided advice on procedures they have witnessed in the past, experienced elders do not force host communities to repeat them. Rather, they practise flexibility in ritual processes, appropriate to

---

22 One *îchiaro* man was killed in a road accident in 2016, soon after the *ûtaara ngeere* in Anjarû. It was rumoured his death was due to his misuse of *îchiaro* power at the ceremony. Some believed he had received cash in exchange for overlooking someone's hidden possession of witchcraft items. It is also said that an elder of the Antûbalînkî clan, whose brother was one of the invited *îchiaro* men in the May 2016 *ûtaara ngeere*, died due to his abuse of power. The elder was sent by an Anjarû clan member to recover a debt from a man of the same clan – on the basis that the claim could not be refused as it had been incurred by an *îchiaro*. However, the elder apparently accepted a bribe from the debtor not to curse him, even if he failed to re-pay his debt. Another death was reported after an *ûtaara ngeere* in Anjarû – it was said that a woman died because her husband refused to jump over the sheep sacrificed on 28 May.

the nature and context of the problems they are asked to address. For example, M'Mauta [7] of the Akachiû clan noted differences between his experiences with the Antûambui clan in Mwithûne in 2016 (Case 3.1) and three other cases: Anjarû in May 2016 (Case 3.2), Antûambeti in September 2015 (Case 3.3), and his own natal clan in the late 1990s (Case 3.4). M'Mauta reported that, in the latter cases, the sacrificed sheep was not placed on the fire until the *îchiaro* men had interrogated every member of the community, each member had sworn that he or she possessed no harmful items, and each member had literally 'passed over' (*ûtaara*) the sacrificed animal. Conversely, in Mwithûne, the community members actually 'passed by' the sheep; doing so *after* it had been reduced to ashes. Several other of my interviewees have reported similar variations.

Case 3.4: Clan revival in Akachiû

This chapter has so far demonstrated *ûtaara ngeere* as either a means to instigate an entire clan's revival, or simply a short-term method of addressing the woes of a particular community. In an entirely different case, the Akachiû clan in Nthare underwent *ûtaara ngeere* in the late 1990s (Case 3.4) but did not engage in organisational reform or clan revival until 2013 – in response to several deaths in the community, which necessitated a structured response. These deaths had been attributed to events that, according to several elders, occurred around one hundred years earlier.

The story goes that Kibire, a man of the previous Gîchûnge age-class,[23] decided to migrate to Athîrû Rûûjîne, taking with him several head of cattle from Nthare. However, after Kibire's arrival, his agnate Nkarichia – who was of the same age-class – decided to return one bull to Nthare. Despite warnings from the Athîrû Rûûjîne *îchiaro* to keep the

---

23 According to my schematic calculation (See Chapter 2, Table 2.2), the previous Gîchûnge age-class was first circumcised in 1885.

bull alive, Nkarichia slaughtered it for meat, which he shared with his agnates – in the knowledge that disobeying instructions could lead to a curse.

In 2013, the Akachiû concluded that Nkarichia's disobedience, and the resulting curse, had led to the current spate of deaths. Their chairman – Mwasimba of the Mîrîti age-class – discussed how to remedy this suffering and, under his leadership, the clan arranged to confess their sin and return a bull to their *îchiaro* in compensation for past sins, as well as to purchase another animal for an inter-clan feast. Mwasimba was anxious about the expense of contributing two bulls, together with other items for cleansing and blessing purposes, but decided to proceed nonetheless.

On 18 April 2013, a horn was blown to announce the Akachiû's inaugural clan meeting. By the end of June, enough money had been collected to purchase the two bulls, and in August they invited their *îchiaro* counterparts from Anjarû to lead the reparation, cleansing and blessing. Ever since, the Akachiû have continued to hold meetings for their own welfare – the clan having been revived as the result of a fundraising drive.

The Akachiû organised themselves as the Akachiû Clan Welfare CBO (community-based organisation), in order to register at the appropriate government office. Meetings were thenceforward held on the 15th and 30th day of each month, to hear disputes, make public announcements, engage in discussions and share information – in the same vein as the Antûambui clan. Each member of the clan was also issued with a certificate.[24]

The Akachiû have since invited their *îchiaro* counterparts from the Anjarû, Aîri and Naathû clans to attend the second meeting of the month, in order to curse ill-wishers within their communities. I attended one such meeting on 30 August 2016, which was announced by sounding a horn at the Kaani-ka-Gîchûnge open field. I was then handed a printed

---

24 Since membership is open to all willing neighbours, regardless of their biological clan affiliation, I was granted ordinary membership at the August 2016 meeting.

Photo 3.10 The Akachiû clan meeting on 30 August 2016

Photo 3.11 The author gives a speech at the Akachiû clan meeting

copy of the timetable, with the redressal of witchcraft-related cases reported by clan members as the main item. Three *îchiaro* men performed collective cursing in the *kwiita rwîî* style. These included an elder brother to Karea (the above-mentioned chairman of the Anjarû clan in Athîrû Gaiti) and Ntuala [3]. As a visitor, I was offered the opportunity to address the participants.

Decentralised agencies in clan revival: Historical lessons

As previously discussed, *ûtaara ngeere* are highly organised events, requiring strong leadership. They may be held simply for remedial purposes, as with the Anjarû and Antûambeti clans (Cases 3.2 and 3.3), or to initiate organisational reform and clan revival, as with the Antûambui clan (Case 3.1). Further, clan revival may be initiated without *ûtaara ngeere*, as with the Akachiû clan (Case 3.4). The concluding section of this chapter addresses the nature of the leadership behind both *ûtaara ngeere* and clan revivals, and the role of various chiefs in this process.

In addition to community members and invited *îchiaro* men, the three *ûtaara ngeere* held in the 2010s – by the Antûambui, Anjarû and Antûambeti (Cases 3.1, 3.2, and 3.3) – were all attended by administrative chiefs. I observed that these men – whose permission was required to organise any meeting, and who undoubtedly supported the events' organising leaders – were more deeply involved in the cursing ceremonies than they would have been in ordinary meetings.

M'Mauta ([7] in Table 3.1) reported to me that he understood all the above *ûtaara ngeere* to have been organised by administrative chiefs, in cooperation with the clan communities. Indeed, the Antûambui invited their area chief, as well as three assistant chiefs of their own and neighbouring sublocations, to their ceremony, with only one failing to attend. Further, the Anjarû held their *ûtaara ngeere* in an open field in front of the assistant chief's office, while the Antûambeti's ceremony was arranged on the initiative of an administrative chief within the Îgembe Southeast Division.

One of the assistant chiefs, who delivered an opening speech at the Antûambui's *ûtaara ngeere*, told me the government administration supports such grassroots initiatives, as they may contribute to peacemaking in local villages. He also indicated they were consonant with the Nyumba Kumi community policing programme, as reintroduced by the Kenyan government in 2013[25] – in accordance with statutory provisions

---

25 According to the *4th Draft Guidelines on Community Policing*, the initiative was first launched in April 2005 by the Kenyan Government. Notably, a government

of the National Police Service Act. The main goals of the programme are the 'elimination of the fear of crime and social disorder, through joint problem solving and prevention of crime' (Kenya 2015, 4).

This did not constitute a new approach on the authorities' part, as administrative chiefs, for example, had historically worked collaboratively with people at the grassroots level for security purposes by appointing their subordinates – called 'sub-areas' – from local residents. It is also debatable whether the Nyumba Kumi community policing programme is literally a community based initiative, given that studies (many focusing on urban settings) have found that, since its introduction in the 1990s, it may have served only to reproduce or reinforce the undemocratic nature of directed community security (Ruteere and Pommerolle 2003; Matsuda 2016).

Policing in Africa is generally 'not a monopoly of government', but rather 'a complex pattern of overlapping policing agencies' (Baker 2004, 218 & 205). Undoubtedly, the authority of chiefs and assistant chiefs facilitated the strong leadership necessary for the organisation of the *ûtaara ngeere* in Cases 3.1, 3.2, and 3.3. However, the revivals of the Antûambui and Akachiû clans should not be predominantly attributed to the chiefs' authority, but rather more to the continuous everyday efforts and personal competence of new leaders from within the clan communities; especially those of the Mîrîti age-class. As noted in the previous chapter, the Mîrîti has been the ruling elderhood in the entire Îgembe community since August 2014 and, by my observation, the Antûambui and Akachiû clans' revivals would have been impossible without the commitment of their respective Mîrîti leaders – James and Mwasimba.

---

journal, *The Administrator*, includes a review of community policing in its first issue, published in January 2008 (Kenya 2008). According to Ruteere and Pommerolle (2003, 594–595), the concept of community policing had been mentioned in police reports as early as the 1990s. The Kenyan government began to introduce local peace committees (LPCs) at the village level in the late 2000s (mainly after the 2007 to 2008 post-election violence), the mandates of which were initially different from but 'increasingly conflated with', the Nyumba Kumi community policing programmes (Kioko 2017, 28).

Strong emerging leadership is a prerequisite to clan revival and the development of self-determined, democratic and sustainable community policing. The Antûambui and Akachiû clan communities now enjoy such leadership, and it seems this *is* associated with greater local political autonomy. For example, one Antûambui young man was elected as a member of the county assembly (MCA) in the August 2017 general election, standing against ten other candidates in the Athîrû Gaiti ward. This young man, in his late twenties, was of the Gîchûnge age-class and his grandfather was once the assistant chief of the then Thaichû Sublocation (the present Îgembe Southeast Division). He alone had been given the opportunity to make a speech following those of Mûturi [9] and the administrative chiefs at Mwithûne village's *ûtaara ngeere* opening ceremony. Although further observation may be needed to qualify this, it seems it was the revival of the Antûambui clan that led to clan members' organised support to the young man and his success at a competitive election.

Although the Antûambui and Akachiû have both revived and strengthened their clans to improve their welfare, neither their communities nor their officials have sought socio-political supremacy over their neighbours. Rather, they have relearned lessons from the past, involving their ancestors' exploitation and harm of neighbours, which may have been overt, covert, unconscious or even in ignorance of shared *îchiaro* relationships. All such misdeeds, the Antûambui and Akachiû have concluded, backfire, leading to retribution against and serious misfortune befalling those responsible, together with their family members – either via *îchiaro* or other forms of cursing. Indeed, the clans now openly share knowledge of past harm and retribution, including the following three cases, as related by the Antûambui:

I) One day in the 1970s, the Antûambui clan invited their *îchiaro* men from Akinying'a to settle a case. They erected a clan house and slaughtered a he-goat as part of the usual preparations for the *îchiaro*'s reception. However, it was soon observed that one portion of the meat was missing. An announcement was made that the thief would be cursed if he or she failed to confess. No-one confessed. The community was aware that a man had stepped into the clan house on the previous night, but he was not suspected since he was believed to be of high integrity. The *îchiaro* men then uttered cursing words against the unidentified culprit and, two days later, the 'man of integrity' was found bleeding, having been pierced by a tree stump. He was rushed to a hospital in Maûa and, en route, confessed to stealing the meat. He later died from his haemorrhages.

II) A man from the Antûambui clan visited an *îchiaro* counterpart from the Akinying'a clan. Although the host had mead in his home, he did not wish to share it since there was not enough to go around. A few days later, one of the Akinying'a man's sons developed a mental illness. The father sought advice from the clan elders and learned the sickness had been caused by *îchiaro*. He then admitted to not sharing his mead. The elders instructed him to invite the Antûambui man back, along with other Antûambui *îchiaro*, to cure his son. The host then slaughtered a he-goat and brewed mead in preparation for his guests. Upon receiving his invitation, the Antûambui man said he did not want many others to be present, since he wanted to keep the sharing of the meat and mead to a minimum. He then took the victuals inside his host's house, to feast alongside several of his own friends – to the exclusion of the Akinying'a clan. In anger, the Akinying'a shouted, 'Let the man from Antûambui remain locked inside his house!' After returning home, the Antûambui man indeed locked himself in his own house, remaining there for six months. At long last he was removed by force, but died within a few months.

III) A man from the Antûambui clan visited a friend from the Akachiû clan. On his way home, he suddenly felt the need to defecate, and requested the latrine key at a nearby canteen. The owners, however, refused him; suspecting him to be a man of questionable character who intended to install a harmful charm inside the latrine. The man's resolve eventually failed and he defecated in front of the building. The canteen owners forced him to remove his own waste and, ashamed at having to carry it, he threatened to bewitch his humiliators. Frightened by his threats, the owners reported the matter to their clan, requesting a solution. The clan then summoned the Antûambui man for interrogation but, when he failed to appear, invited an *îchiaro* man from Akinying'a to curse him. The man soon developed a mental disorder, and eventually died.

*

This chapter has examined clan revival – instigated in the name of peace and social unity – among farming communities of Îgembe Southeast Division. I have focused on two *ûtaara ngeere* (collective cursing ceremonies) organised to remove unidentified sorcerers from the Antûambui and Akachiû clans' neighbourhoods and, in a wider context, initiate their revival under the leadership of the Mîrîti age-class. This process has accommodated the Kenyan government's community policing programme which, introduced in 2013, aimed to enhance security at grassroots level and contribute to local political autonomy (the polar opposite occurred during the COVID-19 pandemic: see the Postscript for a discussion of the Numba Kumi incident on 24 August 2021).

My research has shown that the socio-political power achieved via clan revival is decentralised in the local context. Although the authority of government appointed chiefs has facilitated the organisation of *ûtaara ngeere,* this is not the predominant factor behind the Antûambui and Akachiû revivals. Rather, they have succeeded due to the continuous efforts of new leaders within the clan communities. Further, those leaders have learned from history that, if they do not behave altruistically in both local and wider contexts, their achievements will come at a heavy price.

Chapter 4
The Athimba: Fifteen years of clan making in a local context

This chapter explores, at grassroots level, the various factors involved during fifteen years of clan-making among the Athimba, focusing on the homicide compensation system in Mûringene village. The concluding sections also consider political and socio-cultural influences – specifically the Njûrincheke chairmanship of the entire Îgembe community, land distribution legislation and a conflict over the ownership of Athîrû Gaiti's largest public dispensary.

Under Kenyan criminal law, homicide is an offence to be prosecuted and judged in the state law courts. However, the concerned parties may seek additional means to achieve peace and justice, especially when homicide occurs between neighbours within a locality.[1] In the cases I observed from 2001 to 2015, the agnatic Athimba clan was involved as a responsible party in receiving and paying compensation under the indigenous law of the Îgembe.[2] Athimba elders emphasise that indigenous law prohibits any individual from settling homicide compensation by private transaction – the clan is the only legitimate entity authorised to handle reparations.

---

1 See Appendix 1 for discussion of social contexts and conditions of homicide, and provisions for homicide compensation under Kenyan law.
2 Lambert (1956, 115–120), Middleton and Kershaw (1965), Rimita (1988, 76–77) and M'Imanyara (1992, 91–93) have described homicide compensation in the greater Amîîrû community. Although the above works provide information relevant to this chapter, they are too generalised to be directly applicable. I agree with Richard Abel's critical comment on rule-oriented approaches and his claims concerning the case method – e.g., 'Few, if any, of the numerous ethnographic accounts contain any descriptions of actual cases. Either investigators failed to observe or to inquire about cases, or else they deleted all information about the actual controversies from their reports' (Abel 1969, 574). However, where Abel's case-oriented research on customary law focuses on court records, my research explores cases at the grassroots level. Abel's comment was made with reference to Charles Dundas's documentation of homicide compensation among the Bantu-speaking communities of the Kenyan central highlands (Dundas 1915; see also Dundas 1921).

In total, I observed four cases of homicide compensation (*kûrea kîongo* – literally 'to pay a head') in the Athîrû Gaiti community. This chapter details Cases 4.1, 4.2 and 4.3, with Case 5.1 presented in Chapter 5. The cases vary in terms of the victims' social status. Case 4.1, which transpired between 2001 and 2002, concerned the murder of an agnate, with the Athimba due to receive compensation from the offender's clan. Case 4.2, in 2011, addressed the murder of a woman from another clan, with the Athimba due to pay compensation to her natal family. An Athimba agnate was injured in the same incident and the reconciliation of 'brothers' became a central issue in maintaining clan solidarity. Cases 4.3 and 5.1, in 2013 and 2015, concerned the murder of a second-generation immigrant from other clans who had long been assimilated into the Athimba. It is quite common in Îgembe for an agnatic clan to include members from various backgrounds, and the involvement of allcomers in clan affairs imparts a reflexive sense of solidarity.

For various reasons, the three cases illustrated in this chapter were discontinued without reaching their final stage – as opposed to Case 5.1. In Case 4.2 the victim's family declined compensation – claiming instead some outstanding bride-price items – while in Cases 4.1 and 4.3 a number of intra-clan disagreements resulted in the abandonment of proceedings.

In all cases, the Athimba organised the compensation process via inter-clan negotiation, and in cooperation with the Îgembe's other two indigenous institutions: the *îchiaro* brotherhood and the Njûrincheke council of elders. During this activity, the Athimba accumulated knowledge of indigenous law while also developing a sense of clanship – in the context of a widely shared structural history and the regional politics of the Îgembe community.

Introduction to Mûringene village

Located in Athîrû Gaiti, upper Îgembe Southeast Division, Mûringene village consists of around 40 households. Although the Athimba clan appears dominant (Figure 4.1 and Table 4.1 show Athimba clan households only), families of other clan affiliations also reside there. In general, agnatic clans are not localised in Îgembe and branches may be found over a wide area, as the result of minor migrations. All branches of a clan retain their original names. Thus, members of the Athimba, for example, are ubiquitous in the Îgembe and even Tigania communities.[3] Some Athimba who have tracked the migration of their relatives may maintain inter-regional communication with other branches. Generally, clan meetings within a given locality attract members from the same neighbourhood.[4]

Athimba members in Mûringene village sometimes refer to themselves as *nyumba-ya*-Mwitari or *mûchiî-jwa*-Mwitari (literally, 'Mwitari's house' – meaning 'Mwitari's offspring'). However, Mwitari is not their common ancestor, but one of the wealthy agnates of the former Bwantai age-class who were circumcised in the late 19th century. The Athimba people of Mûringene do not constitute an independent lineage founded by a single ancestor. Rather, its members come from various families whose genealogical links are untraceable.

Mûringene village, which is now densely populated, was widely open to immigration until the 1950s. For example, an elder of the Akinying'a clan and Mîchûbû age-class purchased land from the Ncheme clan in 1951 and migrated from his natal village to Mûringene.[5] Another elder, of the Antûamûtî clan and Lubetaa age-class, remembers that his grandfather (of the former Gîchûnge age-class) was allocated land by an elder of the Ncheme clan, in recognition of their friendship. The amity between the two families continued over the generations, and one of the beneficiary's

---

3   Goldsmith (1995, 29–30) notes, 'Culturally homogenous clans cluster into tribes, but clan relations with other groups can transcend tribe.'
4   Clan meetings in Mûringene village, for example, summon members from within the Athîrû Gaiti community.
5   This man's wife is a cousin (father's brother's daughter: FBD) of M'Lichoro (H29), who is an Athimba elder of another village. M'Lichoro was involved in the homicide compensation processes observed from 2001 to 2002 (Case 4.1) and in 2013 (Case 5.1).

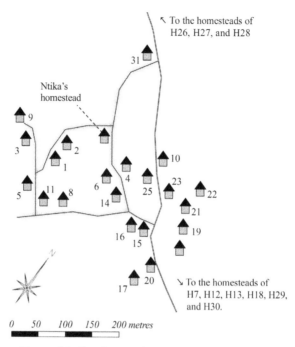

Figure 4.1 Sketch map of Mûringene village, 2012
Note: This map shows the households of Athimba clan members only

sons assumed the role of *îthe-wa-njûri* (literally, 'Njûrincheke father' – meaning 'supervisor of the Njûrincheke initiation') to the donor's son.

Figure 4.1 and Table 4.1 include only agnates and migrants who were given land in Mûringene by the Athimba; they do not include non-Athimba residents and migrants. Nchee (H20) and his brothers (see Table 4.1), including Kîberenge (H19), Mwaambia (H21) and Meeme (H22), are second-generation migrants from the Antûambûi clan of Laare, which is *îchiaro* to the Athimba (see Figure 1.1). Although more than 60 years have passed since their father M'Ikîrîma's migration, Athimba clan members still remember the brothers' biological origin and fear them because of their indelible *îchiaro* relationship (see Chapter 5 for further discussion).

When Mûringene's Athimba clan members call a meeting, they summon both local agnates and those from other villages in Athîrû Gaiti.

The Athimba   97

Table 4.1 Athimba households in Mûringene village and its neighbourhood, 2012

No	Branch	Husband's profile			Wife's clan	Land properties by means of acquisition (acres)			
		Age-class	Circumcision year	Marriage		Inheritance	Purchase	Clan	Other
1	A	I	Lubetaa	1959	1968	Anjarû	3	1	5	0
2			Mîrîti	1976	1991	Antûanthama	4.5	0.25	4	2
3			Mîrîti	1985	1990	Amwari	4	0	15	0
4			Mîrîti	1984	1996	Antûambeti	2.75	0	0	0
5		II	Mîchûbû	–	–	Antûambeti	2	0	0	0
6			Lubetaa	1959	–	Antûborîî	1.25	0.5	0.25	0
7			Lubetaa	1959	1975	[Gîkûyû]	0.25	2.5	3.5	0
8			Lubetaa	1966	1973	Akinying'a	4.5	0	0	0
9		III	Lubetaa	1966	1974 1990	Amwathi –	3.5	0	0.5	0
10			Mîrîti	–	1980	Amwari	2	0.1	0	0
11			Mîrîti	1985	1990	Antûambeti	0.5	4.25	1.5	0
12		IV	Lubetaa	1965	1985	Bwethaa	7	0	3	0
13			Lubetaa	1972	1982	Amakûû	3	3	0	0
14	B		Ratanya	1957	1967	Akachiû	5.5	0	2.5	0
15			Ratanya	1949	1952 1969	Antûbalînkî Antûamûtî	25	0	0	0
16			Bwantai	–	–	–	13.5	0	0	0
17			Lubetaa	1965	1972	Antûamûtî	3	0.5	10	0.75
18			Mîrîti	1975	1993 1998	Anjarû [Tigania]	6	0	0	0
19	Migrant 1		Lubetaa	–	–	Antûamûliûki	1	0	0	0
20			Lubetaa	1959	1978 1984	Akinying'a Anjarû	1	3	2	0
21			Lubetaa	1962	1977	Antûamûtî	0.5	1	0	0
22			Mîrîti	1976	1982	Antûambeti	4	0	1.5	0
23	Migrant 2		Ratanya	1948	1956 1968	Bwethaa Athimba	0	9.5	0	0
24	Migrant 3		Lubetaa	–	–	Bwethaa	2.5	1.5	0	0
25	C		Ratanya	1954	1963	Antûambeti	5	0	0	0
26			Ratanya	1957	1973	Antûbochiû	3	1	4	0.5
27	D		Ratanya	1948	1957	Akachiû	8	3	1	0
28			Ratanya	1954	1961	Antûambeti	10	0	0	12
29	E		Ratanya	–	1950s	Amwari Antûbaiga	3.5	0	9.5	2
30			Lubetaa	1964	1968	Antûbalînkî	0	4	0.5	0.5
31	F		Mîrîti	1976	1990	Antûambui	0.5	0	–	0

Notes:
(1) This table includes some Athimba households beyond Mûringene village; limited to families included in Chapters 4 and 5's case studies.
(2) H20 refers to the husband/male head of household no. 20. All the husbands were alive at the time of research, except for H5, whose widow was the head of her homestead.
(3) The Athimba clan in Mûringene has several branches whose genealogical relations are relatively unknown. The four members of branch A-I are biological brothers. H6, H7 and H8 are the biological sons of H5 (deceased), who is the father's father's brother's son (FFBS) of H1, H2, H3 and H4. H9, H10 and H11 are biological brothers and FFBSS of H1, H2, H3 and H4. The genealogical relationships between A and B are unknown.
(4) Age-class affiliation and circumcision years in this table are based on my interviews with villagers. I have noticed, but not resolved, inconsistencies between data in this table and those in Table 2.2, in terms of the relationship between age-class affiliation and circumcision year.
(5) H19, H20, H21, H22, H23 and H24 are migrants of other clan origin who have been assimilated into the local Athimba host clan.
(6) Gîkûyû and Tigania, in the square brackets, are the names of ethnic groups. The wives' clan names are unknown.

Elders such as M'Barûngû (the father of H12 and H13) and M'Lichoro (H29), for example, are from the lower slope, while Mûteethia (H26) hails from the north-western end. When a third party is needed from either the Antûambûi or Andûûne *ichiaro* clans (or from both), Ngatûnyi – Nchee's father's brother's son (FBS) – of the Antûambûi clan in Laare, or Mpuria and Mbiti of the Andûûne, are often invited. On several occasions, when the Athimba elders have met to discuss demanding problems, Ngatûnyi has been summoned as a representative of the Antûambûi clan whose opinions should be listened to, respected and followed (see also Chapters 5 and 7).

Case 4.1: First experience of homicide compensation

In the 1980s, Îkundi of the Aîri clan killed another young man – Mûtwîri of the Athimba. Both were residents of Athîrû Gaiti. Following the official law courts' verdict, Îkundi was sentenced to around ten years in prison. However, despite the sentence, the victim's kin still required Îkundi's relatives to pay compensation. The two parties were close neighbours and the restoration of their relationship was more important to them than the legal punishment.

This case illustrates how homicide compensation was claimed and awarded under indigenous Îgembe law. It also shows how the substance of the compensation was established, and how the concerned parties organised themselves. The case represents the first time in fifty years that the Athimba clan of Mûringene village was party to the homicide compensation process. Given the novelty of their involvement, the Athimba invited a well-known Kîmîîrû expert from a distant village, who was well experienced in such matters. Kîthia (H3) of the Mîrîti age-class – secretary of the Athimba clan – documented every detail of the proceedings, and the clan record became an important source of information during subsequent cases in 2013 and 2015.

Kûrea kîongo

Case 4.1 came to my attention on 11 October 2001 when, during an interview, an Athimba elder mentioned an ongoing homicide compensation process in which he was involved. I closely followed proceedings until early January 2002 and was then absent for a period of seven months, after which I resumed my research. Because Kîthia (H3) had kept handwritten records of the compensation transactions, I was able to form a comprehensive understanding of the process. Table 4.2 provides a chronology of the case, which took almost twelve months to resolve.

As illustrated above, each transaction has a particular Kîmîîrû name. In general, homicide compensation is called *kûrea kîongo*, which means 'to pay the head [of a murdered person]'.[6] When a person of clan 'A' kills a person of clan 'B' an inter-clan compensation process arises, with four mutual requirements:

(1) Elders must represent both clans.

(2) Clan houses must be built to accommodate the elders of each clan.

(3) Appointed messengers (*atûngûri*) must conduct mediation between the parties.

(4) The Njûrincheke council of elders must be consulted.

In this case, the Athimba built a clan house at Ntika's (the victim's father's) homestead (see Figure 4.1) to show clan unity, but the Aîri built nothing. The absence of a second clan house caused controversy among the elders, who belonged to neither clan, but nobody else showed much concern; being more occupied with a speedy resolution. Since the Athimba's clan house served limited purpose, it was built simply, with a cover of banana leaves and corrugated steel sheets.

---

6 '*Kîongo*' means 'head', while '*kûrea*' means 'to pay'. In his personal communication, Stephen A. Mûgambi Mwithimbû noted that *kûrea nyamuurû* means 'to pay compensation'. Elders of Mûringene village explained that *kûrea nyamuurû* is required as compensation for the theft of goods, such as livestock. *Kûrea tharike* ('to pay blood') is a general term for compensation paid after inflicting a bodily injury.

Table 4.2 Chronology of homicide compensation, August 2001 to August 2002

Date	Process
3 August 2001	**First transaction**: Messengers (*atûngûri*) from the Aîri (paying party) bring a she-goat (*mparika ya ûtumûra moota*) to the Athimba (recipient party).
8 August	[Athimba] Each clan member contributes 200 shillings for preparation fees and builds a clan house (*nyumba ya mwîrîa*) in which 18 elders spend their first night.
14 October	[Aîri] First meeting to organise the fundraising committee.
24 October	[Athimba] Clan meeting to achieve unity (*ngwantanîro*).
28 October	[Aîri] Committee meeting to prepare for a fundraising party.
18 November	[Aîri] Fundraising party.
24 November	[Aîri] A representative purchases animals (a ram, a ewe, a she-goat and a heifer) at the Kangeta livestock market. [Athimba] Clan meeting to discuss elders' complaints.
25 November	[Athimba] A ceremony to bless their unity (*kwîkîra nyumba mûkolo*), performed by elders.
26 November	[Aîri] A representative purchases a bull at the Kangeta livestock market.
29 November	[Aîri] Kalûma, a *Kîmîîrû* expert, visits Athîrû Gaiti.
5 December	**Second Transaction**: Messengers bring a ram (*ntûrûme ya ûtûria ina mukuû nyumba*) and a ewe to the Athimba clan.
7 December	**Third Transaction** (*nkiria*): Messengers bring a bull, a heifer and a she-goat to the Athimba.
18 December	[Aîri and Athimba] Joint meeting to discuss the payment process.
27 December	**Fourth Transaction**: A bull (*ndewa ya ûkundia rûûî*) is brought and slaughtered at a joint feast.
15 March 2002	[Aîri and Athimba] Advisors of both clans visit the Njûrincheke council at Athîrû Gaiti to discuss payment of *rûraachio* (the main part of homicide compensation).
22 March	[Aîri and Athimba] Both parties attend Njûrincheke meeting.
6 June	**Fifth Transaction**: A cow, a bull and a she-goat are paid as *rûraachio*.
20 June	**Sixth Transaction**: A cow, a bull and a she-goat are paid as *rûraachio*.
3 July	**Seventh Transaction**: A cow, a bull and a she-goat are paid as *rûraachio*.
August	[Athimba] Elders leave the clan house.

The transaction process consisted of two phases: preliminary payments and main reparation (*rûraachio*).[7] The first to fourth transactions in the above table represent the former, while the fifth to seventh represent the latter. Strictly speaking, the first phase transactions do not count as part of the compensation, but rather as a necessary preliminary to *rûraachio* – fulfilling the need to first restore relations between the two parties.

The four animals required as payment during the first phase are as follows:[8]

(1) *mparika ya ûtumûra moota* ('a she-goat to lay down a bow' or 'to be disarmed').

(2) *ntûrûme ya ûtûria ina mûkuû nyumba* ('a ram to bring the mother out of the house').

(3) *nkiria* ('a milking cow to comfort the mother').

(4) *ndewa ya ûkundia rûûî* ('a bull to give water').

The above list is flexible and variations may occur according to circumstances – e.g., when a homicide is committed *within* a clan, a bull and a cow may be paid to the victim's *muntwetû* (mother's brother). Further, the substance of any given payment may be subject to negotiation between the two parties, as illustrated in the following section.

---

7 The noun *rûraachio* is derived from the verb *kûraachia*, meaning 'to bring livestock' [as in a bride price]. The main part of homicide compensation is also termed *rûraachio*.

8 In the first, second and fourth instances, the sex of the requisite animals is clear: *mparika* means 'she-goat'; *ntûrûme* means 'ram'; *ndewa* means 'bull'. The *nkiria* of the third payment does not literally refer to a particular type or sex of animal. However, many elders believe that a combination of a milking cow and a calf constitutes *nkiria* in homicide compensation (see Rimita 1988, 76), and I have followed this definition.

A cow without a name: Elders debate compensation items

On 7 December 2001, the messengers (*atûngûri*) from the Aîri clan brought a small bull, a heifer and a she-goat to offer as compensation items (see Table 4.2). This caused controversy among the Athimba elders, who argued that, at the current stage of transactions, a payment should have been made of a milking cow and a calf, as *nkiria*, and that this stage had been omitted. The elders maintained that if the payment of *rûraachio* (the main part of homicide compensation) had already commenced, the animals brought by the messengers would have been appropriate – as *rûraachio* consists of a bull, a cow and a she-goat. On 18 December, the representatives of both parties held a meeting to discuss this point. The Athimba invited Îkotha – a famous Kîmîîrû expert (*mûkirîra*) from beyond Athîrû Gaiti. For their part, the Aîri invited an expert named Kalûma.

The following four dialogues derive from a preliminary discussion among the Athimba, and from the Athimba-Aîri joint meeting – both held on 18 December (see Photo 4.1).

In the first dialogue, M'Lichoro (H29) of the Ratanya age-class acts as the Athimba's principal spokesman (*mwaambi*). Ntika of the Mîchûbû age-class is the victim's father (and H17 and H18's father). M'Barûngû of the Mîchûbû age-class (H12 and H13's father) is the chairman and eldest member of the clan. As key representatives of the Athimba, they discuss the role of experts and the omission of *nkiria* from the compensation process.

Dialogue 4.1 Preliminary discussion among Athimba elders

> M'Lichoro: I have met Kîbaati (the offender's uncle – father's brother – and the main person responsible for payments) near his place. I am sure that he has no problem. A Kîmîîrû expert known as Kalûma has arrived. Indeed, Kîbaati has also invited another elder from Maûa. The second person is from the Îthaliî [age-class]. So, even if Kalûma fails to

	come, Kîbaati can proceed. He says he will pay everything as required. I told him, 'There is no discount'. Our main interest is to know why *nkiria* has been omitted.
Ntika:	We can't alter our law. Mîori (the headquarters of the Njûrincheke council of the Îgembe – see Figure 1.1) is the place where our law is amended.
M'Barûngû:	[The law is changing.] For example, a bride's father used to be given seven cows, but now îeembe (the Njûrincheke council of Îgembe) has reduced the number to five cows. Even in Thaichû,[9] when a girl was impregnated before marriage, her father used to be given ten goats. But nowadays, three goats are enough.
Ntika:	What we need is seriousness. This is our fifth month [since starting negotiations with the Aîri clan]. We are getting tired. I pray to God that we will be friends again as we complete this payment. Whatever we will receive, may it be small or big, let us share please. We have negotiated with Kîbaati for a long time.
M'Lichoro:	There's no need for enmity. It's just a matter of sitting down and paying things.
Ntika:	If *nkiria* came first, then we wouldn't have any problem. After *nkiria*, there should be *ndewa ya ûkundia rûûî*. When we need to know more about these things, we can talk to experts. They can come and tell us what kind of animals should be paid. If there is something unfamiliar to us, experts can tell us.
M'Lichoro:	We wish our expert (Îkotha) a good journey up to this place. I heard that he is always sick. May God help him!

---

9   See Chapter 1 for a comparison between the Îgembe proper and the Thaichû.

Photo 4.1 Athimba clan meeting, 18 December 2001

At noon, some two hours after the above dialogue, Îkotha – the Athimba's advisor – arrived. The Athimba and the Aîri then took two hours to decide on a venue for their joint meeting; eventually opting for Ntika's homestead. The following dialogue derives from the meeting, which began at 2.30 pm with both an invocation to divest the participants of any evil intentions[10] (Photo 4.2) and a Christian prayer to bless the gathering. Next M'Barûngû of the Athimba raised the meeting's main question: why had *nkiria* been omitted? Îkotha stated that, in his opinion, a milking cow and a calf constituted *nkiria*. Kalûma (the Aîri's advisor), however, bypassed any definition of compensation items – saying only that he represented Kîbaati, whose sole interest was in the quantity of the items to be paid.

---

10 The invocation was made by Îkotha, together with a Njûrincheke elder, in the manner of *kwiita rwîî* (see Chapter 3).

The Athimba

Photo 4.2 Invocation to remove evil intentions, 18 December 2001

Dialogue 4.2 Experts at the Athimba-Aîri joint meeting

M'Barûngû: We are the Athimba. Ntika called us to come here. He told us that the Aîri killed his son. Thus, he slaughtered *nthenge ya mbûri iîlî* (a mature he-goat as big as the sum of two goats) and built a clan house. Our representative (M'Lichoro) was sent to the Aîri. We told them to pay the homicide compensation. Soon thereafter, they came with a she-goat (*mparika ya ûtumûra moota*) and said they accepted our claim. They asked us to wait for payment. We waited for four months. To date, we have been given a ram (*ntûrûme ya ûtûria ina mûkuû nyumba*). Then, the Aîri came again with a heifer and a bull, but their messenger didn't tell us what they stood for. The heifer has no name. That's why we called an advisor. This is the point we have reached.

Kalûma: Let me ask you this: after you were given a cow, a bull, a goat and a ram, what's next?

M'Barûngû: Since the cow has no name, they didn't follow the correct way, so I said that we should see an advisor. As I am a man of Kîmîîrû (*mûmîîrû*), I know that *nkiria* comes after a ram, and the *nkiria* consist of a cow and a calf.

Kalûma: Your advisor should tell me that.

Îkotha: I would like to thank the clan members and everyone here. My advice is only for the victim's side. Thus, I can't ask my fellow advisor (Kalûma) a question. According to Kîmîîrû, if a person kills another person, a clan house should be built [to organise homicide compensation]. Yet now, in your case, while one party has built their own house, the other party has not, so I can't say that things are properly arranged. I have never heard of compensation payment being made in an open field without clan houses. But I won't ask you any more about this point. I am supposed to talk about *nkiria*. They say that a ram and a goat were brought. What about *nkiria*?

Kalûma: Are you claiming that *nkiria* has not yet arrived?

Îkotha: You certainly brought certain animals, but they were not *nkiria*. *Nkiria* should be paid with a cow and a calf. The day before yesterday, there was another payment in M'Imaana's village in Nthare, a payment was recently made (see Table 3.3 for M'Imaana and Case 3.4 for Nthare). Furthermore, during another payment in Kîthetu (northeast of Maûa town), Kalûma and I were invited as advisors. Kîmîîrû states that advisors should teach those who do not know how to pay compensation the way to do it. They (the Athimba) argued that they received all the animals except *nkiria*. Please tell us where it is. If you have brought it here, please say so and

	we will name it. I ask you this. Both parties should have discussions separately and come to a conclusion.
Kalûma:	You (Athimba clan members) should talk and tell us the number of animals you want. We will pay.
Îkotha:	Even in law courts, you can't make a judgement. A judge does it.
Kîbaati:	I want to know the number of cows or amount of money required.
Îkotha:	I am not the one to tally it. That's why I say you should talk. Do you understand my point?

Upon Îkotha's advice, the two parties held short, separate discussions, then resumed the meeting. There followed an exchange between their principal agents: Ntika of the Athimba and Kîbaati of the Aîri. As shown in the dialogue below, Ntika confessed the 'real' reason why the Athimba – who had argued for *nkiria* – refused 'the cow without a name'; saying that they could not overlook the fact that the cow seemed weak, and they were thus seeking another animal.[11]

Dialogue 4.3 Exchange between the parties' principal agents

Ntika:	We are going to agree with Kîbaati. The messenger could have told Kîbaati that those animals were not the best. I told the messenger that I refused the cow because it seemed very weak. It may die anytime. He told me that I should sell it [because it was in a bad state]. Furthermore, those animals were not *nkiria*.

---

11 Isak Dinesen (Karen Blixen) related a similar story in *Out of Africa*, Chapter 2: A shooting accident on the farm. A shotgun, fired by mistake on Dinesen's colonial farm in Kenya, killed one boy and injured another. The shooter's father paid a cow and a heifer calf to the injured boy, in compensation. The boy's grandmother, however, disputed the payment as, in her eyes, the cow was too old (Dinesen 1938, 151–154).

Kîbaati:	If I can't get a milking cow with a calf, what should I do? Can you accept any cow if it is not sick?
Ntika:	Anyway, we will agree. Advisors should direct us. Kalûma and Îkotha will tell us and we will agree.
Kîbaati:	If I take back the cow and bring another one, can it be *nkiria*?

At this point, some of the elders took Ntika and Kîbaati aside for a short, confidential talk (*nkilîba*).[12] In the dialogue below, the elders Mîchûbû, M'Imaana and Ntongai speak as third parties.

Dialogue 4.4 Conclusion of the dispute

Mîchûbû:	Both Kîbaati and Ntika have talked in a good manner. We are the Amîîrû. Let us proceed without worrying too much about cows. If there is love, a sheep can be counted as a cow.
M'Barûngû:	I saw a small cow together with a small bull. Let us regard it (the combination) as *nkiria*. I don't mind if a milking cow is there or not. I myself agree.
M'Imaana:	I had a previous experience of being involved in a compensation payment. A heifer and a small bull were paid as *nkiria*.
Ntika:	Since many people have participated in and witnessed occasions of the same kind, I also agree.
Ntongai:	Any animal can be *nkiria*. We have agreed that *nkiria* has arrived. They are here in our place. The *nkiria* is OK. So, let us proceed to the next stage of *ndewa ya ûkundia rûûi*. After that, Kîbaati will call the Njûrincheke council of elders to discuss further steps.

---

12 A confidential talk (*nkilîba*) is often invoked when key speakers at a meeting are required to reach a unanimous decision on a dispute.

After this dialogue, Mîchûbû announced the Athimba had decided to accept the cow brought by the Aîri as *nkiria*, so bringing the dispute to an end.

The controversy over 'a cow without a name' is interesting in that, to some extent, the negotiation between parties allowed for flexible interpretation of the law, via the exchange of views. This negotiation was far from ad hoc; being informed by indigenous law experts from beyond the two villages involved. Thus, the inter-village exchange of expert knowledge contributed to the formation of Îgembe common law.

Personal interest and clan solidarity

In Case 4.1, the Aîri's reparation transactions were organised personally by Kîbaati (the homicide perpetrator's uncle).[13] The Athimba, in contrast, represented themselves as a corporate group. The Athimba elders argued that indigenous law required homicide compensation to be paid in a formal inter-clan deal – an argument founded on the fact that all Athimba clan members stood to receive a share of Ntika's (the victim's father's) compensation, which promised to be many head of livestock. Indeed, many of Ntika's agnatic relatives assembled at the Athimba's clan house whenever a meeting was held, to monitor the case's progress. The Athimba's argument for clan solidarity may thus be seen, at least in part, as based on a desire to pursue their personal interests. Conversely, the Aîri clan collectively did not stand to pay any compensation; with this responsibility falling personally to Kîbaati. Thus, with no incentive, the Aîri showed little concern for adherence to indigenous law.

---

13 The Aîri form one of the smallest clans in Athîrû Gaiti and occupy many acres of tea plantations on the northwest hill slope of Îgembe Southeast Division. The Athimba, in contrast, are one of the largest clans and hold several fertile farms on the division's southeast plain.

Kîbaati pays compensation

Kîbaati decided to organise a fundraising party to pay for the homicide compensation items. Since the Aîri had very few agnatic members in Athîrû Gaiti itself, he was forced to look for support beyond his clan; relying on his personal network, as opposed to his agnatic membership. The following is the main text of a typewritten letter Kîbaati sent to neighbours and friends, near and far.

> Original Kîmîîrû text: *Mbere nî nkethi ndene ya Mwathani wetû Jesû Kristo. Nîngûkûromba wîîje wakwa mûchîî tarîki 14/10/2001 thaa kenda kûthuranîra maketha nîûntû bwa kûrea kîongo kîa 'Mûtwîri' ûrîa waûragîrwe nî mûthaka wetû 'Îkundi'. Kwîîja waku nî kûtharimi mono. Nîni waku...*

> English Translation: First of all, my sincere greetings in the name of our Lord, Jesus Christ. I ask that you come to my place on 14 October 2001 at three o'clock to arrange a fundraising event; it is for homicide compensation for Mûtwîri, who was murdered by one of our young men, Îkundi. Your attendance would be blessed. Sincerely yours...

Kîbaati arranged a meeting on 14 October 2001 to organise a fundraising committee. He expected more than 200 people to attend, and so prepared 100 loaves of bread as a light meal. Only 50 people arrived. Nevertheless, a committee was formed, and the fundraising party was set for 18 November. During the meeting, Kîbaati and the committee calculated the funds needed to pay for the compensation items – arriving at the figure of 100,000 shillings or more. Kîbaati and his relatives would pay some of this from their own pockets but could not afford the full amount. Thus, Kîbaati composed a second typewritten letter, in the hope that more than 500 well-wishers would make small contributions:

> Original Kîmîîrû text: *Makethene ya gûtetheeria kûrea kîongo kîria kîûmba gûtumîra ta Kshs. 100,000 irîa îkethîrwa îrî tarîki 18/11/2001*

The Athimba

Photo 4.3 Fundraising party, 18 November 2001

ntukû ya kîûmia Anjarû kîanine thaa inyanya chiongwa (2pm). Kwîiya na kweeyana gwaku kûrî na gîtûmi mono.

English translation: A fundraiser to help out with the compensation payment, which may cost around 100,000 shillings, will be held on 18 November 2001, Sunday, at the Anjarû open field at two o'clock (2 pm). Your attendance and contribution would be very meaningful.

The party was large (Photo 4.3), with the committee spending around 10,000 shillings on meals for the guests.[14] Most of the attending committee members, well-wishers and guests came from outside the Aîri clan. Although the transaction of homicide compensation was regarded as an inter-clan issue, Kîbaati was held personally responsible. The neighbours, friends, business partners and relatives he mustered to help pay the fine did not constitute a clan in any true sense.

Donations from attendees came to 54,000 shillings, with contributions over the following week raising this to around 70,000 shillings. Although the 100,000-shilling target was not met, Kîbaati and other Aîri members

---

14 Purchased ingredients included rice (100kg), Irish potatoes (one sack), peas (20kg), beef (15kg), cooking fat (2kg), sugar (4kg), tea (500g) milk (20,000ml), and an unrecorded quantity of salt, carrots and tomatoes.

were fairly satisfied with their achievement. On 24 and 26 November, a representative of the Aîri purchased some of the compensation animals from Kangeta livestock market, and *ntûrûme ya ûtûria ina mûkuû nyumba* was given to the Athimba on 5 December (Table 4.2).

Demands of the Athimba elders

On 8 August, following their advisor's counsel, the Athimba built a clan house (*nyumba ya mwîrîa*) at Ntika's homestead. This proved to be more than a symbol of their solidarity, as the clan elders spent many nights sleeping inside – which necessitated the assistance of junior clan agnates and the ongoing contribution of food and money.

After the first transaction on 3 August, progress with the homicide compensation process stalled until mid-October (see Table 4.2). In the interim, a dearth of resources developed into a serious problem for clan members. Ntika, together with M'Lichiro (H29), the clan's head spokesman (*mwaambi*) – and other clan elders, became tired and dissatisfied with the uncooperative attitude of their junior agnates. The clan held a meeting on 24 October, during which the elders requested they provide more contributions, but this proved only partially successful.

When the Athimba elders were informed that Kîbaati of the Aîri clan was ready to restart the payment process, they organised a meeting for 24 and 25 November (Photo 4.4), with the primary aim of reinforcing clan unity before receiving the compensation items. However, the elders at this meeting remained very much concerned with the way they were being treated by their junior agnates.

On 24 November, M'Lichiro and Ntika argued that clan members should make another contribution to pay various expenses. M'Lichiro angrily threatened that the elders would curse their juniors. Mûteethia (H26), who shared Ratanya's age-class, delicately helped him to calm down, and tried to persuade his young peers to cooperate. The clan's Lubetaa and Mîrîti age-class members agreed to this but the elders remained dissatisfied, as it had not been explained exactly how they

The Athimba

Photo 4.4 Athimba clan meeting, November 2001

would be supported. Ntika then announced that another 200 shillings should be contributed by the juniors, and that *îchiaro* men would be sent to visit any uncooperative agnates. This decision was supported by Mûteethia, and so the meeting concluded.

The above agreement represents a common means of employing *mwîchiaro* in the Îgembe community. For example, when one individual (A) requests financial support from another (B), A may send B's *mwîchiaro* to him or her as an agent. This is because B cannot refuse his or her *mwîchiaro*'s plea. The Athimba have two *îchiaro* clans: the Antûambûi and the Andûûne. Theoretically, there is no difference between them in terms of social function. However, the Athimba have historically used Andûûne *mwîchiaro* to request financial support, and Antûambûi *mwîchiaro* for other reasons (see Chapter 5 for further discussion).

Dialogue 4.5 Discussion of sending *îchiaro* men to uncooperative agnates

Ntika: Young people are supposed to help old people, but you are always drunk. We have waited for your response for three months; that is too long to answer a question. [In August] each of you contributed 200 shillings and we received a lot of money. The total amount was 11,550 shillings. For the past three months, since then, all the money has been used up. We bought two Land Rover-loads of firewood with the money. Now we don't have firewood and we don't know where we can get firewood or money to buy it.

I am answering a question from the young men who ask where the money goes. I am the one who keeps track of the money, and it can't be misused until the compensation payment is complete. These are the current circumstances. Advisors told me that we need five he-goats for the messengers (*atûngûri*). We eat two today for our brothers. I have contributed six goats from my shed. The amount you contributed has been used up.

Elders are using my money. I just ask my sons to give 500 each to cater to elders. For the owner of this *mîraa* shamba, I asked him for 1,000 shillings, and I have never seen him. I told him to give elders some money for tea, but he never appeared... So, 200 shillings should be paid, and our leader (*mwaambi*) should be keen on this. The Aîri people will soon come with livestock, and of course we will slaughter a goat for them. We will also give them mead. So, we should know where to get money. If you agree, everything will be over. Failing that, I will go back to Antûambûi to call on our brother (*mûtanoba*)...

Mûteethia: We, the clan, have discussed the matter and found that we have a lot of people who are not all that concerned with our affairs. We are very sad about what happened at Ntika's place. If you don't unite with the clan, you know that if you have any issue you will give us a lot of problems. We have said that those who brought 200 shillings will again add another 200 shillings, and for those who have not contributed, they should pay 400 shillings. Failing that, our brothers from Andûûne will be taken to your homestead.

On 25 November, after the meeting's conclusion, I observed the performance of *kwîkîra nyumba mûkolo* (to put a ram's skin ribbon on a house). This ritual consisted of five phases. (1) In the morning, the skin of a ram – slaughtered the previous day – was cut into a long strip (*mûkolo*). (2) Two elders poured diluted honey into the stems of castor oil plants (*mwaarîki*; *Ricinus communis*) and buried them individually at the front door and four corners of the clan house (both within and without). (3) The two elders sprinkled black millet over all the walls of the house (within and without), while clan members stayed inside. (4) The two elders attached the leather strip to the house (Photo 4.5) – fixing it to the tops of wooden poles that had been cut from a *mûtûngûû* tree[15] and placed at the house's four corners. (5) The two elders each held one mouthful of diluted honey and sprayed it over the walls of the house (within and without) (Photo 4.6).

The earlier mandate that junior members provide material assistance to their seniors at the clan house may be seen as an affirmation of clan solidarity. That solidarity was consolidated by the *kwîkîra nyumba mûkolo* ritual, during which all members confirmed their unity before receiving and distributing several animals, in compensation for the homicide that triggered this case. Throughout this process, arguments rooted in the economic interests of both the whole clan, and the clan elders as a distinct body, were integrated into indigenous law surrounding homicide reparations.

---

15 Any tree could be used in this case. *Mûtûngûû* (*Commiphora zimmermannii*) is one of 'the plants that thrive well in or around places inhabited by people. These plants can be found on farms, homesteads or along pathways' (Thuku 2008, 78).

Photo 4.5 Clan house surrounded by a leather strip

Photo 4.6 An elder sprays honey from his mouth across the walls of the clan house

An unexpected conclusion

Before reaching its final stage, the homicide compensation process was halted by a disagreement among the Athimba. Some clan elders complained that, because the clan house was demolished before the compensatory items could be delivered, they had been secretly consumed by a certain circle of Athimba members, instead of being properly distributed. (See Chapter 6 for Mûrîangûkû's – Ntika's son's – plea for forgiveness and blessings in September 2015.) The case should have concluded with the payment by the Aîri of a ram, a he-goat, a she-goat and *ndewa ya ûkûrîra kîongo* (a bull to call for a head). The bull should then have been slaughtered at a joint feast of the Athimba, the Aîri and the Njûrincheke council of elders. Furthermore, the ram should have been slaughtered for *waakana mauta* (the smearing of ram's fat) to celebrate the two clans' reconciliation (see also Case 5.1).

If the outstanding compensatory items had been paid, the total number of livestock received by the Athimba would have totalled twenty, including ten head of cattle and ten head of goat and/or sheep.[16] The same count of livestock was claimed in Case 4.3. However, in Case 5.1 the two contesting parties agreed on a discount, in recognition of their existing affinal relationship. Notably, in both Cases 4.3 and 5.1, the number of livestock paid as *rûraachio* was the same as in Case 4.1, but the offerings were designated differently – indicating that the Athimba's knowledge of homicide compensation under indigenous law had developed between 2001 and 2015.

The elders of the Mîchûbû age-class – including Ntika (the victim's father) and M'Barûngû (the clan's chairman and eldest member) – all passed away in the years following Case 4.1. They were succeeded by elders of the Ratanya age-class – including Mûteethia (H26), M'Mauta (H27) and M'Lichoro (H29) – who came to supervise their junior peers in the handling of clan matters.

Case 4.2: A victimised agnate

In 2011, I observed another homicide compensation case that centred on the Athimba clan but differed from Case 4.1 in two key respects. First, it

---

16 Rimita (1988, 76–78) described another case of homicide compensation payment as follows: 'The compensation consisted of 20 heifers, 12 goats and one cow called *nkiria*. Nkiria in Kimeru means the one that stops the mother of the deceased and other relatives from crying. This was the first payment to be made and had to be a good milker.'

involved both the murder of the offender's wife, who was from a different clan, and the injury of another Athimba man, who was of the offender's age-class – leaving the Athimba responsible for both compensating the wife's family and seeking reconciliation between the 'brothers'. Second, rather than claiming compensation, the wife's parents demanded the payment of outstanding bride price (*rûraachio*) items, for which the Athimba father-in-law was responsible.

The wife was buried at her marital homestead and, in the event, the two families agreed that the payment of compensation items should be organised on an inter-family, as opposed to inter-clan, basis – since marital transactions are not a clan matter. For the Athimba, the key issue in this case (which the clan elders spent hours debating) thus became the 'brothers'' reconciliation. Strictly speaking, the elders were not even concerned with reconciliation, but rather the importance of the injured agnate forgiving the offender. For weeks, this proved too difficult for him to accept.

From homicide compensation to bride price payment

In January 2011, the offender, Kabeeria, ambushed his wife, Gakii, and his 'brother', Daniel, in Maûa town. Kabeeria, of the Bwantai age-class, was the son of Mîrîti (H10). Daniel, a son of Kamenchu (H14), was of the same age-class. Daniel escaped death by a hairsbreadth, but Gakii died from a serious knife wound. Kabeeria had earlier suspected Daniel, who was working as a mechanic in Maûa, of conducting an intimate, clandestine affair with Gakii – and so Daniel became the target of his revenge. However, by coincidence, Gakii was at the scene of the ambush and became a victim of the ensuing violence. Kabeeria was eventually arrested while hiding in a nearby village.

Gakii's parents first visited the Athimba clan on 18 March 2011, to attend the second case meeting. Some of the elders I interviewed in March 2011 had initially understood that Gakii's family might claim homicide compensation. At the meeting, however, the parents said they would only request their remaining bride price items, including five goats, a ewe, a cow and a bull, which were standard to ordinary marital transactions. They noted that they had previously received items including a ram for Gakii's mother, a he-goat for her father, a bundle of *mîraa*, a drum of honey and two suits. Upon hearing the parents' representation, the Athimba came to understand that they wished to perpetuate their affinal relationship with the offender's family. Both parties took account of the fact that Kabeeria and Gakii had a child.

Mwîchiaro involvement in reconciliation

Having accepted that Gakii's case was not a clan matter, the Athimba shifted their focus to meeting Daniel, the injured agnate, for intra-clan reconciliation. This did not prove easy. Neither Daniel nor his father attended the case's first and second clan meetings; Daniel apparently feeling too victimised to respond to a summons he received.

On 28 March, Ngatûnyi – a *mwîchiaro* from Laare, of the Antûambûi clan –attended the third meeting upon the Athimba's invitation. Ngatûnyi explained that he had visited Daniel and his father on the day of the second meeting, together with the parents of the murdered woman. The party had been welcomed, and both Daniel and his father said they would attend the meeting. In the dialogue below, which focuses on Daniel and his father's continuing absence, Ngatûnyi is bemused that they have not appeared at the third meeting.

The elders who contribute to the conversation include Mûteethia (H26; the acting chairman of the Athimba clan), Matî (H9; the clan secretary who replaced Kîthia, H3), Ntongai of the Lubetaa age-class (the clan treasurer), M'Lichoro (H29, the eldest member), M'Mauta (H27) and Kabithi of the Ratanya age-class. Ntongai, M'Lichoro and Kabithi both travelled from the distant lower slope area.

Dialogue 4.6 The elders discuss Daniel's absence

Mûteethia: I have seen him driving a vehicle.

Matî: Yes, he was the one who was driving a vehicle, but he didn't ask for anything from us.

Ntongai: Did you call upon him to meet with clan elders?

Mûteethia: Yes, we told him to come. We didn't see the young man (*mûthaka*) today. Even the assistant chief did not [find him]. We didn't see him, and the letter said we should meet here at the clan's meeting place (*mwîrîeene*).[17] We should meet with the chief here. The messenger didn't come back to check whether the letter reached the intended person.

M'Lichoro: Was the letter eaten by rats, or what?

Mûteethia: No.

M'Mauta: Chairman, let me ask you a question. If that person doesn't come with the assistant chief giving him the letter, was there any case with the chief? What happened?

Mûteethia: There is no case with the chief, but our case (*îamba*) will continue.

M'Mauta: Let the young man and his father be. We shall continue with our case.

Ngatûnyi: M'Mauta, you have asked a very good question. You have asked, do we have a case with the assistant chief? No. We have a case with this person. Now just tell M'Mauta that we are using our assistant chief so that we can reach the person (Daniel). Now, Mr Chairman, there is a person who can roam in the bush and continues roaming. His roaming

---

17 '*Mwîrîeene*' means literally 'at a clan's meeting place', but implies 'at a clan house' if such a building has already been constructed.

	occurs when he is alone and, when he reaches the person who has called or summoned him, his roaming ceases. Now we want him to come before us and talk with him slowly; he will calm down because we sent the assistant chief, and we shall beseech him. And you, M'Mauta, you must ask: if he doesn't come to us, what shall we do?
Kabithi:	Greetings to the entire clan and again, greetings. I am saying that an aggressive bull can be calmed down. As we are trying to beseech this bull, even though it is trying to kick us, we shall also kick it. You have sent me several times, and this is the third time. Now, we should try beseeching him.
Ngatûnyi:	Now, Mr. Chairman, we came from far away due to your calling. I always come not for my problem, and we advise each other.[18] We always come here, but this time, we don't understand the reason for coming.

As the dialogue continues below, Mûteethia briefs Ngatûnyi on the nature of the murder case. Ngatûnyi, however, is not fully satisfied, as he already knows how the case developed. Rather, he wishes to learn about Daniel's absence. M'Lichoro of the Ratanya age-class then becomes angry about the mismanagement among the clan that has confused Ngatûnyi. He advises his younger agnates to properly fear their *mwîchiaro*, and to treat them well.

Mûteethia:	I am wondering if you were informed of all the issues. I would like to explain the purpose of this calling, and what you are asking about.
	Mîrîti's son (Kabeeria) married a woman in Maûa and had a son with her. They were living in Maûa town, not at their homestead. His brother (Daniel) used to sneak around

---

18 This phrase denotes that the *îchiaro* relationship between clans is always reciprocal.

secretly when the husband was not present. They used to stay like this. The husband became angry, and secretly crept upon Daniel and his wife with a knife and stabbed them both. The woman died of her wounds, but the man was only injured. She died upon arriving at the hospital, but the man was discharged.

After that, he planned to sue his brother for stabbing him. Our leader said we should contribute something big to convince the father [of the woman to pursue reconciliation], and we should visit him. We contributed something big so that we could convince the father. We should be aware of what move the father might make, or if he might be planning to claim that the head should be paid (i.e. homicide compensation). The contribution was taken along with a he-goat.[19]

The father was convinced and told us that the daughter was ours, and to take and bury her at our homestead. We organised the burial ceremony back home. Yet after the burial, we heard that Daniel wanted to sue Kabeeria in the law courts.

That's why we have called you (Ngatûnyi) to stop Daniel from prosecuting the young man. Please tell him to stop this case, because Kabeeria is his brother (*mûtanoîthe* – literally 'his father's son'; here meaning that Kabeeria is Daniel's agnate of the same generation). Apart from this issue, there is nothing else we have called you for.

Ngatûnyi: OK, where is the person we are talking about?

Mûteethia: He is not here.

---

19 *Nthenge ya mîraa* ('a he-goat of *mîraa*'). During the first stage of marriage negotiations, a bundle of *mîraa* should be presented to the bride and her father. If they accept it, *nthenge ya mîraa* should immediately follow.

Ngatûnyi: We went to his homestead, and he was not there. Now whom shall we talk to?

M'Lichoro: As for me, I have lived many years and seen many cases. We did this when we went to build our clan house at Conguri (another name for the Akûi village in the Îgembe Southeast Division). When you go to call upon your brother (meaning *mwîchiaro*), you must inform him of everything. I don't know whether you are thinking from a childish perspective to solve this case. Let me use the method which was used before by our forefathers of the Îthaliî age-class to inform you that our brother (*mûtanoba*; meaning *mwîchiaro*) is bigger (more powerful) than the chief. The chief is employed for a period of time, then leaves the office, but our brother shall remain and can help in paying the head. As for me, I am telling you how our forefathers solved their cases.

Ngatûnyi next instructed Kabithi to seek out Daniel at home and summon him. The Athimba elders responded that Ngatûnyi should accompany him, as Daniel would fear his *îchiaro* power and be unable to refuse. As the dialogue continues below, Mûteethia argues that Daniel and his father should both be summoned, as only the latter truly understands the *mwîchiaro*'s power. Ngatûnyi adds that Daniel welcomed him when he visited on 18 March.

Mûteethia: The reason for calling Daniel's father, Kamenchu, is that he knows the consequences of *îchiaro*. If the son is asked about *îchiaro*, he doesn't know. Kamenchu had an elder brother. When he was asked about *îchiaro*, he said, 'Let them fry the *îchiaro* for me, and I will eat it when it is fried and sweetened.' [Kamenchu's brother died soon after this disrespectful utterance.]

When our family is caught by *ichiaro*, every member of our family will perish. Please, let's just call upon him first, because he will call upon his son for us. Please come, and let his presence be seen. M'Lichoro, I am telling you this.[20] We shall not stay any longer. Otherwise, we shall make this family poor by making them always give us food [to feed the clan members who are meeting at their homestead], as if we are doing anything for them. Today, we shall find a final solution, because we shall not come here again. The solution is, 'Let's go to Daniel's homestead and he will meet us, whether he accepts us or wants to chase us away'. If Daniel has been refusing to come for two weeks, and since he refuses to come today, I shall not come here again.

Ngatûnyi: I was at the place where you sent me before. I met him at his home, where you had sent me on the 18th of this month. We talked with him in person and told him that I would go back to the clan meeting to inform them that he would be coming soon. His response was good, and he welcomed me.

In time, Ngatûnyi and Kabithi returned with only Kamenchu, since Daniel was away when they visited. Kabithi then informed the clan members that Daniel would not come. The dialogue below presents statements given by Mûteethia, Kamenchu and other elders. Mûteethia argues that brothers should not fight each other; i.e., that Daniel should withdraw his case. The elders also request that Kamenchu try to help his sons reconcile.

---

20 When a clan member makes a lengthy speech, he may physically address it to an individual – most likely one of the key elders – but in fact he is addressing everyone present. The individual being addressed is expected to make responses of assent. Mûteethia often employs this method of dialogue.

The Athimba

Dialogue 4.7 The injured man's father speaks

Mûteethia: We were waiting for Kamenchu due to some issues behind the murder case. How can we just sit here, waiting for the two heads to die?[21] That is why we have called you, our brother. We want to inform you that both children are yours, and if the right hand (*njara ya ûrîo*) hurts the left hand (*njara ya ûmotho*), what will happen? Please tell us the solution which you can make as a parent. The one who is deceased is not a problem. Even the one who is left is not a problem. If he is taken to court, he can be sentenced to ten years or more, which is like being dead. But now, you (Kamenchu) are the parent of both parties. Please tell us your advice. If a son files a case against his brother, it is like killing a person.

Kamenchu: I heard that Kabeeria issued a very harsh statement that Daniel should not survive as long as his wife died, and he would die also. Daniel remembers well how he was stabbed. Daniel is now saying, 'Why should I die? Let me sue him at the police station'. This is his statement and my son, Daniel, does not ask Kabeeria for anything. Daniel informed me that he had used 12,000 shillings to pay the hospital bills. He said, 'I am not asking to be refunded. Please tell me what the conflict was for, because I am innocent'.

M'Lichoro: Daniel was trying to figure out the real reason why his brother stabbed him, because Kabeeria had uttered some statements saying, 'I have not done (killed my enemy), but I will do'. Now we are asking you, our brother, and we are saying that when we meet here, we should find peace (*thîîrî*). Please, we are telling you that we shall pay the head

---

21 'Two heads' here may be referring either to: i) Gakii (already dead) and Kabeeria (as good as dead if imprisoned); or ii) Daniel (if attacked again by Kabeeria) and Kabeeria (as good as dead if imprisoned).

together. Daniel should come so that he can know how to reconcile with his brother because, as clan members, it is your responsibility, as well as mine, to pay the head.

Ngatûnyi: Kamenchu, I went to his homestead, but when I arrived there, he wasn't there. But if he has come before the clan, let him tell us what is in his heart, so that we can sort things out as one unit (*kîntû kîmwe*), as a clan.

Mûteethia: Many of us are asking why we have called upon Kamenchu. He is not the one we have a case with, and he is not the one who was stabbed. Does anyone have feelings like this? But remember, Kamenchu is an old person and has fathered many children. Young men of this age don't understand their brothers or sisters. How does one call the other 'my brother' (*mûtanochia*) while they fight for a wife? This is like the right hand hurting the left hand, and he (Kamenchu) is the one who we called upon to find a solution (*kîorio*).[22] If we come together, we can find a lasting solution. That is why we have called Kamenchu to the clan. I confirm that I will assent to what the clan agrees upon, together with our brother Kamenchu.

Kathia: Greetings to the clan. I am saying that Kamenchu has done a good thing by responding to our summons. Kamenchu is like a bridge (*ndaracha*)[23] that all people shall use in order to get Daniel to meet with us.

The Athimba elders, including Kamenchu, then agreed that they should hold another meeting, with Daniel present. This was scheduled for 4 April 2011.

---

22 *Kiorio* literally means 'medicine' but in this context denotes a solution to a problem.
23 Originating from Kiswahili, *ndaracha* means 'bridge' in English and *ûroroo* in Kîmîîrû.

The long process of forgiveness

The fourth meeting went ahead as planned, at Mîrîti's (H10) homestead. Those attending included two *ichiaro* men, Ngatûnyi and Nchooro; the latter hailing from the Andûûne clan. Daniel, however, did not appear and the elders were unable to proceed with the reconciliation. They scheduled another meeting, for 8 April, to be held at Kamenchu's homestead. Kabithi, Ngatûnyi and Nchooro were sent to summon Daniel.

Daniel finally appeared at the fifth meeting, with Ngatûnyi and Nchooro again present. He indicated that he could not forgive Kabeeria and explained how he had been injured. On the day of the incident, he said, Gakii – the murdered woman – and other individuals, had asked him to take her to Maûa on his motorbike. Just after he had dropped her at her house, and was ready to depart, he heard people screaming loudly inside. Daniel decided to find out what was happening and met Kabeeria. Kabeeria then suddenly stabbed Daniel with a knife. Daniel escaped death but, to his dismay, later heard that Kabeeria had let it be known that Daniel forced him to kill his wife and would not leave him be. From that point on, Daniel was convinced Kabeeria was his enemy.

A sixth meeting was held on 28 April, at which the Athimba elders set a date – 7 May 2011 – to send clan members to visit the murdered woman's parents and discuss a way forward with the bride price payment. The elders were unable, however, to make any progress on intra-clan reconciliation at the meeting, as neither Daniel nor Kamenchu were present.

On 14 May, a seventh meeting was held, attended by the *mwîchiaro* Nchooro. The elders who had visited the murdered woman's natal home announced that each clan member should contribute 300 shillings toward the bride price. One clan member suggested that they should summon Daniel, his father and Kabeeria's father. M'Lichoro opposed this and, along with other elders, sought an alternative way forward.

At the eighth meeting, on 10 June, Daniel appeared again with his father. Kabeeria's father, Mîrîti, was also present. Daniel said he was still unable to forgive Kabeeria. Together with other elders, Mûteethia (the acting chairman) strongly requested that Daniel forgive Kabeeria when he came back to the village, and instructed Mîrîti to persuade his son to return. Mîrîti then promised he would bring his son back to the clan, and Daniel finally concurred that he would try to forgive him.

On 24 June, at the ninth meeting, Daniel declared in front of fifty clan members that he had forgiven Kabeeria, who had failed to appear at any of the hearings. Although, to date, the clan claims that they have been reconciled, it remains difficult for Daniel to accept Kabeeria as a 'brother'.

Case 4.3: A failed experiment in homicide compensation

This case differs from Cases 4.1 and 4.2 in that it concerns the failure of a homicide compensation action due to both the plaintiff's behaviour and wider political and socio-historical concerns. Beginning in March 2015, the proceedings, conducted between the Athimba and Amwari clans, concerned the murder of a young man following his involvement in *mîraa* theft.

The victim's father – a member of the Athimba – built a clan house at his homestead on 25 March to receive compensation items (Photo 4.7). The early stages of the case proceeded quickly and, by the end of April, the father had received five head of cattle and five head of goat and sheep (equivalent to almost half the total claim), and the two clans had held a joint feast. However, the process then stagnated, due to financial difficulties among the Amwari.

After a three-month hiatus, the impatient father – who had failed to attend any clan meetings over the previous fifteen years – decided on an alternative plan to avenge his son's death. The Athimba elders severely criticised this. Worse still, at the end of August 2015, they noticed the father had removed the clan house from his homestead with neither their knowledge nor permission. This constituted a slight against the Athimba and their accumulated knowledge of homicide compensation procedures. Consequently, the clan ceased working with the father.

Photo 4.7 Clan house at Karatho's homestead (10 August 2015)

The victim's background

The murdered man, Gîtonga, was a second-generation immigrant – in common with the victim in Case 5.1. His father, Karatho (H24), of the Lubetaa age-class, was born in Nairobi in 1954. Gîtonga's grandfather was from Mwîmbî[24] but worked in Nairobi as an administrative officer under British colonial rule. He eventually migrated to Athîrû Gaiti to work as an agricultural officer and, some years later, the Athimba gave him the piece of land in Mûringene village, where the family's homestead is still situated.

According to the Athimba clan elders I interviewed, Gîtonga's father, Karatho, and grandfather were ordinary immigrants who assimilated into the clan. Soon after their arrival, the grandfather married for a second time; to a woman from the neighbouring Antûamûtî clan. The woman

---

24 Mwîmbî is one of greater Amîîrû's nine subgroups (see Figure 1.1).

gave birth to Karatho's younger siblings and behaved as a mother to Karatho. After the grandfather died in the 1960s, a member of the Athimba 'inherited' his wife.[25] The siblings recognised this man as their father and were accordingly embraced by the Athimba as clan members.

Experienced elders

Karatho heard from neighbours that Gîtonga was discovered one night stealing *mîraa* from a *shamba* (farm) near Kîraone market. He was then severely beaten by three sons of Nkiiri – a farm owner of the Amwari clan's Lubetaa age-class. Gîtonga was taken to hospital but eventually died. Karatho strongly condemned Nkiiri and his sons, who initially denied responsibility for the death but later admitted that they had captured and beaten Gîtonga. Karatho claimed homicide compensation, together with all the expenses he had paid for medical care and the funeral. He also warned he would request that the Njûrincheke council put Nkiiri and his sons into *kîthiri* (literally 'a pot'; here indicating the secret *kîthiri* oath – see Chapter 3, footnote 20) if they refused to pay what he claimed. Although Nkiiri believed his sons' actions were a form of self-defence against *mîraa* theft, he decided to pay the reparations.

Seeking advice on the compensation process, Karatho first visited a Njûrincheke elder named Kauo – a man of the Lubetaa age-class, from another administrative division of the Îgembe South. Karatho then called upon the Athimba clan, which held its first meeting on 3 March and, upon his request, appointed Kauo as their advisor (*mûkîrîra*).

Table 4.3 shows the four members of the Njûrincheke council of elders who were appointed as *mûkîrîra* and *mûtungûri* (messenger) in this case. Baariu, the *mûtûngûri* for the Athimba, had previously acted for the Bwethaa clan in 2013 (Case 5.1). Kathia was said to be an Akachiû clan member by biological origin. However, he had previously been initiated

---

25 The term *kûrîa ûkûa* (to eat the dead) means that, of a deceased man's surviving brothers, one may inherit his properties, a wife being considered property.

Table 4.3 Elders appointed as *mûkirîra* and *mûtûngûri* for homicide compensation

Name	Role	Age-class	Clan
Kauo	*mûkirîra* for Athimba	Lubetaa	Antûbochiû
Baariu	*mûtûngûri* for Athimba	Lubetaa	Bwethaa
Mîchûbû	*mûkirîra* for Amwari	Ratanya	Akachiû
Kathia	*mûtûngûri* for Amwari	Lubetaa	Athimba

Table 4.4 Chronology of homicide compensation, March–April 2015

Date	Process
3 March 2015	[Athimba] First clan meeting to discuss arrangements.
23 March	[Athimba] Second clan meeting to discuss building a clan house.
25 March	[Athimba] Third clan meeting to build a clan house.
26 March	[Athimba] Chairman sends a message to the Amwari clan to indicate that that they are ready to receive items.
30 March	[Athimba] Fourth meeting.
8 April	[Athimba and Amwari] **First transaction** at the joint clan meeting; the representatives of the Njûrincheke council of elders receive the compensation items.
17 April	**Second Transaction**
27 April	[Athimba and Amwari] A bull (*ndewa ya ûkundia rûûî*) is slaughtered at a joint feast.

into the Athimba in order to receive a piece of land. Both Baariu and Kathia were well-known as senior officials in the divisional Njûrincheke house of the Îgembe Southeast.

Table 4.4 provides a chronology of the compensation case. At the 3 March meeting, the Athimba specified the initial offerings – a ram, a ewe, a she-goat and *nkiria* (a milking cow and her calf, named *atang'atang'i*) to comfort the mother of the deceased. The clan record noted, 'When these items come, the clan will build a house, attach a leather strip (*mûkolo*) to it, then seek compensation for a person (the victim).' However, the clan house – the basic structure of which was the same as in Case 4.1 – was built at Karatho's homestead on 25 March, before the items arrived. The ritual of *kwîkîra nyumba mûkolo* (to put a ram-skin ribbon on a house) and the sprinkling of finger millet and honey were then performed (see

Photos 4.5 and 4.6). Each clan member contributed 300 shillings, and Karatho provided a he-goat to be slaughtered for the guests.

At the 26 March meeting, the Athimba specified the items – including preliminary payments and the main part of the reparation (*rûraachio*) – to be given before the concluding ritual of 'calling for a head' (*ûkûrîra kîongo*).

In the list below, items 5, 6 and 7 – each of which were due to be presented along with a cow and a she-goat – represent *rûraachio*. These were allocated new names, such as *ntaa kîî*, which were not used in Case 4.1.

(1) A she-goat (*mparika ya ûthoni*).

(2) A ewe, a she-goat and a he-goat.

(3) *Nkiria* and *atang'atang'i*.

(4) A bull to give the clan water (*ndewa ya ûkundia rûûî*).

(5) A small bull to exorcise death (*ntaa kîî*).[26]

(6) A bull for the clan (*ndewa ya mwîrîa*).

(7) A bull for uncles [of the victim] (*ndewa ya ba muntûoo*).

On 30 March, the clan also instructed Karatho to provide *nthenge ya mbûri iîlî* (a mature he-goat as big as two goats) and 5,000 shillings, to be taken to the Njûrincheke council of elders.

At the joint meeting on 8 April, both parties, along with the representatives of the Njûrincheke council of elders – 43 elders in total – witnessed the first preliminary payment being delivered by the Amwari clan. These included two she-goats, one ram, a milking cow and her

---

26 *Ntaa kîî* – literally 'one which exorcises death' – may be paid together with one he-goat, ram or small bull. The name first appeared in a homicide compensation case of 2013 (Case 5.10).

calf, and a third she-goat for the messenger. The remaining preliminary payment of one bull, one cow, one heifer and one she-goat was made on 17 April, with 29 elders in attendance. The fact that the delivered items did not tally with those specified at the 26 March meeting was not considered to be problematic. On 27 April, both parties, together with the representatives of the Njûrincheke council of elders, met for a joint feast, which included 'a bull for water' (*ndewa ya ûkundia rûûî*). A total of 74 elders attended.

Demolition of the clan house and its consequences

After the joint meeting on 27 April 2015, progress with the homicide compensation payments stalled for three months, due to financial difficulties among the Amwari clan. When I visited Karatho at his homestead on 10 August, he told me he could wait no longer for them to proceed to the next stage, and that he would be better off taking revenge for his murdered son with *kîthiri*. I noticed that Karatho's anger was never easily tamed. He also told me he had already sent one of his sons to be initiated into the Njûrincheke council of elders, under the instruction of Kauo, the Athimba's advisor.[27] This action later aroused intense criticism from local Njûrincheke elders, who believed it was wrong for Karatho's son to be initiated in a village of the Îgembe South Division, from where Kauo originated. They argued that any candidate should instead be initiated at his place of residence.

When I interviewed Karatho on 10 August, the clan house still stood at his homestead (see Photo 4.7). On 13 August, I interviewed him again for two hours, prior to the beginning of the next clan meeting, which he said he would attend to demand that the Athimba demolish the building. Its existence indicated the compensation process was still in progress, whereas destroying it would mean the process had ended. Karatho did not

---

27 This was in order for Karatho's son to witness *kîthiri*, which is administered in secret by the Njûrincheke council of elders.

want to wait any longer to be paid, and it was in his interests to demolish the house so that he could proceed with *kîthiri* against Nkiiri and his sons.

The 13 August meeting was held principally to settle a case of finger compensation (*kûrea kîara*). At the end of June 2015, a son of Kubai (of the Athimba clan) had used a *panga* (long-bladed knife) to chop off a woman's finger at a midnight bar in Athîrû Gaiti. The woman's father, M'Anampiû (of the Bwethaa clan's Lubetaa age-class) accepted Kubai's apology, and both parties agreed he should pay 40,000 shillings for expenses such as hospital bills. When I visited M'Anampiû on August 17, he said he required only an amicable settlement, in appreciation of Kubai's sincere approach after the incident, and their families' long history of friendship. Kubai initially paid M'Anampiû 20,000 shillings and was preparing to pay the rest as soon as possible.

The finger compensation meeting on 13 August – held at Kubai's homestead – was the third such since 30 July. At the previous meeting, the clan had decided each member should contribute 300 shillings towards the full amount. Their target was 40,000 shillings, including 1,000 shillings each from Kubai and his brothers. Kubai prepared meals for guests, expecting many to attend the meeting. All clan members were informed they should arrive by 11 am. I also attended the meeting. In the event, only a few elders appeared on time, with others arriving one by one. Karatho came at around 12.45 pm and spoke briefly with Kîthia, the chairman of the Athimba clan.[28]

The meeting finally began a few minutes before 1 pm. After an opening prayer by another attendant, Kîthia gave a speech to brief everyone on the day's agenda. In the following dialogue, he first addresses the issue of finger compensation, and then Karatho's request that the clan house be demolished.

---

28 Kîthia was elected clan chairman at the election on 14 August 2014, which I attended (see Chapter 7).

The Athimba

Dialogue 4.8 Finger compensation and the response to Karatho's request

Kîthia: Greetings, clan. Greetings, a person who doesn't die. Greetings, a person who eats his own.[29] I am grateful for the prayers, and I say that God shall bless the prayers among us.

We started meeting here at Kubai's place on 30 July. That was when we started meeting here because his son cut M'Anampiû's daughter's finger off. That's the reason we are meeting here, even today, to help to pay the expenses that M'Anampiû has asked for, which is 40,000 shillings.

As elders of the clan, we said on 6 August that every clan member was to contribute 300 shillings, brothers should give 1,000 shillings each, and Kubai himself should pay 10,000 shillings. That is what we said as the Athimba clan, according to the expenses.

Today is the day to contribute. The way we have come, the only path forward is to make a contribution (*marita*). I can see that some are coming to contribute.

Now, we beg for forgiveness from God in terms of the way we started contributing money, without giving thanks and praises. I give many thanks to those who have reached out and even to those on their way [to the meeting]. God is able to make you reach your goal.

The secretary is writing the names and continues to record the names of those who contribute money. Even if a person sends someone [with money], the name shall be written.

Karatho has an agenda. He has told me about the clan house, which he built at his compound, and he can't sleep

---

29 See Chapter 3 for greetings commonly used at clan meetings.

well because of the clan house. He wants us to set a date to demolish it according to the Kîmîîrû tradition, so that he will be able to proceed with his own issues.

It's like a person suffering from a toothache; when you're suffering, it aches all the time. Karatho is like a person suffering from a toothache. Whenever he sees the clan house, he feels uneasy. Now, my clan, we have to deal with those matters I have told you about, and you're welcome. If anyone has other issues, you can talk and feel welcome.

While the chairman was speaking, Kubai began serving lunch, alongside several women who had come to help with the cooking. Mûteethia, the former acting chairman, arrived at 1.15 pm, while the clan members were eating and chatting. Kîthia then explained the day's agenda once more. Mwenda, of the Lubetaa age-class, who speaks in the following dialogue, was not an Athimba clan member but often attended meetings out of curiosity. The clan welcomed any outsiders who could help settle their problems and it was Mwenda who gave the aforementioned opening prayer.

Kîthia:	Today is the day for making contributions. We said that every clan member should contribute 300 shillings, Kubai's brothers should contribute 1,000 shillings each, and Kubai himself should pay 10,000 shillings. While today is a day for making contributions, Karatho also has another agenda. He wants the house at his homestead to be demolished. Karatho says he is going to bring a ram for this purpose.
Karatho:	Yes, I will buy a ram this Saturday.
Mwenda:	Karatho says that he will buy a ram this Saturday.
Mûteethia:	Now, Mwenda, I hear that we have such an issue (Karatho's case); however, that is not an issue to be quickly resolved.

>Rather, as a clan, we should hold a *nkilîba* (confidential talk) slowly, then find a solution. Today, I want the contributions to continue, because we have finished a *nkilîba* [for Kubai's case]. Now I only want contributions.

Some elders, including Kîthia and Mûteethia, were cautious in dealing with Karatho's proposal, for two main reasons. First, since demolishing the clan house would signify the end of the transaction, they needed to go carefully through all the proper steps. Second, it was the clan's first meeting since they had become aware of Karatho's controversial initiation of his son into the Njûrincheke council of elders. These issues engendered the elders' need to hold a *nkilîba*.

At 3.10 pm, after discussing the finger compensation case for one and a half hours, key elders went aside for the *nkilîba*. These included Kîthia (the chairman), Matî (the secretary), Mûteethia (the former acting chairman), Mwenda (a third party), and M'Mauta (the eldest member), among others. After forty minutes, they announced their conclusion: Karatho was to return on the following Thursday, 20 August, to hear the date of the clan house's demolition.

Mwenda: We just had a *nkilîba* and listened and talked very nicely with each other. We have decided that Karatho should remain silent until the day we arranged, Thursday, which is when we shall tell you when the house will be demolished. Then we can give you a date to remove the house. On Thursday, you should come, and the clan will set a date to demolish the house.

Mûteethia: My friend, when a person goes to ask permission [for marriage], that is not the day to get a wife. Today you have asked permission and the clan has heard that Karatho wants the house to be demolished. That's why they say the day [we will meet] will be on Thursday. They shall bring you a report. Just stay calm, the way you are. Now, we are finished.

The next clan meeting was held on 20 August, again at Kubai's homestead, to collect more contributions from clan members. Karatho did not appear. By then, by his own volition, he had demolished the clan house. During his opening speech, Kîthia (the chairman) referred briefly to this issue, saying he had received a phone call from Karatho, who told him what he had done. He continued that, although Karatho had asked him to visit in person, he refused, because issues concerning the entire clan should not be addressed by personal communication. Karatho's actions ultimately worsened his situation, with the elders halting any discussion of homicide compensation for his son. By the end of the meeting, the case had been abandoned.

Political turmoil in Îgembe

The sudden termination of Case 4.3, without reaching its final stage, was similar to Case 4.1 – in that it was caused by disagreements between the victim's father and other Athimba clan elders. The context, however, differed. By my observation, the disagreement in Case 4.3 stemmed not only from mutual misunderstanding and conflict over private and common interests, but also from regional power politics concerning the Njûrincheke chairmanship of the entire Îgembe community.

As reported by the Kenyan press, from February 2015 onwards the Njûrincheke council of elders of the entire Amîîrû community became involved in regional politics – splitting into two factions over the issue of leadership within the greater Meru region. According to a story published on the *Daily Nation*'s website on 13 June 2015,[30] one of the factions had visited President Uhuru Kenyatta at the State House – following the ousting of their leaders from the council and their replacement by a newly appointed chairman and secretary.

---

30 'Njuri Ncheke faction stages coup, gets President's support'; 13 June 2015, *Daily Nation* website; http://www.nation.co.ke.

Both the former and newly appointed chairmen of the council were of Îgembe origin, and Njûrincheke elders from all administrative divisions of the region were inevitably caught up in the power struggle over their election. It seems that those involved in factional strife became more and more concerned with state-level politics – which involved senators and the county governor – and that this affected village-level social relations.

In March 2015, at Karatho's request, the Athimba clan appointed Kauo (from the Îgembe South Division) as their advisor on homicide compensation. However, as the political confrontation described above heated up, the local branch of the Njûrincheke council – to which Kauo belonged – came to be recognised as a political opponent of the Athîrû Gaiti branch's elders. It was under Kauo's guardianship that Karatho, in August 2015, controversially sent one of his sons to the Îgembe South branch to be initiated into the Njûrincheke council. Both Athimba clan elders and Njûrincheke elders from Athîrû Gaiti criticised this and political differences, at least in part, led to Case 4.3 being abandoned.

Land adjudication and a church controversy

This chapter has described three cases of homicide compensation between 2001 and 2015, all of which were abandoned before reaching any conclusion. During this time, the Athimba accumulated knowledge of indigenous law, reinforcing their sense of clanship. Further, as the clan grew, its members were influenced by both a widely shared structural history and the regional politics of Îgembe society. Two other historical factors also had a major impact on the Athimba clanship – namely, land adjudication issues that began in 1989 and a dispute over the Kîraone community dispensary in 2006.

In March 2015, the Kenyan government began to issue official land title deeds to the people of Athîrû Gaiti and its neighbouring communities. The Îgembe Southeast Division (formerly the Athîrû Gaiti, or Thaichû, Sublocation) had first been declared an adjudication section in 1966 but, due to staff shortages, land adjudication was not initiated until 1989.

This transpired under the Land Adjudication Act (Cap 284), when a government demarcation officer was stationed in every adjudication section to register all plots and draw up maps of land boundaries (see Chapter 1).

In the 1990s, during the initial phase of the adjudication process, the clan was allocated a significant role in determining land boundaries in sparsely cultivated areas of the lower plain, known as *rwaanda*. In densely populated areas, it was relatively easy to identify which land plots were under private ownership. However, this proved more difficult in the vast virgin land of the lower plain, which was first demarcated into 'clan lands' and then distributed among clan members. The Athimba were one of several beneficiaries to claim and receive a large share of *mbûrago* (ancestral land). Intra-clan land distribution continued until the early 2000s and, during this time, the development of clanship among those Îgembe who lived in adjudication sections (including the Athimba) was associated with their interests in land resources.

The distribution came to an end in the early 2000s, when, by my observation, the people of Îgembe became generally less conscious of their clanship. The Athimba proved an exception to this – at least partially – because of their experience of homicide compensation from 2001 to 2002 (Case 4.1). Another critical incident occurred in 2006 – which also led to clanship being taken more seriously – namely, a dispute over a dispensary.

In 2006, a conflict arose over the ownership of Athîrû Gaiti's largest public dispensary which, in 1984, was built as part of a church compound at Kîraone market – with financial support from the World Bank and the donation of land, construction labour and materials by the local community. During its first decade, the dispensary was managed by the Maûa Methodist Hospital – the most advanced medical institution in the Îgembe region, which fell under the jurisdiction of the Methodist Church of Kenya. The church represented the largest, most established denomination in the Îgembe Southeast Division.

The ownership dispute began in 1996, with confrontations between those who claimed the hospital should remain at the same location as the dispensary, and those who argued that the Methodists should leave. The latter accused the hospital of consistently overcharging for medical services and argued that the dispensary should fall under community management, with government support. Matters intensified in 2006, when youths set fire to several private buildings in the Kîraone compound. In 2010, the dispute was taken to court. The whole affair enmeshed the Athimba in a deep internal conflict which threatened to split their community in two.

It was widely thought that in 1983 the clan had donated several acres of land to the Athîrû Gaiti community for the dispensary plot but, during the court case, one of the contesting parties stated that the Athimba had donated the land to the church. Further, both Mûnoru (H12) and another clan member were accused by their agnates of taking sides with the church hospital against the people's will (see Chapter 7). It was during this internal dispute that contention over the Athimba's chairmanship arose.

Although the Athimba held meetings from 2006 to 2007 (see Chapter 5), they did not openly address the dispensary matter – focusing instead on issues such as family disputes. Neither was the issue discussed during 2011's meetings, which dealt with the reconciliation of the two 'brothers' in Case 4.2. Indeed, I came to understand that the dispensary dispute was too sensitive to be discussed as part of an open agenda (see Chapter 7 for further developments in this case).

Fifteen years of clan making in a local context

The homicide compensation cases described in this chapter required that the Athimba work together as a clan, but during a time when unity and clanship were often in dispute – as exemplified between 2001 and 2015 by political controversy, land adjudication issues and the dispensary dispute. Indeed, reaching mutual intra-clan agreements proved more difficult than achieving inter-clan reconciliations – as in Cases 4.2 and

4.3. Moreover, the Athimba's clan chairmanship was never properly determined during this period. This may be largely attributed to their being enmeshed in the dispensary case. Finally, though, some resolution came in August 2014, with the appointment of Kîthia of the Mîrîti age-class as the Athimba's new chairman, in the culmination of the process described below.

On 9 August 2014, the Njûrincheke elders of all Îgembe communities organised a general meeting at their headquarters in Mîori, to commemorate the official transfer of power from the Lubetaa to the Mîrîti age-class (see Chapter 2). The Athimba clan also underwent such generational change, with the handing over of power to and from the Lubetaa age-class over the previous fifteen years.

Various elders of the Mîchûbû age-class, such as Ntika and M'Barûngû, were still alive in the early 2000s. In the 2010s, after they had passed away, elders of the Ratanya age-class, such as M'Lichoro (H29) and Mûteethia (H26), became the oldest clan members. Mûnoru (H12) of the Lubetaa age-class (one of M'Barûngû's sons) was appointed chairman in 2003 but replaced by Ntika's son (H18) of the Mîrîti age-class in November 2006. Due to a years-long dispute that arose among the Athimba over this matter (see Chapter 7 and Case 5.10), Mûteethia served as acting chairman for around eight years, until 14 August 2014. Kîthia (H3) of the Mîrîti age-class was then elected as clan chairman (see also Chapter 7) – having worked as clan secretary and documented every detail of the homicide compensation payment in Case 4.1.

Chapter 5
Clanship and îchiaro: The individual, the depersonalised and the indeterminate

In the communities of Îgembe, each clan has a reciprocal *îchiaro* relationship with two others. People related by *îchiaro* address one another as *mûtanoba* (brother; literally, 'son from the same father'), while biological brothers address one another as *mûtanochia* (brother; literally, 'son from the same mother'). This inter-clan fellowship has existed for many generations and cannot be altered, because no individual may change their ascribed, or biological, status. Clan members are conditioned to fear and respect their *îchiaro* counterparts – also known as *îchiaro* or *aîchiaro* (singular *mwîchiaro*) – and vice versa.

The previous chapters documented several cases in which *îchiaro* from distant villages were invited to serve as third-party advisors, witnesses or mediators. This chapter illustrates how *îchiaro* who long ago migrated to their counterparts' villages now experience a sense of indeterminacy, or otherness.

The sons of M'Ikîrîma – the late Kîng'angi, Nchee, Kîberenge, Mwaambia and Meeme (see Figure 5.1) – are key figures in the complex cases discussed below. Hailing from the Antûambûi clan in Laare (see Figure 1.1), in the 1950s they migrated with their father to Mûringene village, where they were allocated land by the Athimba, their *îchiaro* counterparts. They have since assimilated into the clan but their *îchiaro* status remains to some degree. While certain Athimba understand M'Ikîrîma's sons to have become full clan members – because they have shared the same water for several years – others maintain that they remain *îchiaro*. These viewpoints derive from different contextual considerations.

This chapter also discusses how the egalitarian principle of *îchiaro* relationships functions in local conflict management. When an individual from another clan is invited as *mwîchiaro* – for the purposes of mediation or cursing – they should neither identify themselves as an expert with private capacities nor use their power for their own purposes. In other words, they serve only to represent their clan. Accordingly, in Case 5.10, below, when *îchiaro* men come face to face, they depersonalise themselves in their speech. While the first nine cases in this chapter are only described in outline, the last case (Case 5.10) describes the interaction in detail. The depersonalising scene will be revealed in this last case.

Case 5.1: Homicide compensation, April to June 2013

In May 2013, the Athimba clan received homicide compensation from the neighbouring Bwethaa, following the murder of Kîng'angi in the late 1990s by an unnamed suspect. Kîng'angi was a second-generation migrant from the Antûambûi clan of Laare and had lived for many decades in Mûringene village.

This section focuses on two issues: (1) The role of the *kîthiri* oath in homicide compensation; (2) The question of to whom and to which clan (Athimba or Antûambûi) the compensation should be paid.

The compensation process for Kîng'angi's murder was completed in less than two months – a significantly shorter time than in Case 4.1. When Kîng'angi's corpse was found in his compound, the suspect – of the Bwethaa clan – initially denied responsibility. He was then put in *kîthiri* (meaning literally 'a pot'; indicating here the *kîthiri* oath – see Chapters 3 and 4) and cursed by Ngatûnyi at Njûrincheke (the council of elders). The suspect was subsequently murdered during a robbery in 2006 – long before the Bwethaa addressed Kîng'angi's homicide. His family also befell grave misfortune, with two of the suspect's brothers being seriously injured in a traffic accident, and another brother and a nephew succumbing to illness and dying. According to the Athimba, the suspect's remaining brothers believed the *kîthiri* oath was responsible for these tragedies. However, the brothers argued that the true perpetrator remained unknown and *kîthiri* was not responsible for their family's afflictions. Nevertheless, they disliked the damaging local rumours and, given that one of the brothers was wealthy, agreed to pay compensation to ensure the curse be removed and their reputation restored as soon as possible.

Below, I describe the process by which, following the negotiation of homicide compensation during inter-clan meetings between the Athimba and Bwethaa, reparative items were distributed to Kîng'angi's relatives – and the significance of clan identity to this.

Kîthia (H3; Table 4.1), the Athimba's clan secretary, recounted Kîng'angi's clan history to me. Kîng'angi was the eldest biological brother of Nchee (H20), Mwaambia (H21) and Meeme (H22). When M'Ikîrîma, Kîng'angi's father, first came to Mûringene, Kamanja (biological grandfather to H1, H2, H3 and H4) and his younger brother Mûmama served as hosts. Kamanja and Mûmama (each of the Kîramunya age-class) welcomed and donated land to their *îchiaro*, in a process named *ûkîlua kîthiana*. M'Ikîrîma and his sons thereafter lived among the Athimba clan. From a biological perspective, they were still Antûambûi, but from a sociological perspective they became Athimba. Kîthia's point of view was that the brothers' status as *îchiaro* had weakened because they had been assimilated into the Athimba.

Table 5.1 shows the compensation items paid between April and May 2013. The numbers in square brackets refer to Figure 5.1, which identifies individuals by their genealogy.

Kîng'angi's close relatives were given five of the eight head of cattle brought by the Bwethaa.[1] Kîng'angi's mother's *ntaû*[2] [9] was given a ram, which was slaughtered at his brother Mwaambia's homestead for a feast that included six granddaughters. Mwaambia [2] received a milking

---

1   This included 16,000 shillings cash that was paid in lieu of a calf.
2   *Ntaû* denotes the relationship between two persons who share the same name. In Amîîrû tradition, children are named after one of their older relatives (see Chapter 6). In this case, Kîng'angi's mother's granddaughters, who were from the same neighbourhood, were invited to a feast as *ntaû*.

Table 5.1 Distribution of compensation items

Date	Items	Recipient
April 2013	One she-goat for a chief elder (*mparika ya mûaambi*).	M'Lichoro (H29) (*mûtûngûri*) [Athimba].
13 May	A bundle of *mîraa* (*nchoolo ya mîraa*) [paid in 5,000 shillings cash].	Distributed among clan members [Athimba].
	One ram for respect (*ntûrûme ya uthoni*).	Kîng'angi's mother's *ntaû* [9] c/o Mwaambia.
	One ewe for respect (*mwatî ya ûthoni*).	Meeme [4].
	One she-goat for respect (*mparika ya ûthoni*).	Ntongai (*mûtûngûri*) [Athimba].
14 May	One milking cow with a calf (*nkiria na atang'atangi*.	Mwaambia [2] (*atang'atangi* for Ngatûnyi from Laare [1]).
	One heifer (*mwari*).	Kîng'angi's son [8].
	One she-goat (*mparika*).	Îrukî [Mûmama's house] [Athimba].
17 May	One bull for giving water (*ndewa ya rûûjî*).	Slaughtered for a joint feast at a clan house [Athimba and Bwethaa].
	One calf for the clan (*njaû ya mwîria*) [paid in 16,000 shillings cash].	Distributed among clan members [Athimba].
	One she-goat (*mparika*).	Mbanga (H15) [Athimba].
28 May	One small bull for exorcising death (*ntaa kîî*).	Ndatu [6].
	One heifer (*mwarî*).	Kajuuju (Kîng'angi's son's wife) [7].
	One she-goat (*mparika*).	Murithi (Kîng'angi's sister) [5].
30 May	One bull for calling for a head (*ndewa ya ûkûrîra kîongo*).	Slaughtered at Njûrincheke (hide given to Mwaambia's wife [3]).
	One ram for smearing fat (*ntûrûme ya waakana mauta*).	Slaughtered at Njûrincheke.
	One he-goat (*nthenge*).	Slaughtered at Njûrincheke.
	One she-goat (*mparika*).	Ntongai (*mûtûngûri*) [Athimba].

cow, which should have been accompanied by the calf (*atang'atangi*) which, in the event, was given to Ngatûnyi [1] (Kîng'angi's FBS).

Ngatûnyi is a biological father's brother's son (FBS) to the late Kîng'angi and his brothers: Kîberenge (H19; Table 4.1); Nchee (H20); Mwaambia (H21); and Meeme (H22). However, he continues to reside in their native Laare as *mwantûambûi* (an Antûambûi clan member) and thus retains his status as *mwîchiaro* to the Athimba. By this reckoning, it appears that an Antûambûi clan member received homicide compensa-

Clanship and *ichiaro*   147

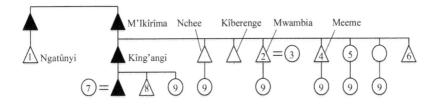

Figure 5.1 Distribution of compensation items among M'Ikîrîma's sons

tion. However, during the compensation process, Ngatûnyi was assumed to be of the Athimba.

Aside from the distribution of compensation items to individuals, one of the nine bulls was slaughtered for another feast at Mwaambia's homestead, where a clan house (*nyumba ya mwîrîa*) had been built for the elders. The last animal was slaughtered on the day of *ûkûrîra kîongo* (calling for a head), when both parties met to reconcile in the presence of the Njûrincheke council of elders. As part of a ritual cleansing, Ngatûnyi of the Antûambûi clan and Gitonga (biological brother of the suspect) of the Bwethaa smeared ram's fat on each other (*waakana mauta*).

In April 2013, Baariu of the Bwethaa clan was sent with a she-goat to M'Lichoro (H29) of the Athimba. Both were Njûrincheke elders. M'Lichoro was consulted because he was regarded as a *mûaambi* (spokesman or chief elder) of the Athimba and because his mother belonged to the Bwethaa. The two men agreed to a discount on the number of compensatory cattle to be paid, taking into account the affinal relationship between the two parties.

On 18 April, soon after the consultation, the eleven Athimba elders met at M'Lichoro's homestead. They comprised Kabeeria (H21), Ndatû (H18), Kîthia (H3), Kîthia's brother (H2), Mûteethia (H26), M'Lichoro (H29) and five other elders from Mûmama's house. The clan sent Mwaambia (H21) and another elder to Laare to inform Ngatûnyi (of the Antûambûi). The Athimba record, dated 25 April 2013, notes that the 'sons' (descendants) of both Kamanja and Mûmama would inherit the deceased's properties (*kû-ria ûkûa*).³ This implied the Athimba were 'brothers' of the victim and should thus receive compensation.

Items given to the Athimba elders included: (1) a she-goat for M'Lichoro, the chief elder (*mûaambi*); (2) two she-goats for Ntongai, as messenger (*mûtûngûri*); (3) a she-goat for Îrukî, chief elder of Mûmama's house; (4) a she-goat for Mbanga (H15), who had previously contributed a he-goat for a feast at Mwaambia's homestead; (5) 21,000 shillings in cash (5,000 shillings for a bundle of *mîraa* and 16,000 shillings for a calf), to be shared among the clan. Beside these payments, the Athimba elders present were treated to the meat of two he-goats and a bull; both of which were slaughtered at Mwaambia's residence.

Three important facts emerged from the above compensation process.

First, the Athimba, including Kîng'angi's brothers, were orientated towards confession-based conflict management; understanding that the *kîthiri* oath should be directed towards the Bwethaa clan, to obtain an admission of guilt over the homicide.

Second, although Kîng'angi and his brothers were second-generation *îchiaro* migrants from Laare – and Ngatûnyi (Kîng'angi's FBS) remained in Laare as a member of the Antûambûi – the Bwethaa regarded them as Athimba and duly paid them compensation.

Third, the compensation items were not distributed equally between Kîng'angi's brothers. The Athimba regarded Mwaambia – one of Kîng'angi's younger siblings – as the family representative, and therefore requested that, for the duration of the case, he provide the elders with sustenance and a clan house (*nyumba ya mwîrîa*) at his homestead. Accordingly, Mwaambia was given the largest share of compensation from the Bwethaa. Two elder brothers, Nchee and Kîberenge, received nothing, because they had made no contributions to the elders; their reasoning being that such expenditure may have cancelled out the value of any compensation they received.

---

3   As per Chapter 4, footnote 25, the phrase *kûrîa ûkûa* ('to eat the dead') indicates that the surviving brothers of the deceased will inherit his properties.

Clanship and *îchiaro* 149

Incidentally, when I interviewed Mwaambia, he told me that he would share his compensation with Nchee and Kîberenge.

Cases 5.2–5.9: Athimba clan record, June 2006 to November 2007

When the Athimba clan members met in Mûringene village, Kîthia (H3) – who served as clan secretary for some years and became chairman in 2014 – usually recorded the proceedings. Entries for the clan record book from 12 June 2006 to 20 October 2007 summarise eight further cases heard by the clan elders, which are presented below.

Case 5.2: Dispute between Nchee's wives, heard on 12 June 2006

Nchee (H20), of the Lubetaa age-class, was first married to Kaario, with whom he had a son and two daughters. Kaario left the family in 1984, and Nchee remarried to Miriam, with whom he had two sons and two daughters – each of whom remained single. Kaario suddenly returned to Nchee in 2006, upon the marriage of their son. At this point, a property dispute between the two wives erupted and the clan elders instructed them to summon their *mwîchiaro* to seek reconciliation. They were also required to clarify the conditions of Nchee's *mîraa*-leasing contract, so that a part of his property could be allocated to Kaario. Mwaambia (H21) – Nchee's brother – bore witness (*mûkûûjî*) to this settlement. Twenty-eight elders, including the area assistant chief, also attended the hearing.

Case 5.3: Land inheritance dispute between two brothers and their sister's son, heard on 11 August 2006

M'Barûngû[4] (of the Mîchûbû age-class) allocated land to his daughter's son (of the Bwantai age-class). However, M'Barûngû's two sons, of the Lubetaa age-class – Mûnoru (H12) and his brother (H13) – plotted to

---

4 M'Barûngû, who passed away in 2010, was also involved as clan chairman in the homicide compensation process of 2001 to 2002 (Case 4.1).

chase the recipient off. Ultimately, the clan elders supported M'Barûngû's decision over land allocation.[5]

Case 5.4: Dispute between clan members over a ram, heard on 11 November 2006

Mbanga (H15; of the Ratanya age-class) consumed a ram belonging to his eldest brother's son, Îrukî (H14's brother; also of the Ratanya age-class),[6] who argued that Mbanga should replace it. Kîberenge (H19; of the Lubetaa age-class), attended the hearing as *mwîchiaro* from the Antûambûi clan, and testified that he had witnessed Mbanga consuming the animal. Mbanga confessed and promised to provide a replacement. Fearing the family's *mwîchiaro*, Mbanga's son Richard (H16; of the Bwantai age-class) then made an unexpected confession of irresponsible behaviour – that, having taken a lease on the *mîraa* plants growing in his cousin Îrukî's field, he had neglected to harvest their shoots. This left the plants vulnerable to damage unless the situation were quickly remedied. Ultimately, both Mbanga and Richard's cases were resolved, in the presence of 36 elders.

Case 5.5: Land dispute, heard on 11 November 2006

Kînyûûrû (of the Mîchûbû age-class) sold communal property without seeking the clan's consensus. The elders then sent Mpuria (a member of the *îchiaro* Andûûne clan's Mîrîti age-class) to Kînyûûrû's residence on the lower slope. Mpuria summoned Kînyûûrû to a clan meeting on 25 November 2006 but he failed to attend. At a further meeting on

---

5 Matsuzono (2020, 43–48) interviewed fathers who had allotted land to their daughters; be they married, unmarried or divorced. Some of the elders I interviewed recognised that both daughters and sons should receive their share of land.

6 It sometimes occurs that a man and his brother's son belong to the same age-class. Mbanga was circumcised as Ratanya Nding'ûri in 1948 (by the majority of the Ratanya elders' recollection; in 1949, by Mbanga's recollection), while Îrukî was circumcised as Ratanya Kabeeria in 1957 (see Table 2.3). Mbanga, the youngest of the family's brothers, was born near the time of Îrukî's father's circumcision. Peatrik (2019, 89) notes, 'A first underlying rule lies in the domain of the family: as soon as a son or daughter is (was) initiated, their parents must stop having children.'

November 29, the elder M'Barûngû declared that Kînyûûrû would not respond to any summons and that the case should instead be taken to the land office.

Case 5.6: Land dispute, heard on 25 November 2006

The neighbours Ciomûthoi (H5; wife to the late M'Mwambi of the Mîchûbû age-class) and Kîeri (see PN4, Chapter 6),[7] of the Amwari clan, became embroiled in a land dispute. They requested the clan elders to invite their *mwîchiaro* to settle the case by planting a cursing shrub at the appropriate land border. First, however, a third neighbour was consulted, who knew that the border was marked by a particular tree stump. This worked against Kauo's claim and Mpuria – a *mwîchiaro* of the Andûûne clan (see Case 5.5) – determined that Kauo should end his quarrel with Ciomûthoi. The clan elders ruled that no *mwîchiaro* curse was needed, as the case had been resolved.

Case 5.7: Case of an uncooperative *mwîchiaro*, heard on 27 January 2007

Nchee (H20) and Mwaambia (H21) – the sons of M'Ikîrîma (of the Antûambûi clan) – were allocated a piece of land in Mûringene village. However, the brothers failed in their duty to assist the Athimba – their *îchiaro*. Some clan members insisted they should be fined one bull, but the clan elders ruled this would be inappropriate for a *mwîchiaro*. In accordance with Kîmîîrû tradition, the brothers were instead instructed to pay *nkome* (a token of apology) to the clan, in the form of 500 shillings each.

Case 5.8: Dispute over land resale in Ngawa, heard on 27 January 2007

M'Imaana (of the Amwari clan's Mîchûbû age-class) sold land in the lower slope area that had been gifted to him many years earlier by Baitumbîrî (father of H1, H2, H3 and H4). To recruit M'Imaana to Njûrincheke, Baitumbîrî assumed the role of his *îthe-wa-njûri* (Njûrincheke father),

---

7   The husband of a woman who was accused of witchcraft and took an *îchiaro* oath during her case in 2005 (see Appendix 2).

after which the pair developed a strong friendship. Following Baitumbîrî's death, his son Kîthia (H3) became M'Imaana's guardian and, later, when M'Imaana sold the lower slope land, he presented Kîthia with a goat's head (*mûtwe*) as a token of his appreciation. However, Mûnoru (H12), Mûteethia (H26) and another elder claimed M'Imaana should also have presented them with gifts. Kîthia explained his family connection to the land and said the three elders had no grounds to suggest M'Imaana was in their debt. Nevertheless, on 22 September 2007, M'Imaana and Kîthia paid *nkome* of 500 shillings to the clan, to restore harmony (*ngwataniro*).

Case 5.9: Land dispute, heard on 20 October 2007

When Matî (H9) sold a hilly part of his land in the lower slope area to another farmer, local land board member Chege tainted the transaction with illegal activity. Matî and Ndatû (H18) reported this to the land office and were told to visit Maûa police station to obtain a warrant for Chege's arrest. Chege was subsequently detained.

Cases 5.3, 5.8 and 5.9, which were summarised in the record book alongside the other five cases described in this section, did not require the invocation of *îchiaro*. Specifically, in Cases 5.3 and 5.8, members resolved their land disputes within the clan; while in Case 5.9 – another land dispute – a state agency was called on. The following discussion focuses only on those cases in which *îchiaro* was invoked.

As presented above, Cases 5.1, 5.2, 5.4, 5.5, 5.6, 5.7 and 5.8 reveal local theory of biological determinism in the *îchiaro* relationship. While the power of *îchiaro* is based on biological status in terms of clan affiliation, in practice it is conditioned by social and historical processes. For example, Nchee (H20) asserts to outsiders that he is a member of the Athimba clan but, from a biological perspective, he and his brothers belong to the Antûambûi – one of the Athimba's two *îchiaro* clans. Ever since their father was allocated land by the Athimba, the brothers have lived in Mûringene village but, because the Athimba elders remember their biological origin, in certain cases their power of *îchiaro* is invoked for dispute settlement.

Nchee is a key figure in Cases 5.2 and 5.7 in this section, and Case 5.10 in the following one. Because he and his brothers appear as disputants, they are not called upon to serve as *îchiaro*. Case 5.2 concerns a conflict between Nchee's two co-wives, during which the Athimba instruct Nchee to allocate shares of his property to them. In Case 5.7, Nchee himself is the defendant against other clan members, who challenge his unique position as an *îchiaro* migrant. Nchee and one of his brothers (Mwaambia) are publicly blamed by their *îchiaro* counterparts – the Athimba clan elders – for ignorance of their obligation to respect their host clan. Although the brothers are not subjected to any direct disciplinary action, they are requested to pay cash as *nkome*.

In Case 5.4, the presence of Nchee's biological brother Kîberenge sparks the defendants' admission of responsibility, as they are afraid of giving false testimony before him as their *mwîchiaro*. Kîberenge is also generally feared by the Athimba for his eccentric personality. Having remained single for a long time, he often relies on his Athimba neighbours for food and lodging. The neighbours cannot refuse Kîberenge, because of his *mwîchiaro* status, but some find his behaviour somewhat disturbing.

Cases 5.5 and 5.6 describe Mpuria – of the *îchiaro* Andûûne clan – serving as *mwîchiaro* to settle a dispute at an Athimba clan meeting. Mpuria's homestead is around three kilometres from Mûringene village, and he travels there only in special situations. His father, the late Kiwanthi (of the Mîchûbû age-class) was widely known as Thirua (a type of wildebeest), and was feared by the Athimba for his aggressive, stern demeanour. These traits made him indispensable as a *mwîchiaro* counterpart because, in certain situations, a hostile *mwîchiaro* is more suitable than a placatory one – especially when elders use the power of *îchiaro* against fellow clan members. After Kiwanthi's death, Mpuria inherited his role, but he too soon died and was succeeded by his biological brother, Mbiti, as described in the next section.

Case 5.10: Group cursing at Nchee's residence, 7 September 2012

On Friday 7 September 2012, six *îchiaro* men visited Nchee's homestead to place a curse. The meeting was organised to remedy a series of misfortunes Nchee had suffered since 2010, when his first son succumbed to a short illness and died. In 2011, one of Nchee's goats either was lost or stolen, and a suspicious object was placed on his *kîlaa* (*mîraa* tree) by an unknown person. In 2012, Nchee's dog was poisoned, also by an unknown person.

The conflict between Nchee's wives recorded in Case 5.2 resurfaced at this point, with Nchee's first wife, Kaario, accusing his second, Miriam, of being a sorcerer (*mûroi*) and causing the family's misfortunes. Miriam denied the allegation, which was neither substantiated by any evidence nor supported by relatives and neighbours.

Case 5.10 differs significantly from Case 5.2 in that it was viewed not only as a dispute between wives but also as one of malicious damage by an unknown person. To ensure the offender was sanctioned, every clan member who might have been involved was put under a conditional curse by his or her respective *mwîchiaro*. Six men were summoned to conduct the ceremony, each of whom shared *îchiaro* relationships with either Nchee's wives or neighbouring clans. Kaario, Nchee's first wife, belonged to the Akinying'a. Her *mwîchiaro* was Nderi of the Antûambui (as distinct from the Antûambûi, to whom Nchee and his brothers originally belonged). Miriam belonged to the Anjarû. Her *îchiaro* included Njou and Kîûa of the Akachiû, and Nderi of the Antûambui. Three Njûrincheke elders were also summoned: Reuben of the Antûbakîthoro; Mbiti of the Andûûne; and Kaumbu of the Antûamûtî.

The elders listed in Table 5.2 – Reuben, Mbiti and Kaumbu – attended as *mwîchiaro* to Mûringene village's major clans: Amwari, Athimba and Antûambeti. However, because other, minor clans – to which Nchee's wives belonged – also resided in the village, they were required for the conditional curse to be effective. Some people also believed the Akachiû had a special function because they shared an *îchiaro* relationship with

Clanship and *îchiaro*

Table 5.2 The six *îchiaro* men summoned for group cursing

Name	Clan	*Îchiaro* clans
Reuben	Antûbakîthoro	Amwari
Mbiti	Andûûne	Athimba
Kaumbu	Antûamûtî	Antûambeti
Nderi	Antûambui	Akinying'a and Anjarû
Njou	Akachiû	Anjarû and all other clans in Athîrû Gaiti
Kîûa	Akachiû	Anjarû and all other clans in Athîrû Gaiti

not only the Anjarû but all other clans of the Athîrû Gaiti community (see Case 3.4).

The cursing ceremony was hampered by a series of absences. Miriam (Table 5.3 [3]) was away from home at the time and, since her presence was essential, the *îchiaro* men told Nchee to locate her. Ngatûnyi (Nchee's FBS) of the Antûambûi clan was called but could not attend due to illness. Nchee's biological brothers – Kîberenge (H19), Mwaambia (H21) and Meeme (H22) – were also absent, although Meeme's wife did attend. Mwaambia and Meeme's non-attendance was not seen as problematic, while Kîberenge complained after the event that he had not been informed of the meeting.

Several Athimba clan members also attended the ceremony. Kabwî (Kînyûûrû's brother's son; see Case 5.5), who was the meeting's organiser, and Mûnoru (H12), the self-proclaimed clan chairman, appeared as elders. Immediately before the meeting, the pair began to quarrel (Table 5.3 [2]) because the *îchiaro* men had left the compound without informing Kabwî, and Mûnoru wanted to know why. Although they soon realised the men were occupied with making arrangements outside Nchee's homestead, abusive words were exchanged. Mûnoru blamed Kabwî for mismanagement, while Kabwî criticised Mûnoru, saying he seemed to be drunk and had never been recognised as clan chairman. (As noted in Chapters 4 and 7, a disagreement over the chairmanship had resulted in some Athimba elders recognising the need for an election.)

Table 5.3 Timeline of the group cursing

Time	Process
2.20 pm	Guests are served lunch at Nchee's homestead.
2.34 pm	The group of *îchiaro* men leave to find cursing plants (*kûramûka kamwari*) [1].
3.18 pm	Mûnoru arrives at the compound and begins to quarrel with Kabwî [2].
3.35 pm	The *îchiaro* men traverse Nchee's homestead and find that Miriam is absent [3].
4.17 pm	The *îchiaro* men order Nchee to find Miriam.
4.27 pm	Nchee and Mbiti visit Miriam's hut.
4.30 pm	Miriam arrives.
4.31 pm	The *îchiaro* men are asked to stand in a line, and are then placed under a conditional curse by Nchee's wives and Kabwî [4].
4.34 pm	Each clan member present, irrespective of their connection to sorcery, is interrogated by one of the *îchiaro* men, who is holding a small bundle of cursing plants [5].
4.43 pm	The *îchiaro* men place a curse on the unknown offender [6].
4.50 pm	The *îchiaro* men gather and tie the small bundles of cursing plants into a larger bundle [7].
4.57 pm	The *îchiaro* men traverse Nchee's homestead for a final observation.
5.13 pm	The placing of the curse concludes with *kwiita rwîî* [8].

Table 5.3 presents the timeline of the cursing ceremony, as per my observations. After lunch, the *îchiaro* men left Nchee's homestead to find cursing plants (*kamwari*) – an activity known as *kûramûka kamwari*[8] (see Photo 5.1 and Table 5.3 [1]). The plants included *mûroo* leaves (*Dovyalis abyssinica*), *îoka* grass (*Cynodon dactylon*), *mûtoongu* root (*Solanum incanum*), *mûooru* leaves (*Pycnostachys umbrosa*) and *rûthirû* (fern). These were tied into bundles.

The group cursing consisted of four parts, as detailed below. Each was essential because only when all concerned parties had been subjected to a conditional curse could it take effect on the actual miscreants.

---

8   *Kûramûka kamwari* literally translates as 'to go and collect a small daughter.'

Clanship and *îchiaro*

Photo 5.1 The *îchiaro* men collect cursing plants

The *îchiaro* men are placed under a conditional curse

Kaario and Miriam (Nchee's wives), together with Kabwî (the meeting's organiser) placed the *îchiaro* men under a conditional curse (Table 5.3 [4]). Due to their inexperience, Mbiti instructed them to repeat his words while using a bundle of *kamwari* to circle each of their *mwîchiaro*'s necks (Photo 5.2). Mbiti named this action both '*ku-thîînja*' ('to slaughter') and '*ku-iita nkingo*' ('to cut the neck'). Kaario performed the ritual on Reuben and Nderi, Miriam performed it on Njou and Kîûa, and Kabwî on Mbiti.

The following dialogue demonstrates how Miriam was instructed to place both herself *and* her *îchiaro* men under the conditional curse. Initially, she flailed under Mbiti's instruction, but in time achieved success.

Mbiti: You just slaughter [you and your *mwîchiaro*] while we are watching… [Miriam appears confused.] What kind of woman is this? Who is your *mwîchiaro*?

Photo 5.2 'Cutting the neck' of the *mwîchiaro*

Miriam: I don't know who is mine.

Reuben: She is from the Anjarû clan and a daughter of M'Mpara. Her *îchiaro* is Akachiû.

Miriam: Now listen, if I have something that can harm someone's child, let me perish! And if you secretly come at night or day, your seeds of boys and girls should be poured on the ground!

Mbiti: You have not cut him in the way we wanted (*ûtaiitana bûûra tûkweenda*). Tell him, 'If you try to go at night or daytime or you spit saliva without my knowledge, you should be cut like this!' (*wîyîkia wîîta ûtukû kana mûthenya kana ûaikîa mataa ntîkûmenya ûrotuîkaa ûû!*)

Miriam: If you try to go at night or daytime or you spit saliva without my knowledge, you should be cut like this!

Clanship and *îchiaro*

Photo 5.3 Participants being interrogated by *îchiaro*

Interrogation of attending clan members

Next, each attending clan member was interrogated over whether they practised witchcraft (Photo 5.3). After replying no, they were told to spit on the cursing plant held in their *mwîchiaro*'s hands. They were then considered to have been placed under a conditional curse by all six *îchiaro* men (Table 5.3 [5]).

Placing a curse on unknown perpetrators

The *îchiaro* men, led by Reuben and Mbiti, next recited a curse against the unknown perpetrators (Table 5.3 [6] and Photo 5.4) facing south towards the sacred volcanic hill of Kîrîmakîerû (the White Hill; see Chapter 1).

Reuben:	Please, now the sun, you rise from below, then set on the Nyambene Hill. Now I tell you, witches. If you know you possess witches or charms and you are left with it, surely I don't leave you in this compound, but I leave you at Kîrîmakîerû. Now surely, I ask for everything. I also ask for charms, and I ask with our herbs (*kaarî*),[9] and I ask with everything that is required in the Kîmîîrû tradition. Surely, if there's someone who sends a person to this homestead using money so that this home can collapse or who likes to see this home destroyed or wants to see the home in shabby condition, surely I won't allow him in this homestead. I exile him to Kîrîmakîerû, and I am standing on one leg (*ndakinya îruu*). We will leave him in the wilderness, and his flesh will be eaten by vultures.
Îchiaro men:	[Each standing on one leg] We will leave him in the wilderness, and his flesh will be eaten by vultures.
Mbiti:	Stand on one leg, all of you.
Reuben:	Surely, if anyone knows what killed a son of this family, and he knows the secret… We will exile him to Kîrîmakîerû, and he should be eaten by a lion (*tûmûtia kîrîmakîerû aroriwa nîî simba*).
Îchiaro men:	He should be eaten by a lion.
Mbiti:	He should be hit by a vehicle, and the one who was sent should be hit by a motorcycle. He should be killed by a python (*ndatû*).
Îchiaro men:	[Each standing on one leg] He should be hit by a vehicle, and the one who was sent should be hit by a motorcycle. He should be killed by a python.

---

9   The term *kaarî* literally means 'small girl' (see footnote 8).

Clanship and *îchiaro*

Photo 5.4 *Îchiaro* men placing the curse while standing on one leg

Photo 5.5 An *îchiaro* man turns his back to the large bundle on the ground

Reuben: Let him fall on the white grass (*nyankine înjarû*)[10] and be consumed by wild animals… [The cursing continues.]

The *îchiaro* men then gathered the small bundles of herbs they had been holding, to form one large bundle – known as the 'cursed object'. This was bound by a rope of *rûoka*[11] (Table 5.3 [7]). The bundle was

---

10 In this context, 'white grass' refers to Kîrîmakierû (the White Hill) and the plain.
11 *Rûoka* is a variety of grass that can be tied into rope.

then borne jointly by the *îchiaro* men as they pronounced *Tûmûkundîka* ('We tie him').

> Reuben: We tie him. We send him away to Kîrîmakîerû (*tûmûtaa Kîrîmakîerû*). We tie him with rûoka (*tûmûkundîka rûoka*)! We throw him away!

After placing the bundle on the ground, the *îchiaro* men lay down over it in turn, cursing the anonymous offender with the words, 'I turn my back to him (*Nkûmuutatîra*)' (Photo 5.5). In the following dialogue, *mpangaa* (cursed object) and *kiimba* (dead body) both refer to the bundle.

> Reuben: Come here, *îchiaro*. Let them see the cursed object. Now we are going to turn our back (*twetaa kûtatira*) [to the cursed one].
>
> Nderi: Now he's in the wilderness.
>
> Reuben: I turn my back to him. I turn my back to him.
>
> Mbiti: Surely, this person is cursed. I turn my back also to his children, boys and girls. Let them perish. Surely, I turn my back to him. I even incite him to lose control of his bowels (*nkûmuutatîra, nkûmûringîra kinya mai*).
>
> Nderi: He isn't left by the powerful *îchiaro* (*atatîlwa nîî îchiaro îtûnga*).[12] Surely, they do not permit him here, and now the sun is going to set. Let it set with him.
>
> Kaumbu: Surely, we turn our backs to him, and even his wife should not menstruate (*kinya mûka wake akorona mweri*). I turn my back to him.

---

12 The term '*îchiaro îtûnga*' indicates that the *îchiaro* hold more power as a group than individually.

Clanship and *îchiaro*

Njou:	Uui, I turn my back to him. Let him die. Let him get lost in the wilderness. Let his wife eject placenta (*mwekûrû wake aromiaa thiirii*). I have left him in the wilderness of hyenas (*rwaanda rwa mbiti*).
Kîûa:	Let him live like a rat (*mbîa*). I turn my back to him. Let his head be broken by his son.
Reuben:	Now, *îchiaro*, let all come and give me this person (the cursed object). When you are lifting him, make a loud cry.
All:	Uui, uui, now he's dead.
Mbiti:	Now the corpse (*kiimba*) we are going to throw away (*rîu kiimba kîî tweeta ûtaa*).

Kwiita rwîî to conclude the group cursing

The cursing concluded with *kwiita rwîî* (clapping of hands) by the whole meeting (Table 5.3 [8] and Photo 5.6). In the dialogue below, the *îchiaro*s' cursing words emphasise that each has attended as *mwîchiaro*; as opposed to as a private individual. For example, Mbiti represents the Andûûne clan, but neither in his own name, nor as an Njûrincheke elder, nor as a skilled mediator.

Mbiti:	Now we are closing the homestead. If anybody says I was here as Andûûne, his boys and girls should perish like this! [All clap.]
Reuben:	Now I say as Nkula or Antûbakîthoro. It was the clan that sent me; it was not the son of M'Thîrîbî.[13] Whoever says that I was the one here with this occasion, his sons and daughters, let them perish! [All clap.]

---

13 M'Thîrîbî is widely known in the neighbourhood as Reuben's father. Reuben's pronouncement indicates that to call him 'son of M'Thîrîbî' would fail to depersonalise him.

Photo 5.6 Clapping of hands to conclude the group cursing

Nderi: If anybody says I was the one as Antûambui, we do not allow him here! [All clap.]

Kaumbu: I am saying this as Antûamûtî. If anybody comes back and says I was the one who was here and if he got bribed to destroy this homestead, I won't allow him here. I will chase him to the wilderness! [All clap.]

Kîûa: I am saying this as Akachiû. I was here, but it was the clan that sent me. I won't leave him here. I chase him out to the wilderness! [All clap.]

Njoua: I am saying this as Akachiû. I was here, but it was the clan [that sent me]. I won't allow him here! [All clap.]

Clanship and *îchiaro* 165

With the group cursing over, the cursed object was taken by the *îchiaro* men to a secret place known only to them. The matter was then closed for the time being, with the intention that, whenever the unknown offender came forward to take responsibility for his or her crimes, the victim would receive ample justice and compensation. The *îchiaro* men would then also cleanse the cursed object to remove its power, which would otherwise continue to harm both them and their property.

Findings from Case 5.10

Four important findings emerged from my analysis of Case 5.10, which are presented and discussed below.

First, in the communities of Îgembe, even if the identity of a crime's perpetrator is unknown, there is an imperative to curse him or her. This case initially appeared to arise from a dispute between Nchee's wives, with Kaario accusing Miriam of witchcraft. Because Nchee was unable to resolve the issue himself, the wives' *îchiaro* men were invited to mediate. However, Nchee then argued that his misfortunes were actually the responsibility of anonymous neighbourhood miscreants, who had maliciously damaged his property. He thus attempted to resolve the issue by involving a group of men who stood as *îchiaro* to neighbouring clans. Notably, Mbiti of the Andûûne clan was invited in his capacity as *îchiaro* to the Athimba to place them under a conditional curse. Also of note is the fact that neither Nchee's nor his brothers' power of *îchiaro* against the Athimba was deployed in this case.[14]

Second, the Îgembe believe that curses against unknown perpetrators should be effective against all possible targets. As described above,

---

14 Another group cursing was held in the Mûringene village neighbourhood in August 2013. Those invited as *mwîchiaro* to the Athimba included Denis, of the Bwantai age-class – M'Ikirîma's last-born son and stepbrother to the late Kîng'angi – along with Kîberenge (H19), Nchee (H20), Mwaambia (H21) and Meeme (H22). This matter is of interest because the *îchiaro* power of M'Ikirîma's sons was invoked for dispute settlement (see Case 5.4, in which Mbanga and his son confessed their faults because they feared Kîberenge (H19) as their *mwîchiaro*).

the group cursing at Nchee's residence consisted of four parts: (1) the *îchiaro* men were placed under a conditional curse; (2) all those present were interrogated by the *îchiaro* men as to whether they harboured evil intentions and, in the process, were also placed under a conditional curse; (3) the *îchiaro* men placed a curse on the unknown perpetrator; (4) *kwiita rwîî* was performed to caution clan members not to identify the *îchiaro* men in their individual capacities. The first two steps were taken to ensure that neither the *îchiaro* men nor any clan members present intended to harm anyone else. The third step targeted the anonymous offender. These three forms of cursing left no-one exempt. Moreover, the group cursing was reciprocal in that the *îchiaro* men cursed all parties present, and those parties returned the curse to them. This reinforces the notion of *îchiaro* reciprocity, as expounded elsewhere in this book.

Third, the Îgembe maintain that those who deliver curses should not be identified in any personal capacity – see (4) above. Indeed, the *îchiaro* men in this case emphasised that it was not they as individuals, but rather the clans in their entirety, who held the power of *îchiaro*. Their status was based not on any personal achievement or expertise, but rather on their ascribed or biological status as *îchiaro*. Notionally, any member of the *îchiaro* men's clans could have assumed the same role – the power of *îchiaro* being, in theory, universally and equally distributed among the people. Such egalitarianism theoretically extends to gender equality. It should, however, be noted that I have never observed a case of *îchiaro* counterparts inviting women to participate in conflict management.

Fourth, the Îgembe are strongly oriented towards materialism. During the *îchiaro* men's cursing, words alone would not have sufficed. Rather, the bundle of herbs used at the meeting served as a physical manifestation of their imprecations. From this it may be inferred that *visible* evidence of action by third parties (such as a group of *îchiaro* men or of Njûrincheke elders) supersedes the importance of *actual* evidence of a crime.

Local theory of biological determinism

In cases of conflict management, Îgembe communities do not rely primarily on specialists, professionals or experts. Neither are disagreements adjudicated in the context of unilateral relationships between accuser and accused, or arbitrator and disputant. Further, third parties do not convict disputants; instead, conditional curses – using the power of *îchiaro* – are deployed. These curses provide a more elevated and less hasty mechanism than human reasoning, enabling disputants to bide their time in recognising and confessing to responsibility for a given dispute. Conflict management among the Îgembe may thus be seen as confession-oriented process that leads to social harmony; but not at the immediate expense of contesting parties (see Appendix 2).

Îchiaro conflict management is egalitarian to the extent that, in theory, every member of the Îgembe holds *îchiaro* power. For example, anyone born into the Athimba clan automatically becomes *mwîchiaro* to the Antûambûi and Andûûne clans. Such biological determinism is key to identifying and understanding *îchiaro* relationships. However, some individuals – such as Ngatûnyi of the Antûambûi clan and Mbiti of the Andûûne clan – are held to wield greater *mwîchiaro* power than others, and are prioritised in representing their clans. That said, *îchiaro* men should never elevate themselves as experts in a personal capacity, as shown in Case 5.10. Biological determinism may invest individuals with power, but it also depersonalises their role within *îchiaro*.

To conclude, clan affiliation is conditioned by socio-historical facts but also interpreted circumstantially by clan members – as outlined earlier in this chapter. Knowledge of that affiliation is central to both biological determinism among the Îgembe and to *îchiaro* as a generalised theory (or set of norms) that imparts egalitarianism to conflict management. For these reasons, clan affiliation and *îchiaro* may be seen as stabilising, productive forces – both throughout Îgembe history and in modern society (although, as mentioned above, the limitations of gender inequality should also be recognised).

Chapter 6
Feathers and guardians: The perpetuation of shared personhood

On the afternoon of 29 August 2018, a small bird – known as *kanyîrî* in Kîmîîrû language[1] (see Photo 6.1) – flew into my hotel room on the outskirts of Maûa, the headquarters of Îgembe district. At that moment, I was daydreaming about a baby girl, also named Kanyîrî. The coincidence seemed preternatural.

Earlier in August, I had interviewed Kanyîrî's father – Mwasimba (PN10[2]) (of the Mîrîti age-class), who was chairman of the Akachiû clan in Nthare – a village bestriding the boundary of the Îgembe Southeast and East Divisions (see Case 3.4). Mwasimba told me that the *kanyîrî* has long, white tail feathers; traditionally worn by Îgembe dancers. He also quoted a Kîmîîrû proverb – *Kanyîrî kainachua nî mweene* – which means, 'The long tail feathers of the *kanyîrî* can only dance with their owner' (i.e., the bird itself).[3]

Baby Kanyîrî was born in March 2018, to Mwasimba's delight, and her name was registered in her official birth certificate. Mwasimba and his wife Margaret, however, understood that for the name to be recognised within the village it would also need to be authorised in the proper Kîmîîrû manner. Mwasimba thus organised a name-giving ceremony for the following September, during which relatives and neighbours were entertained with a surfeit of food and drink, while Mwasimba and his

---

1. The *kanyîrî*'s common English name is the African paradise flycatcher. See epigraph and Introduction.
2. PN numbers refer to the individuals discussed in this chapter. Mwasimba (PN10) appears further on, as the tenth and final PN example.
3. In general usage, *kanyîrî kainachua* (*kainagua*) *nî mweene* connotes that every treasure is revered by its guardian, although in some contexts the feathers represent a woman who is faithful to her husband. Mwiti (2004, 37) translates this proverb as, 'A champion is advertised by the owner'.

Photo 6.1 The *kanyîrî*

mother, Kathao, petitioned them. The event was a success and Kanyîrî's name was accepted.

Among the Îgembe, the Kîmîîrû phrase for name-giving is *kûchia rîîtwa* – literally, 'to give oneself a name'. During Kanyîrî's naming ceremony, Kathao – the grandmother – first assumed the responsibility of giving *herself* a name, to represent her character and social attributes, before transferring it to the baby girl. With no objections raised, Kathao was then recognised as the baby's *ntaau* (namesake). Indeed, grandmother and granddaughter now address one another as such and are believed to share the same personhood.

*

The first section of this chapter introduces three of my age-mates in the Athîrû Gaiti community; detailing their various personal names (*marîîtwa*). The second section outlines the four principles of the Kîmîîrû naming system and explores how their names were arrived at.

The third section presents case studies of seven more interviewees from various backgrounds,[4] describing how their (and their family members') names came to be allocated, and how those names are shared with friends and relatives of preceding and proceeding generations. I also discuss how my subjects' names have proved significant in their personal histories.

The fourth section demonstrates how the Kîmîîrû naming system – particularly the allocation of *ntaau* – affects the very fabric of life in Athîrû Gaiti and beyond. I describe in detail a visit by Mwasimba (father of Kanyîrî, whose naming ceremony is described above) to his in-laws' home, to meet his wife's namesake and celebrate their families' unity.

The chapter continues with a discussion of how personal names inform and reflect the Îgembe's understanding of personhood, and how they connect individuals in various ways. As illustrated earlier in the book, politico-economic situations are most prominently informed by agnatic membership and seniority. Personal names, on the other hand, can reveal much about matrimonial/affinal, inter-generational and inter-familial bonds, as well as personal friendships.

Specifically, this chapter discusses how personal names are shared between younger and older generations via the reciprocal *ntaau* system – thereby negating the importance of personal identity within any given genealogy and allowing individuals to be survived by their names. As personhood is shared over successive generations, the Îgembe achieve collective immortality.

Three character sketches

When asked for their title, many people give their birth name, their *ntaau* (namesake), their name by Christian baptism or their father's or husband's name. Any of these may appear on their national ID cards. However, in some cases people are also known locally by nicknames.

---

4   From a total of thirty people I interviewed during my research.

In this section, I present three character sketches of my age-mates in Athîrû Gaiti, which inform the principles of name giving expounded in the following section.

1. Born in 1977, my research assistant Bruce (his nickname in Athîrû Gaiti) (PN1) belongs to the Bwantai age-class. His parents address him either by his Christian name or as *nthaka yekwa* ('my circumcised but unmarried son' in Kîmîîrû kinship terminology) – despite the fact that he has a daughter, who is his mother's *ntaau*.

2. Another friend of mine, Mûrûngî (his *ntaau* name) (PN2) – also of the Bwantai age-class – was born in 1981 and works as a *mûrathi* (hunter; meaning 'professional witchman in charge of criminal investigation/prevention'). Mûrûngî has six names, in addition to the three official ones on his ID card. Four of these are business titles, bestowed by former clients. The fifth is a nickname, which came from Mûrûngî's age-mates and relates to where he lives. The sixth is the name his parents gave him, which, by his own volition, he replaced on his ID with 'Mûrûngî' – the name of his father's brother, of the Lubetaa age-class – who thus became his *ntaau*. Very few people beyond Mûrûngî's family know his birth name.

3. Kîthîînji (PN3) – another friend, also of the Bwantai age-class – was born in 1980. In addition to his three official names, he is known by friends as Matîenyawa (a Rastafarian hair style) and Mashangi ('entertainer' in Kiswahili). He also has a third, unofficial, Njûrincheke name: Baimîrongo (literally 'tens'; see next section) which he shares with his mother's brother. This is sometimes used by the village's Njûrincheke elders, to acknowledge that Kîthîînji and his mother's brother are *ntaau*. Because Kîthîînji was his parent's last-born, they often addressed him as *mwana wakwa* ('my child') or *mwîîjî wakwa* ('my uncircumcised boy') – even after his circumcision, until their deaths in the early 2000s.

The four principles of the Kîmîîrû naming system

The Kîmîîrû naming system follows four principles, each of which apply to my three friends, as introduced above.

1. An individual can have more than three names, which may be allocated at different stages in their life (Peatrik 2019, 45–50).

    As previously mentioned, Mûrûngî (PN2) accumulated his four business names after beginning work as a *mûrathi* in 2006. On 12 August 2018, I accompanied him to a job in a village near Maûa, where I observed him being called Kingwetee – a name derived from the verb *kûgwaata* ('to catch criminals by curse'). It might be inferred from this example, together with the seven case studies in the next section, that men garner more names than women because they have greater professional/geographical mobility, and have also preserved gendered institutions such as age-class organisation and the council of elders. However, both men *and* women may be designated nicknames by their friends, in a variety of social contexts, and this may be a more significant factor than gendered spaces in name-sharing across generations.

2. Almost all of Kîmîîrû's personal names bear meanings both literal and dependent on social context.

    Kîthîînji (PN3) was named by his mother and her doctor, just after his birth in hospital by caesarean section. His name derives from the verb *kûthîînja* – 'to slaughter an animal for meat' – in this context meaning 'to cut or operate on a patient'. Another of Kîthîînji's names – Baimîrongo – was shared with his *ntaau*, as previously noted. Baimîrongo derives from the word '*mîrongo*'; literally 'tens' but signifying the counting of money and goods. Like Kîthîînji, Baimîrongo carries contextual meaning – having been designated to Kîthîînjij's *ntaau* (who died in the mid-2000s) by the Njûrincheke council, and reflecting his profession as an accountant for local coffee and tea factories. The case studies in the third section present further acquired names, along with their literal meanings and contextual significance, which reveal information about their owner's family history.

3. Each individual has a reciprocal relationship with their *ntaau*, with whom they may also share personality traits.

   Mûrûngî (PN2; see above) shares a *ntaau* relationship with his father's brother (FB). The two Mûrûngîs – junior and senior – enjoy a jokey camaraderie, which would be impossible if they were not namesakes. The name Mûrûngî derives from the age-class[5] to which the senior *ntaau*'s own *ntaau* – of a still older generation – belonged. An individual may thus gain *ntaau* from both previous and subsequent generations – taking the role of intermediary between their predecessor and successor, with this succession expected to continue ad infinitum.

   On some occasions, a junior *ntaau* may not inherit their senior's actual name, but rather be allocated a name representing the elder *ntaau*'s character, personality or social attributes. My research assistant (PN1) was named Kîrîmi, after his *ntaau* (his mother's brother). This was not his uncle's name but, because he was remembered as a good farmer – or *mûrîmi,* from which Kîrîmi derives – the name was deemed appropriate.

4. Children's *ntaau* alternate between their paternal and maternal relatives, by order of birth (Peatrik 2019, 43).

   First-born sons are named after their father's father (FF), while first-born daughters are named after their father's mother (FM). Second-born children are named after the 'opposite' grandparent – i.e. second-born sons are named after their mother's father (MF) and second-born daughters are named after their mother's mother (MM). This alternation continues with third-borns, although their *ntaau*

---

5 'Mûrûngî' is another name for the former Kîramunya age-class.

may be selected from either a paternal grandparent or one of their father's siblings.

Theoretically, clan affiliation among the Îgembe is agnatically oriented, i.e., children belong to their father's clan. This biological status never changes, even after marriage. The Kîmîîrû naming system, however, is bilaterally oriented, as it allows some children to inherit their father's kin's names and personhood, and others to inherit their mother's. Mûrûngî (PN2), for example, was named after one of his father's brothers, while Kîthîînji (PN3) was named after one of his mother's brothers – as was my research assistant Bruce (PN1).

Land scarcity in Îgembe has sometimes led to family disputes in which clan members argue for agnatic inheritance. However, village elders generally agree that the obverse power of bilateral orientation has historically allowed daughters and their children to reside in their natal homes – and that this system should continue (See also Matsuzono 2020).

The Kîmîîrû texture of personhood: Case studies

Below, I present seven case studies of Athîrû Gaiti residents whose names demonstrate both adherence to and divergence from the four principles of the Kîmîîrû naming system. This section also describes how those names reflect and are woven into the fabric of their owners' family histories and lives.

A man who amassed five names

Kîeri (PN4) was born into the Amwari clan in the early 1950s. Upon his circumcision he joined the Lubetaa age-class. He bears five names: (1) his birth/*ntaau* name, Kîeri; (2) his Christian name; (3) his father's name; (4) his nickname among his age-mates, M'Mweenda; and (5) his official Njûrincheke council name, Matata Baikwîînga.

Kîeri is the third-born of six children, and the second-born of four brothers. In his case, the principle of children's *ntaau* being selected alternately from paternal and maternal relatives was not strictly followed. Rather, his biological father's mentor, Baikwîînga, named Kîeri after himself. Baikwîînga's role as 'substitute' grandfather came about because he supervised Kîeri's father's initiation into the Njûrincheke council. He has no biological relationship with Kîeri, but Kîeri regards him as his father's 'father in Njûrincheke' (*îthe-wa-Njûrî*) and thus as his *ntaau*.[6]

The naming of Kîeri's siblings also involved some divergence from tradition. Two were named after their biological father's parents, two were named after their biological mother's brothers, and two were named after family friends or neighbours.

Kîeri may be addressed or referred to by any of his various names, depending on circumstance. In everyday life, he is known by his birth/*ntaau* name, although his age-mates sometimes call him M'Mweenda. In formal settings, his colleagues on the Njûrincheke council recognise him as Matata Baikwîînga. Kîeri's Christian name, nickname and father's name each appears on his national ID card.

The nickname M'Mweenda – meaning 'a man who loves people' – was conferred on Kîeri by his peers when he contributed a he-goat at an age-class meeting. Kîeri uses this title on his ID card; reflecting his pride in it. Upon joining the Njûrincheke council in 2014, Kîeri received the name Matata Baikwîînga. The name Matata – meaning 'water drops' (from banana leaves, in this context) – came from the fact that Kîeri was initiated on a rainy day. However, because this is a fairly common name, it was appended with 'Baikwîînga' – in recognition of his *ntaau* 'grandfather', who is also his *mwîchiaro* counterpart and a respected Njûrincheke member.

Kîeri joined the Njûrincheke council because he realised he needed to protect himself and his family. I first met him at a case hearing in September 2005, when he was defending his wife Kaario from accusations

---

6   Baikwîînga, who belongs to the Antûamûtî clan, is also Kîeri's *îchiaro* counterpart.

of witchcraft made by their neighbours. His wife denied the allegations and, to prove her innocence, took a *muuma* (oath) before her *îchiaro* (see Appendix 2).

By this time, Kîeri was used to dealing with testing situations. In the early 1990s, he was involved in a land border dispute with his 'brothers' (neighbours of the same clan affiliation). The issue was resolved between the two parties, and their *îchiaro* men were invited to curse anybody who broke their agreement. However, Kîeri later discovered his 'brothers' had seized his land while he was in jail (following a false charge of illegal timber cutting). By his reckoning, they bribed the *îchiaro* men to remove the curse without his consent (which ultimately led to the latters' deaths).

When I met Kîeri again at the Njûrincheke compound in August 2012, he was involved in a case hearing, demanding the original land dispute be settled by *kîthiri* oath. By now, he had realised he must become a Njûrincheke member in order to keep himself and his family safe – specifically because the *kîthiri* oath, as the highest means of dispute settlement, is administered and witnessed by Njûrincheke members alone. To ensure that no conspiracy could be organised against his property, his family or their wellbeing, he needed to join the council. In 2014, Kîeri was ordained into the Njûrincheke, at which point he received his official name, Matata Baikwîînga.

A man named after his ancestor

Kîthia (pseudonym) (PN5),[7] of the Mîrîti age-class, was born into the Athimba clan in the late 1960s. He has been clan chairman since August 2014 (see Chapters 4 and 7) and is also a Njûrincheke member (H3) (see Table 4.1). He has five names: (1) his birth name; (2) his Christian name; (3) his father's name; (4) his *ntaau* name; and (5) his official name in the Njûrincheke council, Baiweeta Atalala.

---

7   I have used the pseudonym Kîthia for this individual elsewhere in the book.

Kîthia is the ninth-born of ten children, and the third-born of four brothers. The children's *ntaau* were selected from among both their paternal and maternal relatives (although not necessarily alternately), except for the last-born brother, who was named after his *mwîchiaro*.

Kîthia's birth name (as opposed to the pseudonym used here) was chosen by his parents upon his delivery at a Catholic hospital in Maûa. It derives from the Kîmîîrû for 'to last' or 'to stay' – because Kîthia remained in his mother's womb beyond his due date. Shortly after his birth, he was given his *ntaau* name, after his mother's father's brother (of the Antûborii clan's Îthalîî age-class). During an interview, he told me that he might have been named after his mother's father, if not for his early death. Kîthia's Christian, birth and father's names each appears on his national ID card.

Since achieving Njûrincheke council membership in 1992, Kîthia has borne the official name Baiweeta Atalala. Baiweeta means 'a self-dependent person who can make his own way forward'. Atalala is the name of one of Kîthia's clan ancestors (of the former Bwantai age-class), who is deemed to have belonged to the first Athimba family in what is now the Îgembe Southeast Division. The conferral of this name upon Kîthia implies he is a direct descendant of that family.

A man who ate many things

Mûriangûkû (PN6) – also identified as H17 in Table 4.1 – was born into the Athimba clan's Lubetaa age-class in the early 1950s. His five names are: (1) his birth/*ntaau* name, Mûrûngî; (2) his Christian name; (3) his father's name; (4) his neighbourhood nickname, Mûriangûkû; and (5) his nickname among age-mates, Mûremera – the first three of which appear on his national ID card.

Mûriangûkû was the first-born of six children, including five brothers. As per the Kîmîîrû naming system, he is *ntaau* to his father's father. The second-born, a brother, is *ntaau* to his mother's father, and the third-born, a sister, is *ntaau* to her father's mother. The naming of the subsequent siblings continued to alternate between the mother's and father's sides.

Kamûrû – Mûriangûkû's father's father and *ntaau* – belonged to the former Mûrûngî age-class (also known as Kîramunya), and passed the same name to his grandson. Kamûrû's actual name derives from the Kîmîîrû word *rûûrû* (westward/highland),[8] indicating his *mûrûûrû* (highlander) origins. Notably, although Kîthia (PN5) and Mûriangûkû both belong to the Athimba clan, they have different ancestral origins.

Because his birth/*ntaau* name is common in Athîrû Gaiti, in everyday life Mûrûngî is known by the nickname Mûriangûkû, which derives from an episode in his family history. Years after their marriage, Mûriangûkû's parents had yet to produce any children and so, in accordance with bygone custom, his mother's brothers presented her with a series of goats, sheep and chickens, until she conceived and gave birth. The nickname Mûriangûkû – 'a man who eats many chickens (*ngûkû*)' – thus suggested itself. Mûriangûkû's other, somewhat derogatory, nickname, Mûremera, translates as 'a man who insists'; originating from the fact that – as Mûriangûkû himself recalls – when he joined the Lubetaa age-class, he would always refuse to contribute he-goats.

The word *mûremera* implies a certain miserliness; a deficit that some also attributed to Mûriangûkû's father, Ntika – who I first met in October 2001, when he was representing the Athimba in a matter of homicide compensation (see Case 4.1). The clan had received restorative items, which some said had been secretly divided among a certain circle of their members instead of being properly shared out (see Chapter 4). Ntika was later accused of misappropriation (although I noted that there were valid reasons why he might have warranted a larger share of the compensation[9]) and, following a spate of mistrust and misunderstanding, he passed away in an atmosphere of village discord.

---

8   The opposite of *rûûrû* is *gaiti* (eastward/lowland).
9   Ntika had in fact helped elders with their living expenses while they were staying in a clan house awaiting the delivery of compensation items.

As the oldest of his siblings, Mûriangûkû was plagued by his father's tarnished reputation, and so took measures to redeem his own name. On 3 September 2015, a clan meeting was organised to fundraise for the hospital bill of a young woman (from another clan) who had suffered a finger injury (*kûrea kîara*) (see Case 4.3 and Photo 6.2). The Athimba were to donate 40,000 shillings – 300 shillings each. In the event, Mûriangûkû helped anyone who came with only 100 or 200 shillings; donating a total of around 3,000 shillings of his own money. He emphasised to his beneficiaries that the funds came from his father, who intended them to be used to help other clan members – and that he, Mûriangûkû, needed their blessings.

Dialogue 6.1 Mûriangûkû's request for blessings

> Mûriangûkû: This is from my father. He left it for me. I am eating it for nothing. Do as I have done for the Athimba clan. You have tried to move me to do something, and now I shock you like hitting your head with a hammer. [Addressing one of the clan officials] Ngore, do you want me to give you something? [Addressing the biological father of a boy who hurt the girl] Kûbai, have I helped you to pay for the finger with my 3,000? Who else wants some? It is the clan I am trying to help. This money will help you pay for the finger. Stop empty talk! If you beat me again, I will stop you with money. Is there anybody left with outstanding balance? That's the reason why I bless you and you bless me. Ûûii!

[Other members speak, and Mûteethia recalls a past clan leader.]

> Mûteethia:[10] Now, you (clan members) tell him, Mûriangûkû, he has done something good, because he has lessened some burden. Let

---

10 Mûteethia, of the Ratanya age-class, served as acting chairman of the Athimba for around eight years, until 14 August 2014 (see Chapter 4).

	his pocket be added. Let his way be straight because his money is for helping others.
Mûriangûkû:	When M'Imaana (a frequent advisor to the Athimba clan) was about to die, he blessed me, and he told me to attend clan meetings and never to abandon the clan.
Mûteethia:	I have blessed you much.
Mûriangûkû:	No! You have not blessed me. Stand there (in the centre of the circle of sitting attendants) and say that you bless me. They have not blessed me, and I want them to say it. Have you blessed me, please?
Members:	Yes, we have blessed you very much.
Mûriangûkû:	Thank you.

Most of the clan members appreciated the goodwill behind Mûriangûkû's donations; blessing him as requested. Some, however, did not believe the money fully covered his longstanding debt. Mûriangûkû was thus required to rebuild the clan house – which had been demolished in 2002 without formal agreement – and to restore the items his father had 'secretly distributed' to the clan. Otherwise, the dissenters said, the clan could neither resolve the homicide compensation case nor bless Mûriangûkû and his family (see Postscript for the final settlement in November 2021).

Incidentally, I met Ntika (Mûriangûkû's father) many times in the early 2000s. An elder of the Mîchûbû age-class, he was also an active church member and soya drink lover and was lame in one leg. He was very kind to me and smiled whenever interviewed. It thus surprised me that, despite his benign personality, there was a hidden, somewhat sinister, meaning behind his third-born child's name, Chiobebeeta, which does not appear on her national ID card. Literally, *chiobebeeta* means 'a woman who clears everyone'. However, in this context it implies 'a woman who kills off every white man and woman'. This reflects Ntika's role as a freedom fighter during the Mau Mau war for independence. The

Photo 6.2 Athimba clan meeting, 3 September 2015

ex-soldier also named his fifth-born child after a famous field marshal in the war, who he held in high esteem.

A woman named after a wild animal

Nkoroi (PN7) was born in the 1930s and belongs to the Nkirinaathi women's age-class. Every morning, she sells bundles of banana fibre for *mîraa* workers at the Athîrû Gaiti open market, alongside three of her age-mates.[11] Nkoroi is her birth name, and she informed me that the only other name people recognise her by in her neighbourhood is her Christian name.

There were two reasons why Nkoroi, meaning colobus monkey, was so named. First, her mother had experienced several miscarriages, and naming her new child after a wild animal was intended to end her cycle

---

11 In local industry, banana fibre is used to tie up bunches of *mîraa* (see Chapter 1).

Feathers and guardians

Table 6.1 Nkoroi's children

Name	Reason name was chosen	Sex	Age-class	Ntaau
Karanyoni	Selling vegetables during pregnancy	Female	none	FM
Meeme	Radios became popular items	Male	Mîrîti	MF
Îrukî	Guarding her maize field against monkeys during pregnancy	Male	Mîrîti	FF
Karîîthi	Grazing cattle during pregnancy	Male	Mîrîti	MB
Mûrûngî	After his *ntaau*'s age-class	Male	Bwantai	FB
Kaumbu	After his *ntaau*'s easygoing, chameleon-like character	Male	Bwantai	MFB

of suffering. This was in the belief that, if a new-born is given such a negative, unpleasant title, it will not be much missed if it dies; or that it might survive without being prey to evil spirits. Second, Nkoroi's mother encountered *nkoroi* several times while pregnant. Such thinking is common in the Îgembe community, where some of the people I interviewed – or their relatives – were named after fauna such as the *mbiti* (hyena), the *îrukî* (monkey), and the *mpaandi* (a type of small insect). Nkoroi's younger sister is named Nchee (porcupine) for similar reasons.

Nkoroi has six children (see Table 6.1). Her first-, third- and fourth-born were named after the daily work she performed during pregnancy, including selling vegetables (*nyoni*), guarding crops against monkeys, and grazing cattle (*kûrîîthia*). Nkoroi's second-born was named Meeme (meaning radio); a device restricted to colonial chiefs prior to independence, which only became generally available in the early 1960s, when Meeme was born. Nkoroi's fifth-born, Mûrûngî, was named after his *ntaau*'s age-class,[12] while her sixth-born, Kaumbu (meaning chameleon) was also named after his *ntaau*, who was known for his easygoing nature.

Nkoroi is now *ntaau* to three granddaughters (the daughters of Meeme, Îrukî and Karîîthi). Each bears a name representing an aspect

---

12 Mûrûngî is another name for the Kîramunya age-class.

of Nkoroi's character: Mûkiri ('a cool and calm woman'), Kîendi ('a beloved woman') and Kathure ('a chosen woman').

A woman who cares for a granddaughter

Kainchua (PN8) was born in the early 1960s, is married with eight children, and lives in Mûringene village. She has three names: (1) her birth/*ntaau* name, Kainchua; (2) her Christian name, Susan; and (3) her husband's name, Kîthûûre – each of which appears on her national ID card. Her birth name – derived from the verb *kûinchia*, meaning 'to close the eyes' – was given after her father's mother, who was blind. Nobody in Kainchua's neighbourhood recognises her by any other names.

Kainchua's father (of the Bwethaa clan's Ratanya age-class) was born and circumcised in the Îgembe Southeast Division. He later moved to Imenti district, where he secured a semi-permanent job as a live-in farmer and was married for many years. Kainchua was her parents' first-born. She has three younger brothers and one younger sister. Two of the brothers' and the sister's *ntaau* were chosen (although not necessarily alternately) from paternal relatives in Îgembe and maternal relatives in Imenti. Kainchua's youngest brother's *ntaau* name, Kîrema, came from their father's employer in Imenti, who supported him for years. The name derives from the verb *kûrema* ('to be obstinate').

Upon her family's return to the Îgembe Southeast Division, Kainchua married her husband (of the Antûamûriûki clan's Lubetaa age-class) in Mûringene village. Her father spent his remaining years at a newly built homestead in the southern lower plain frontier (*rwaanda*) – where land demarcation began in the 1990s – and was buried there.

Kainchua has eight children: five sons and three daughters. Table 6.2 explains their *ntaau* names. It also details the gifts their *ntaau* brought on the day of *kûchia rîîtwa*.

As per Table 6.2, female *ntaau* brought specially prepared gourds full of porridge for the *kûchia rîîtwa* celebration, while the first three male *ntaau* each arrived with either a he-goat or a chicken. Male *ntaau*

Feathers and guardians

Table 6.2 Kainchua's children

Name	Reason name was chosen	Sex	Age-class	Name-sake	Gift items from *ntaau*
Baariû	After his *ntaau*'s age-class (the former Gîchûnge)	Male	Bwantai	FF	Male goat
Kawîira	After her *ntaau*'s people-pleasing (*kwîiria*) character	Female	None	FM	Porridge, cereals
Nkatha	After her *ntaau*'s qualities as a generous woman (*nkatha*)	Female	None	MFBW	Porridge
Kainda	After her *ntaau*'s hardworking character; derived from *îiinda* (early morning)	Female	None	FM	Porridge
Mwîti	After his *ntaau*'s life as a migrant; derived from *kwîita* (to go)	Male	Gîchûnge	MF	Chicken
Mweenda	After his *ntaau*'s all-loving (*kweenda*) character	Male	Gîchûnge	FB	Male goat*, cash
Koome	After his *ntaau*'s good performance at school	Male	Gîchûnge	MB	Cash (porridge brought by his wife)
Kîriinya	After his *ntaau*'s reputation as a man of great strength (*inya*)	Male	Gîchûnge	FF (F's *îthe wa kianda*)	Cash (maize and sugar brought by his wife)

* During an interview, Kainchua recalled this gift as actually being a heifer.

for the youngest two sons brought cash. They were accompanied by their wives, who also brought cooked porridge or uncooked food (maize and sugar). Kainchua explained that, although in recent times traditional items of livestock and porridge have been replaced by cash and raw food products, their meaning remains the same.

Baariû, Kainchua's first son, had two daughters with his former wife who, after their divorce, remarried elsewhere. The two girls – the eldest named Atwîri – still live with their mother but often visit Baariû and Kainchua in Mûringene village. Thanks to the permanency of their *ntaau* relationship, Kainchua continues to care for Atwîri during her stays and, although Baariû's younger daughter's *ntaau* is his former wife's mother, her grandmother welcomes her too.

Atwîri's name, which means 'a woman who gives fodder to livestock', reflects her grandmother Kainchua's hardworking character – especially in the field of dairy production. Kainchua is also *ntaau* to Mûkami (her eldest daughter Kawîira's daughter), whose name means 'milker' – also reflecting her grandmother's solid vocation.

Kainchua's third son Mweenda's *ntaau* (of the Antûamûriûki clan's Mîrîti age-class) is a resident of Mûringene village. Although not Muslim, he is locally known by his Arabic nickname, which was given to him by Somali business friends when he worked in the *mîraa* industry. He loves this title and even wears a *kufi* (Muslim cap) in everyday life.

A woman whose child has no namesake

Born in the early 1970s, Doris (PN9) is a divorced, single mother who lives in Mûringene village. I first met her in 2002, one year after the birth of her third child, when she was working at a small-scale *mîraa* workshop (Ishida 2008, 141–142). She now manages her own, even smaller, workshop.

Doris has three names: (1) her birth name; (2) her Christian name, Doris; and (3) her former husband's name – each of which appears on her national ID card. Having never been given a nickname, in day-to-day life Doris is known by her birth and Christian names. Her former husband's name remains on her ID card.

After being deserted by their mother – who remarried elsewhere – Doris and her younger siblings were brought up by their maternal grandparents in Mûringene village. They know neither the name nor clan of their biological father.

Their maternal grandfather – and hence their mother – belonged to the agnatic Athimba clan.

Doris' first-born was a girl, who was named after Doris' mother-in-law. Her second-born was a boy, who was named after Doris' brother.

After Doris separated from her husband and returned home to Mûringene village, her spouse visited many times, and became biological father to Doris' second son. This child's *ntaau* should have been selected from Doris' husband's side of the family but, by Doris' own report, the separation prevented this and the boy was left with no namesake.

At the time of our interview in September 2018, Doris had two granddaughters, the eldest of whom – Doris's first-born's six-year-old girl – was staying with her. Notionally, this girl's *ntaau* was her paternal grandmother but, when I met the family, her name-giving ceremony was yet to be organised. Doris' second granddaughter, aged three, was her son's first-born. The girl was notionally *ntaau* to Doris, who addressed her as such (and whose nursery fees she paid) – even though her name-giving ceremony was also pending and she had only a Christian name.

A man with three nicknames

Mwasimba (PN10), chairman of the Akachiû clan in Nthare, was introduced at the beginning of this chapter, and reappears in a case study of 'Namesake Day' in the next section. He has five names: (1) his birth/*ntaau* name, Mûng'aathia; (2) his Christian name, Joel; (3) his nickname, Mwasimba; (4) a second nickname, Mûthumo jwa Ndege; and (5) a third nickname, Baithinyai.

Mwasimba's birth/*ntaau* name, Mûng'aathia, came from his maternal grandfather, Mûrîîkî, who belonged to the Ratanya age-class's Kobia subset – which is 'sandwiched' between the Nding'ûri and Kabeeria subsets. The Kobia play a pivotal role in every age-class, as described by its members' names. Mûng'aathia, for example, derives from *kûng'aathia* ('to move'), while Murira derives from *kûrira* ('to protect').

The nickname Mwasimba – meaning a brave, leonine person – was conferred on Mwasimba by his workmates when he was involved in the *mîraa* industry. His second, childhood, nickname, Mûthumo jwa Ndege, means 'the landing gear of aircraft', and was conferred by Mwasimba's friends when he fell from a cliff and landed safely on both legs. Mwasimba's third nickname, Baithinyai, comes from his father but, rather than being conferred at birth, was given by Mwasimba's age-mates – upon his own suggestion.

Namesake Day: The *ûtuunga* celebration

On 24 August 2019, I was invited to join a day trip organised by Mwasimba (PN10) of the Akachiû clan's Mîrîti age-class, to visit his wife Kanjîra Margaret's natal homestead in Imenti district. We travelled in seven Toyota Probox Wagons.[13]

Upon our arrival, I observed a joint-family wellbeing celebration, in the Kîmîîrû way of *ûtuunga* ('to put special attire on leaders, guests or any kind of important person'). The event had been initiated by Nkoroi[14] (meaning colobus monkey), Margaret's deceased grandmother (father's mother) and *ntaau*.

A single parent, Nkoroi was also the founding mother of all the children and grandchildren shown in Figure 6.1 below. In 1971, she left a will specifying that, one day in the future, when both her *ntaau* were married and blessed with children, her son Mûtûma (Margaret's father) should call them back to her homestead for a celebration.

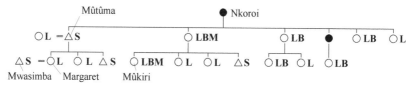

Figure 6.1 Genealogy of Nkoroi's daughters and *ntaau*

---

13 The four-wheel-drive Toyota Probox is often used to transport *mîraa* from the farming villages of Îgembe to the international export hub of Nairobi.

14 The two Nkorois – one here and the other (PN7) – are different persons.

Nkoroi had left Mûtûma two other instructions. First, when his sister Benditah married, he was to take a heifer from her *rûraachio* (bride price), which he duly did. Second, when Mûkiri (Nkoroi's *ntauu* among Benditah's daughters) married, he was to slaughter a heifer, again taken from her *rûraachio*, which he also did. However, Mûtûma avoided arranging the *ûtuunga* for many years because Mûkiri's marriage had faltered and, childless, she had left her husband's homestead to return to her parents' home. The husband's family demanded that Mûtûma pay them back for the heifer he had taken from the *rûraachio*. Mûtûma took Mûkiri's precarious situation seriously, saying, 'I would be caught by a curse… I was tied with a rope because of Mûkiri'.

Mûkiri finally settled back at her husband's home and had two children, and Mûtûma was relieved of his responsibility to compensate for the heifer. Indeed, he received another such animal from Mûkiri's husband's family, as the remaining part of the bride price. Once Mûkiri's marriage had stabilised and she had given birth to two children, Mûtûma realised the time had come to honour Nkoroi's will and hold the wellbeing celebration.

Mwasimba received news of the imminent *ûtuunga* in 2018, via a phone call from Mûtûma. He welcomed the prospect; seeing it as an opportunity to celebrate with his in-laws the arrival of his and Margaret's daughter Kanyîrî, and their first grandson (first son's son; named after Mwasimba). He proposed the *ûtuunga* should be held in August 2019, to give him time for preparations.

When the day arrived, our party reached Nkoroi's homestead at around 2 pm. We were served food and drinks, alongside other guests as they arrived from the neighbourhood. Christian prayers were held at 3.10 pm, followed by self-introductions, both between in-laws and between guests from Îgembe and their hosts from Imenti. At 3.50 pm, Mûtûma delivered a speech to explain the history and purpose behind the day's events. His first words impressed the audience: 'Now, now, now, now … it's now!' (*Naandî, naandî, naandî, naandî…nî naandî!*) – as did the story that followed (see Photo 6.3).

Photo 6.3 Mûtûma giving a speech

Mûtûma: Let me tell you my story. It's my story and nobody knows it. There is no appointment day (*kîatho*) that won't ever come. Now I am telling you that a parent is the second God (*mûruungu wa baîîrî*). As you see, now I am here in front of you. This issue came to me in 1971, and I have lived with it until now. We had stayed here [for many years] with only our mother because my father was abruptly killed by an elephant. My mother told me something one day because of which we are here today. I was told that a heifer for Benditah was mine... Now I am telling you what my mother told me. Kanjîra (Margaret's first name) is named after my mother and the holder of this family...

In her will, Nkoroi had specified to Mûtûma that, on the *ûtuunga* day, Margaret (Nkoroi's *ntaau*) should represent her presence. Accordingly, during the ceremony Margaret wrapped first herself and then Nkoroi's daughters with *leso*, to celebrate their being blessed with children. The daughters included Margaret's biological father's sisters, her biological mother, and Mûkiri (Nkoroi's second *ntaau*). Some of the women were

Feathers and guardians

Photo 6.4 Nkoroi's namesakes and daughters wearing *leso*

Photo 6.5 People holding mattresses with Benditah and Mûkiri

given blankets or mattresses, or both, to symbolise their establishment of a permanent place to settle (see Photos 6.4 and 6.5).

Mûtûma organised the *ûtuunga* and paid for the guests' food and drinks, while Mwasimba took responsibility for buying the requisite thirteen pieces of *leso*, six blankets, two mattresses, ten white shirts for the men and 30 kilograms of honey for mead. For Mûtûma, the event represented a sacrifice for his mother, sisters, daughter and in-laws. For Mwasimba, bringing his family and friends all the way from home, and paying for the victuals, was a token of his appreciation for his wife and in-laws. His contributions were not associated with *rûraachio*, as Mwasimba had previously paid off all the bride price items under his responsibility, including one ewe, one ram, one he-goat, six she-goats, one heifer and some cash. Only *mwari-o-nkûrio*[15] remained to be contributed by Mwasimba's children at a future date.

During an interview in 2019, Mwasimba recalled how, in 1993, he first met his wife at a marketplace in Îgembe district, where he was involved in the emerging *mîraa* industry. Margaret was travelling from Imenti to visit her married sister at the time. The couple fell in love and moved in together but Mwasimba felt as though he was 'stealing a girl', because he and Margaret lived together for more than a year without her parents' knowledge.

Mwasimba's first meeting with Margaret's parents arose from a coincidence. In 1995, he met Derrick – one of Margaret's cousins (her biological father's sister (Benditah)'s son) – in his home village of Nthare. The young man had found a job there splitting timber in the *mîraa* industry, which had increased production in the mid-1990s – offering employment to people from outside the Îgembe district. Subsequently, Mwasimba and Margaret bumped into Derrick in Nthare. Mwasimba contacted Margaret's parents via her cousin and began to purchase *rûraachio* items. In 2019, Derrick attended the *ûtuunga* celebration in Imenti.

---

15 *Mwari-o-nkûrio* are counter-gifts from nephews to those of their maternal aunts who provide them with material support at various stages of their lives, e.g., help with schooling, circumcision and marriage. They do not strictly constitute a part of *rûraachio* (Ishida 2010, 137).

Kîmîîrû concepts of personhood and immortality

Kûchia rîîtwa (the Kîmîîrû way of name-giving) both informs and is informed by the interconnectedness of people of different social attributes and generations. This section discusses the complexity of this process and its implications for collective immortality.

In the village communities of Îgembe, personal names do not necessarily refer only to their bearers. Further, when a name characterises an individual, those characteristics may actually describe someone else. For example, a name may describe someone's mother's experiences during or before pregnancy, or how her child was delivered. Other examples include: Kîthîînji, meaning 'to cut or operate on a patient' (PN2); Kîthia's birth name, derived from the word for 'to stay' (PN5); Mûrîangûkû, meaning 'a man who eats many chickens' (PN6); and Nkoroi, meaning 'colobus monkey' (PN7).

Nicknames bestowed by friends may reveal something about an individual's personality or social attributes – see Mûrîangûkû (PN6), whose nickname Mûremera means 'one who insists'; and his grandfather, whose name Kamûrû means 'highlander'. However, if the same nickname is later given to a *ntaau* child, it does not necessarily foretell their personality – see Kîthîînji, whose nicknames are Baimîrongo (PN2), meaning 'tens' but signifying the counting of money and goods; and Kainchua (PN8) meaning 'one who closes her eyes'. Rather, *ntaau* names engender a reciprocal relationship between namesakes and their descendants (see Mwasimba's visit to his wife's home in Imenti in the previous section). In some cases, a name may 'skip' a generation; passing from one's grandparent to his grandchild, with the individual between performing an intermediate role – see Mûrûngî (PN3), whose name denotes the age-class of the previous *ntaau* but one.

My personal role as *ntaau* to a boy named Kaûme reveals the fluidity of *kûchia rîîtwa* in Îgembe; to the extent that it can occur beyond family relationships. I have been friends with Kaûme's father, Baariû – a *matatu* (minibus) driver/conductor – since 2001 when, after I was swindled out of money reserved for a journey to Nairobi, he kindly offered me a lift.

Following Kaûme's birth by caesarean section in 2007, Baariû asked me to help pay the hospital bill. He later informed me that Kaûme – meaning 'a boy who performs well at school' – had been named after me in appreciation of my generosity, and for my role as an academic. Of all their sons, Baariû and his wife always count on Kaûme to be the first to achieve educational targets. Indeed, Baariû had Kaûme transferred from a local public school to a private one, where he is performing well – apparently demonstrating that namesakes do sometimes share the same characteristics!

In Îgembe, agnatic membership and seniority take precedence in the arbitration of land demarcation, succession and property disputes (see Chapters 1, 4 and 5); whereas the significance of Kîmîîrû personal names is often prioritised in matrimonial/affinal, inter-generational and inter-familial bonds – as well as in personal friendships. The interconnecting functions of such names manifest in various ways; many of them positive. Mwasimba's (PN10) successful visit with his wife to her *ntaau* in Imenti is a case in point. Further, the children of a divorced wife may continue visiting their paternal grandparents or relatives if they share a *ntaau* relationship – see Kainchua (PN8) and her granddaughter. However, if a single mother's children are not recognised by their biological father, it may be difficult to find them a *ntaau* on the family's paternal side – resulting in social fragmentation, as opposed to cohesion – see Doris (PN9) and her child with no namesake.

*

In *African Religion and Philosophy*, Mbiti (1969, 26) writes that, in African communities, an individual will retain their 'personal immortality' for several generations after death, until becoming an 'empty name' with no personality and entering into 'the state of *collective immortality*'.

> The appearance of the departed, and his being recognized by name, may continue for up to four or five generations, so long as someone is alive

who once knew the departed personally and by name... When there is no longer anyone alive who remembers them personally by name ... the living-dead do not vanish out of existence: they now enter into the state of *collective immortality*. (Mbiti 1969, 25–26)

Menkiti (1984, 175) contradicts this, stating that the term 'collective immortality' is 'problematic' as the dead 'cannot form a collectivity of any kind' and that the deceased become the 'nameless dead'. My research, however, reveals that, according to Îgembe philosophy, while a deceased individual cannot be immortalised, their name and personhood are perpetuated over generations; never to die.

The Kîmîîrû saying *muntû nî antû* ('a person is people') implies that 'the person is a function of the group to which he or she belongs' (Goldsmith 1995, 41). Thus, although personal immortality in Mbiti's sense does not endure over generations in Îgembe society, collective immortality does. People do not remember their ancestors' names, and their genealogical depth is relatively shallow as compared to other agnatic societies with strong lineage principles – such as the Gusii of Western Kenya and the Mae-Enga of the New Guinea Highlands.[16] However, the Îgembe are never indifferent to their shared history. Rather than recalling memories of individual ancestors, they speak of the shared past of their communities, Athîrû Gaiti, the Îgembe as a whole, and the greater Kîmîîrû-speaking nation.

Although clan affiliation is agnatically oriented, Îgembe village communities have, over time, accommodated and assimilated people of various origins, leading to complex genealogical relationships. However, the lack of personal commemoration of the deceased means that many people have no recollection of those relationships, or even of their ancestors' personal names. Instead, all individuals are subsumed into

---

16 Among the Mae-Enga, for example, 'every man wishes to see his son's sons before he dies and so take comfort from the hope that they will eventually form a patrilineage bearing his name' (Meggitt 1965, 29).

collective immortality via the namesake system. Peatrik observes the same phenomenon among the Îgembe and Tigania communities where:

> ...there is no belief in life after death; there are no ancestors, no ancestor worship, no genealogical mentality, a state of things that fits well with the absence of descent groups... Perpetuation is achieved through grandchildren, by the gift of a grandparent's name to a grandchild of the same sex, and through the orderly flow of the generations (Peatrik 2005, 295).

There is, however, space for intimate memories to be conveyed ephemerally among and along lines of immediate family, relatives, friends and namesakes (see also Mbiti 1969, 25). In this sense, the Kîmîîrû proverb *kanyîrî kainachua nî mweene* ('every preciousness shines only with its holder' or 'every preciousness is truly praised by its guardian') may hold true for personal names – just as it may for a cherished family photo album (Baba 2020) or a bracelet that was 'an extraordinarily live thing' on a Meru girl's arm (see Dinesen in the epigraph, p. ii).[17]

This philosophy is apparent in the Îgembe's lack of use for gravestones. During their colonial administration, the British introduced the inhumation of corpses; banning traditional Îgembe methods of cadaver exposure[18] (Lamont 2011). In the post-colonial world, the Îgembe continue to bury their dead but have never adopted the erection of permanent gravestones. Rather, it is assumed that the bereaved cannot and should not forget deceased family members – as demonstrated by Mûtûma's speech on the *ûtuunga* day, above (see also Matsuzono 2020). Physical markers are thus irrelevant.

---

17 In an account of her life in Kenya from 1914 to 1931, the Danish author Isak Dinesen wrote that, when she visited Meru, she bought a bracelet from a girl and that, 'No sooner had it come upon my own arm than it gave up the ghost. It was nothing now, a small, cheap, purchased article of finery' (Dinesen 1938, 257).

18 Traditionally, the corpses of of those who died inauspiciously should be carried into the bush, away from the settlement, while the corpses of (accomplished) seniors were laid on the household waste heap to decompose. Only extraordinary people who had 'lived a long time after reaching the final grade' were buried (Peatrik 2019: 57–60).

Although novel to studies of the Îgembe, my findings on notions of personhood and immortality are not unique among African ethnographies. As Lienhardt (1961: 319) notes in the conclusion to his masterpiece *Divinity and Experience: The Religion of the Dinka*, 'Notions of individual personal immortality mean little to non-Christian Dinka, but the assertion of collective immortality means much.' However – in an observation that provides a significant qualification to this chapter's contents – Lienhardt also describes a tension between personal loss and the necessity to relinquish loved ones to collective immortality. On the death of 'a master of the fishing-spear' (religious community leader), he writes:

> It is conceded to the man's close kin – those for whom his own personality has been most significant – that they may indeed break down under the strain imposed, by custom, upon them, in having to control the expression of the sadness they may feel. (Lienhardt 1961, 316)

Chapter 7
Transcending inner conflicts: Election day for the Athimba clan

This concluding chapter begins with a brief summary of Chapters 1 to 6.

Chapter 1 describes the socio-economic life of the Îgembe people, and how it evolved from the late 1980s to the mid-2010s – with the beginning of land adjudication in 1989 and the waxing and waning of the *mîraa* industry until 2014. It was after an extreme decline in coffee prices in the late 1980s that the Îgembe began cultivating *mîraa* as their main cash crop. After land distribution in the lower plain was completed in the early 2000s, farmers began to extend *mîraa* cultivation there. The industry developed steadily with the growth of international exports, until the Netherlands and the UK legislated bans on *mîraa* in 2013 and 2014, respectively.

Chapter 2 deals with generational change in the context of the Îgembe's indigenous age organisation, covering the circumcision ceremonies of the Bwantai age-class from 1989 onwards, the Gîchûnge from 1998 and the Kîramunya from 2013. The Gîchûnge's ceremonies coincided with the boom in the *mîraa* industry and, following the *mîraa* crisis, the people led the community into a new economic era.

Chapter 3 focuses on the revival of the Antûambui and Akachiû clans via the practice of *ûtaara ngeere*, and how this related to both the Kenyan government's introduction of the Nyumba Kumi community policing programme in 2013 and the initiation of the Mîrîti ruling elderhood in 2014. This chapter also demonstrates how justice among the Îgembe is not necessarily reached via confrontational hearings, but may be allowed to 'manifest' over time – with individuals recognising their personal responsibilities in a wider communal context.

Chapter 4 discusses three cases of homicide compensation, which required the Athimba to organise themselves as a clan – a process that began in 2001 and continued for fifteen years. The official transfer of power from the ruling Lubetaa age-class elderhood to the junior adjacent Mîrîti age-class was announced on 9 August 2014 by the Njûrincheke council of elders. Also that August, a Mîrîti man was appointed as the Athimba's new clan chairman.

Chapter 5 describes how the second-generation brothers of a migrant Antûambûi family variously succeeded and failed to assimilate into their host Athimba clan, to whom they were *îchiaro*. This chapter also demonstrated how the local theory of biological determinism depersonalises individuals who are invited to join a clan in their *îchiaro* capacity, and how newcomers experience the manifestation of that theory in social and historical contexts.

Chapter 6 considers how individuals, as members of collective bodies, experience immortality over the generations – via the Îgembe concept of shared personhood with namesakes of their own and other generations. In metaphorical terms, the long tail feathers of a bird are lively and beautifully fluttering only so long as they remain attached to their owner. Once shed, they exist solely as a material object of finery. Similarly, any given person retains their individuality and indispensability only so long as their face and voice are remembered by friends and relatives. In time, that person becomes one of the depersonalised, faceless dead; with only the personhood shared with their namesakes continuing into eternity.

The overall narrative of my book suggests that, despite a certain homogeneity of socio-economic circumstances among the Îgembe people, there has been huge variation and fluidity in clan constitution since the late 1980s. Overarching this is the temporality of communal intention, which transcends the immediacies of the present.

Below, I present case studies of the Athimba clan, which emphasise the Îgembe's inclination to allow matters of justice to be resolved over long timespans – as opposed to by quick adjudication. I have chosen the Athimba for this purpose because their clan's formal operations have remained active over time, where others have lain dormant for long periods.

To conclude, I discuss how the idea of 'protracted' justice might be intimately related to the Îgembe belief in communal intention and shared personhood.

Athimba clan continuity and the temporality of conflict resolution

As described in Chapters 3 and 4, the Athimba clan of Mûringene village is exceptional in Athîrû Gaiti, in that it continued to function formally (although intermittently) throughout the 2000s and 2010s.

In Chapter 1, I noted that, from the initiation of land adjudication in 1989 until the end of the 1990s, land boundary disputes intensified between Îgembe clans, but that, since the early 2000s, such disputes have transpired solely between individuals. Writing on Îgembe communities, Krueger (2016, 431) notes, 'With private property comes an increased emphasis on household decision-making with its compressed patriarchy... As compared to the household, age set and, to a lesser extent, clan have become like ghost institutions.' This observation also applies to Athîrû Gaiti in the 2000s and early 2010s, when many people became indifferent to clanship.

For the Athimba, as discussed previously, the clan did not decline into a ghost institution. Formal meetings were maintained from the turn of this century onwards for the practical purpose of addressing compensation payments (see Chapters 4 and 5). During this time, the Athimba learned from experience how to organise, keep clan records and employ their *ichiaro* counterparts to settle intraclan conflicts. Eventually, this knowledge was used to address all kinds of disputes among clan members (see Chapter 5).

As a body, the Athimba have experienced inner conflicts at different times and in various circumstances. These have included a dispute over the community dispensary in 2006 (Chapter 4, final section), the strained reconciliation of two 'brothers' in 2011 (Case 4.2), the unauthorised demolition of a clan house in 2015 (Case 4.3), and controversies over the chairing of the clan. All these cases took time to resolve, because the Îgembe do not hasten to conclusions – waiting instead for the best moment to address material conflicts. Even when a matter appears to have been resolved, no final outcome may have actually been reached. Further, when the Îgembe issue curses, they are not immediately effective. Two further examples are outlined below, in greater detail.

First, at the Athimba clan meeting on 3 September 2015, Mûriangûkû sought blessings to cleanse his family of its dark past (see Dialogue 6.1) – his late father, Ntika, had been accused by Athimba clan members of wrongly disposing of reparation items from a 2001–2002 homicide case involving the Aîri clan (Case 4.1). To gain absolution, Mûriangûkû shared cash his family had historically received as clan members. This did not, however, represent a final solution. The homicide compensation remains unfinished to this day and should eventually conclude with the slaughter of a bull (*ndewa ya ûkûrîra kîongo*)[1] at a joint feast of the Athimba and Aîri, and the Njûrincheke council of elders.

The second example concerns Mûnoru of the Lubetaa age-class, who became chairman of the Athimba in 2003. According to court records, Mûnoru sent a letter to the District Commissioner on 12 May 2005 declaring that the Athimba clan had allocated three acres of ancestral land to the Methodist Hospital.[2] Mûnoru was subsequently accused by clan members of favouring the church, while Samuel, of the Ratanya age-class – a devoted member of the same church – was accused of complicity. Since this controversy concerned the entire Athîrû Gaiti community, the clan members were unable to address it at their own discretion. Instead, Mûnoru and Samuel were cursed by the Njûrincheke council of elders.

---

1 Literally 'a bull to call for a head'.
2 As noted in Chapter 4, the dispute over the community dispensary went to court in 2010, and the letter was submitted and accepted as evidence to support the hospital's land ownership. However, I could neither trace the source of the letter nor find relevant information in the clan records. Some of my interviewees argued no such letter had been authorised by the clan.

In 2006, further controversy arose around the dispensary case (see Chapter 4, final section) and Mûnoru was replaced by Ndatû of the Mîrîti age-class (H18; Mûrîangûkû's younger brother). However, Mûnoru contested his dismissal and, instead of Ndatû assuming his new role, Mûteethia of the Ratanya age-class (H26) became acting chairman. Eventually, on 14 August 2014, with Mûnoru's case apparently overlooked, Kîthia (H3) was elected chairman.

Mûnoru's contestation of his dismissal remains unresolved. On 7 September 2012, Mûnoru quarrelled with Kabwî over this matter – Kabwi having previously challenged Mûnoru's claim to chairmanship (see Table 5.3 [2]). Mûnoru's case undoubtedly remains in the collective memory and will be resolved when the time is right – perhaps when the Njûrincheke council's cursing takes effect.

An election and a dispute

The Athimba held a meeting on 7 August 2014 to elect clan officials. The election (*kithuurano*) meeting was attended by seventeen people, including me and the three candidates for chairperson – Mûnoru (H12), Ndatû (H18) and Kîthia (H3).

Prior to election day, Ndatû travelled as clan representative to Laare, to engage Ngatûnyi of the Antûambûi clan – a *mwîchiaro* who had previously advised on various Athimba cases (see Chapters 4 and 5). It transpired that he was unavailable, so the 7 August meeting commenced with no *mwîchiaro* present. Seeing that both Ngatûnyi and his own supporters were absent, Mûnoru (H12) argued strongly for postponement. He was initially opposed by Kîthia (H3) but supported, among others, by Mûteethia (H26), the acting chairman, who asserted that every branch of the clan should vote. Finally, the election was adjourned until 14 August, when Kîthia (H3) was voted in as chairman with unexpected ease – simply because he was the only one of the three candidates to attend. The reason for Ndatû (H18) and Mûnoru's (H12) absence was unknown.

Before any votes could be cast, the 14 August meeting was thrown into confusion when a clan member, Meeme, lodged an unscheduled land case against his older brother, Samuel (who had earlier been accused as Mûnoru's accomplice in the dispensary case). The clan had already ruled in Meeme's favour at a meeting on 28 May 2013, which Ngatûnyi from Laare attended as *mwîchiaro*.[3] There, Meeme had claimed a share of land allocated to him by his father which, according to the Athimba clan record, had been wrongly disposed of by Samuel. The clan and the *mwîchiaro* had instructed Samuel to return the land, but Samuel refused; arguing that it was his father who disposed of it, and that Meeme was not really his biological brother. Thus, having achieved no favourable resolution, Meeme requested that the clan discuss his case again and a further meeting was scheduled for 22 July, at which it was decided that the *mwîchiaro* Ngatûnyi should be called once more. However, no date was specified for this.

When Meeme appeared at the 14 August 2014 election meeting, he did so with Ngatûnyi in tow – to the surprise of the entire clan. The clan elders agreed to address his case there and then, for which Meeme paid a fee of 500 shillings. Samuel, however, complained that he had received no advance warning, refused to recognise Ngatûnyi as *mwîchiaro*, and refused to pay any fee. During a heated exchange, Samuel abused Ngatûnyi, saying, 'This is not my brother (meaning *mwîchiaro*). He is a killer (*mworoani*)' – adding, 'Let him (Ngatûnyi) bewitch me and go back home.' Ngatûnyi rose to his feet, stepped forward to come face to face with Samuel and said three times, 'Bring the land of Meeme!' (Dialogue 7.1). He then held out his hand to ask for Meeme's share. Ngatûnyi's words were far more explicit than those during his previous visit, and the clan members understood them as nothing less than a *mwîchiaro*'s curse. Mûteethia thus closed the case – with the clear indication that Meeme should now wait until, in time, Samuel recognised his responsibility.

---

3 The Athimba also received compensation at this meeting (see Case 5.1, Table 5.1).

Dialogue 7.1 *Mwîchiaro*'s direct demand

Ngatûnyi:	Now, let me say one thing now. Let me tell you, Samuel, before I leave this place here. Bring the land of Meeme, my brother! Bring the land of Meeme!
Samuel:	There is none I have. I have none, nothing.
Ngatûnyi:	Is Meeme Karani's (Samuel's father's) son or not his son?
Samuel:	I don't know [indicating that he doesn't care].
Ngatûnyi:	Bring his land, my brother!
Samuel:	Which land? It's my father who sold his land. I was not the one who sold it.
Mûteethia:	Now, it is finished. Now pay your fee because we have done what you wanted… [Samuel again refuses, via a complaint about the way he has been treated.]

Curses do not lead to social ostracism and clan records show that, despite Ngatûnyi's words, Samuel continued to attend meetings until 21 March 2017 (see Table 7.1). He also joined a feast with *ndewa ya ûkundia rûûi* (a bull for water) on 27 April 2015, alongside Meene, as part of a homicide compensation process (Case 4.3). Further, Samuel, Meeme and Mûnoru were among eleven clan members to attend a family dispute hearing on 14 March.

In early 2017, Samuel became unwell and unable to walk. As noted above, he had earlier been cursed by the Njûrincheke council of elders for favouring the church hospital in the dispensary controversy. Some say this curse, together with Ngatûnyi's at the 14 August meeting, caused his sickness – although Samuel would never admit this due to his Christian faith. It might be added that Samuel, who was born in 1939, was by now infirm with old age.

Table 7.1 Attendance record of three agnates and *mwîchiaro*[1]

Date	Agenda	Number of attendants	Mûnoru	Samuel	Meeme	*Mwîchiaro*
22 March 2014	Land administration	9	–	present	present	
28 March	*Mwîchiaro*'s blessing for family welfare[2]	20	–	present	present	M'Ikîrîma's sons
29 March	*Mwîchiaro*'s curse against witchcraft[3]	44	present	present	present	Ngatûnyi Mbiti
8 July	Land dispute	11	–	present	present	–
17 July	Land dispute	19	present	present	present	–
22 July	Land dispute/ election	15	–	–	present	–
7 August	Election	17	present	–	present	
14 August	Election/ land dispute	14	–	present	present	Ngatûnyi
3 March 2015	Case 4.3 (Table 4.4)	13		present	–	–
23 February	Case 4.3/ Family dispute	13	–	–	–	–
23 March	Case 4.3	16		present	–	–
25 March	Case 4.3	23	–	–[4]	–	–
30 March	Case 4.3	10	–	present	–	–
8 April	Case 4.3	43	–	–	–	–
17 April	Case 4.3	30	–	–	present	–
27 April	Case 4.3	74	–	present	present	–
30 July	Finger compensation	16	present	present	–	–
6 August	Finger compensation	21	–	–	–	–
13 August	Finger compensation	23	present	–	–	–
20 August	Finger compensation	21	–	–	present	–
7 March 2017	Land dispute	11	present	present	–	–
14 March	Family dispute	11	present	present	present	–
21 March	Family problem	21	–	present	–	–

Notes:
1 The data provided here are based on clan records. The records for 2016 were unavailable.
2 The wife of Mbanga (H15) had long quarrelled with her sons. She once received a ram from one of them in reconciliation, in the presence of *mwîchiaro*, but nevertheless again started quarrelling and became sick. The 28 March 2014 meeting was convened to cure her sickness. In Case 5.4, M'Ikîrîma's sons (the second-generation brothers of a migrant Antûambûi family) assumed the role of *mwîchiaro* for cleansing.
3 Ngatûnyi of the Antûambûi clan and Mbiti of the Andûûne cursed anyone who bewitched a clan member's children. In this case, the children's father suspected another agnate of the Athimba.
4 Samuel did not appear on the day, having notified the clan of his absence in advance.

Communal intention and shared personhood

In 1999, I conducted fieldwork in a village of the Gusii people, in western Kenya. During this time, I often observed the difficulties elders faced in managing local disputes at lineage meetings. Their judgements did not always satisfy both parties involved and sometimes created further conflicts. During my time in the Athîrû Gaiti community, in contrast, such difficulties did not always transpire, because the Îgembe people have their own means of transcending inner conflicts and personal interests.

One of the Îgembe's guiding principles is that private individuals should not take the law into their own hands, or resort to physical violence to enforce their own perceptions of justice. When crimes such as sexual assault (see Chapter 2), the infliction of large-scale suffering (Chapter 3) or homicide (Chapters 4 and 5) are committed, age-classes or clans organise collectively to achieve justice, in conjunction with, or under the authority of, the Njûrincheke council of elders.

Notably, an age-class or clan is usually considered to be a category, as opposed to a group, while a council of elders is recognised as an established body. Individuals are certainly aware of their own age-class and clan affiliation but may consider these to be dormant 'ghost' entities – as opposed to organisations for collective action. Thus, only when leadership is strong enough to mobilise people in the name of their age-class or clan affiliation will communal intentions materialise. Such leadership – be it strong or weak – is not immutable. Generational changes between age-classes have allowed new leaders to emerge throughout history, and the heads of any established Njûrincheke council must, in time, relinquish power and authority to their juniors.

It seems the Îgembe people live in accord with the African saying, 'I am, because we are; and since we are, therefore I am' (Mbiti 1969, 108–109). This outlook manifests in both the shared personhood of Kîmîîrû names and the *îchiaro* relationship, which curbs inclinations towards individualism. After death, discrete individuals are usually only remembered for any length of time by family members and intimates, whereas shared personhood is immortalised over generations via name sharing (see Chapter 6). Further, when a man, together with his agnates, fears the visit of his *mwîchiaro*, that fear is not of an individual but rather of a social person who symbolises and represents his *îchiaro* clan. Thus, a *mwîchiaro* should conduct his work in an impersonal manner, without employing his power in his own interests (see Chapter 5).

The Îgembe's disinclination to individualism may account for the unique characteristics of their justice system. As previously noted, they recognise the merits of waiting for any current material conflict to be addressed at a future time. For example, the third parties involved in managing civil disputes and witchcraft accusations among family members and neighbours do not provide judgements. Rather, they use conditional curses – which do not take immediate effect – and/or the power of *îchiaro* (see Appendix 2) to enable one of the parties involved to transcend individualism and recognise their responsibility.

The *îchiaro* relationship is reciprocal between clans and, since every clan member is born into the system, it may be defined as biologically determined and egalitarian. Further, because *îchiaro* and cursing do not lead to the immediate or unilateral administration of justice, their use in dispute management may be characterised as more restorative than retributive. The ultimate benefit of this framework is that, rather than providing coercive solutions, it gives space for disputing clan members to transcend the immediacies of the present – to live not only as individuals in the here and now but also to exist within a wider web of identity, which extends across time – from the past to the present and into the future.

Postscript

After a research hiatus due to the COVID-19 pandemic, I revisited Athîrû Gaiti in August–September 2022 and found that momentous events had occurred, for both the source community and this study, during this three-year gap. First, in 2020, young men belonging to the Gîchûnge age-class (see Chapter 2) placed a curse upon their seniors who controlled the local economy. Second, the Nyumba Kumi system of community policing (see Chapter 3) came to be untrusted and paralysed by the local community after a serious incident on 24 August 2021. Lastly, a longstanding question over the disposal of the 2001–2002 homicide compensation (see Chapters 4 and 6) had reached a final resolution within the Athimba clan.

On arrival there, I learned of some sad news. Both Nchee (H20, see Chapter 5), an *îchiaro* migrant of Antûambûi origin, and his younger brother, Mwambia (H21), passed away in 2021 and (June) 2022, respectively. While I am unclear whether their death was related to COVID-19, I heard that they had been very sick in their last days and that many people had died during the pandemic.

The COVID-19 pandemic also had a severe negative impact on the cash crop industry in the Îgembe district. Between 2020 and 2022, when the pandemic spread, exports of *mîraa* to neighbouring Somalia were suspended. When I revisited the community, the cash crop industry was recovering, with exports to Somalia having been resumed since June 2022. Nevertheless, due to a severe lack of rainfall in the first half of the year, many people, including my research assistant, went to work in other areas of the country. Conversely, some people attributed the economic depression in the early 2020s to a curse cast by young men of the Gîchûnge age-class. I met Mwasimba, the chairman of the Akachiû clan in Nthare (see Chapters 3 [Case 3.4] and 6 [PN10]), only to find him preparing for a healing ceremony (*kûoria kîrumi*). According to him, the Gîchûnge young men from his neighbourhood were strongly dissatisfied with their working conditions in the *mîraa* industry, thus they placed a curse upon their ruling seniors in 2020, which caused the breakdown of the local economy. However, the Gîchûnge's rebellion was reported not only from Nthare but also from different places within the Îgembe district in the late 2010s and early 2020s. The new findings show that the Gîchûnge have not remained silent in the sense described in the last section of Chapter 2.

The difficulties faced by the people in the Athîrû Gaiti community were not only economic in nature: one of the Nyumba Kumi units introduced in 2013 began to repeatedly harass local people in the 2020s, culminating with an unprecedented incident on 24 August 2021. People claiming to be Nyumba Kumi members (none of them were involved in this study) suspected a woman of producing and selling illicit brew and beat her to death. However, her family and acquaintances strongly denied this infamy and claimed that it was an unreasonable harassment by those calling themselves Nyumba Kumi members. The victim was the wife of a man of my generation, that is, belonging to the Bwantai age-class, and a mother with children. I have known her husband for 20 years as a cheerful and well-liked man in the community. In my view, his wife could not have been involved in the production of illicit brew. The suspects in this incident were soon arrested, the criminal case proceeded to trial, and the harassment stopped. However, this episode caused a deep-seated sense of mutual distrust within the community. I heard voices of strong discontent with those who had misappropriated the state-backed institution of Nyumba Kumi for their personal benefit or revenge. Although Chapter 3 of this book observed the Nyumba Kumi in the context of materialisation of 'communal intention', its malfunction in the 2020s overturned such understandings.

During the three years of research hiatus, a historical event occurred within the Mûringene village of Athîrû Gaiti. As described in Chapters 4 and 5, the Athimba clan of Mûringene has experienced four cases of homicide compensation since 2001. In August–September 2022, I learned that the first case (Case 4.1), observed between 2001 and 2002, had reached a final settlement in November 2021. The case was interrupted in 2002 when an Athimba elder disposed of some animals his people had received as compensation items and demolished the clan house, a symbol of clan unity, without the clan's permission. In the following two decades, the Athimba clan members did not forget his culpability. With the man already deceased, his sons were left responsible for their father's actions (see Dialogue 6.1 in Chapter 6 for an example of how this manifested in the words and actions of a son, Mûrîangûkû). The moment all clan members had been waiting for finally arrived in 2021. A chain of misfortunes had befallen the sons: one passed away in 2020 and another became seriously ill. The rest of the sons judged the root cause to be a curse of the clan, and at a clan meeting, they accepted the responsibility for their father's actions to have the curse removed. The sons brought cash and two animals, a he-goat (in place of a bull) and a ram, on 5 November 2021. The clan met again on 9 November to rebuild the clan house (as it was in 2001) and demolish it properly, which was the only resolution that would receive the blessing of the entire clan. The son who had been hospitalised for many months recovered and was discharged.

Although I did not directly observe this final settlement, I managed to get an overview of the event through interviews. On the day of demolishing the clan house (*kûthalia nyumba ya mwîrîa*) and blessings (*kûtharimana mwîrîa*), the he-goat, symbolically called a bull, and ram were slaughtered. Five elders from the Athimba's *îchiaro* clans were invited and given the front legs (*lubwatha*) of the sacrificed ram. When the clan house was demolished, the *îchiaro* men uprooted its poles, saying 'We demolish the house for the head (meaning homicide compensation). The family members of Ntika (the responsible person) shall never see this (series of misfortunes) again. We are *îchiaro* and clan. We have uprooted the clan house.' Concluding the function, the *îchiaro* men uttered a blessing phrase, to which clan members responded; the responsorial pair was repeated eight times: four times for men, three for women, and one for the *îchiaro*. Knowing that one of the challenges for the clan was finally solved after 20 years, I was again convinced of the merit of waiting.

In the years to come, the Îgembe communities will make use of their rich natural, cultural and human resources to overcome various challenges and develop a bright future. The time will come when the people of the Bwantai age-class will take the helm of society. No one can or should predict the shape of the future. However, one can talk about their aspirations for the future. Waiting does not mean doing nothing.

Appendix 1

Homicide compensation in Kenya

This appendix briefly outlines the legal context for homicide compensation in Kenya and East Africa as a whole, together with some of the debates surrounding it. It also précises research by three researchers on patterns of homicide in African countries.

Section 175 of the present Kenyan Criminal Procedure Code permits courts to 'order the convicted person to pay to the injured party such sum as it considers could justly be recovered as damages in civil proceedings brought by the injured party against the convicted person in respect of the civil liability concerned'. In Section 176, the code also states, 'In all cases the court may promote reconciliation and encourage and facilitate the settlement in an amicable way of proceedings for common assault, or for any other offence of a personal or private nature not amounting to felony, and not aggravated in degree, on terms of payment of compensation or other terms approved by the court, and may thereupon order the proceedings to be stayed or terminated'. Hence, the relatives of 'the injured party' (a somewhat euphemistic term in cases of homicide) may be awarded 'blood money' under the provisions of both the Criminal Procedure Code and Section 31 of the Penal Code[1], both of which were introduced in the colonial period (Morris 1974, 107) and derived from other British colonies.

The provisions above have, however, long been 'a dead letter' in colonial and post-colonial East Africa (Brown 1966, 35; Coldham 2000, 221–222; see also Bushe Commission 1934, 63–66). One disputed area has been 'the mixing of criminal and civil business in a single hearing', which is generally natural to African societies but not to British oriented courts (Brown 1966, 37). Historically, judges have thus discouraged

---

[1] Section 31 of the code states, 'Any person who is convicted of an offence may be adjudged to make compensation to any person injured by his offence, and the compensation may be either in addition to or in substitution for any other punishment.'

lower courts from using their discretionary power to award compensation in criminal cases, without actually forbidding it (Brown 1966, 34–35 and 39). Morris (1974, 111) questions this, noting that it would be 'clearly advantageous if separate civil suits for blood money could be obviated by an award of compensation being made in the criminal case'. Despite this, the status quo has prevailed in colonial and post-colonial Commonwealth Africa, where 'sentencing was [and still is] based on the principles of retribution and general deterrence and there was a marked reluctance to consider customary notions of compensation and restitution' (Coldham 2000, 220).[2]

Patterns of homicide: Three perspectives

In his March 1970 study of 108 offenders serving sentences for criminal homicide at Kamiti Maximum Security Prison in Kenya, East African law professor Tibamanya Mwene Mushanga concludes that criminal homicide is 'commonly committed by persons against members of their immediate families, domestic groups, friends, workmates and acquaintances' (Mushanga 2011, 94).

In a wider comparative analysis of patterns of murder and offender/victim relationships in seven African countries, Bohannan finds that brother-killing and uxoricide occur in all societies, although the patterns vary among different cultures (Bohannan 1960, 244), and that 'what appears to be the same pattern in wife-killing can be given vastly different expressions' (Bohannan 1960, 253).

Komma (1997) provides a detailed description of local responses to two homicide cases in the Kipsigis community of Western Kenya – where the number of reported murders is relatively low. Further, he compares two ethnic communities in terms of how the killing of a person reveals (or

---

2   See Donovan and Assefa (2003) for further discussion of the awarding of homicide compensation in East Africa, from the perspective of legal pluralism, and Okupa (1998, 63–79) for a general discussion on compensatory justice in Africa (as well as a useful bibliography on this matter).

contributes to) structural clashes. Among the Kipsigis, these fall between state and customary law, while among the Isukha of the greater Luhya (Nakabayashi 1991), they fall between politically autonomous lineages. The Kipsigis' nationwide age system, which cuts across clan borders, contributes to the creation of ethnic common law, which recognises compensation claims only for the killing of a person of the same ethnicity (Komma 1997).

Appendix 2

A witchcraft accusation in Mûringene, September 2005

On Saturday 3 September 2005, approximately fifty members of the Njûrincheke council assembled at the divisional headquarters in Athîrû Gaiti. The main purpose of their meeting was to settle local disputes, some of which had been referred to them by administrative chiefs.

Of the four cases heard, the most serious was between Mwîti[3] (H11) of the Mîrîti age-class and Kaario (Kîeri's [PN4] wife; see Chapter 6), both of whom are agnates of the Athimba, residing in Mûringene village. Mwîti accused Kaario and her friend Margaret of conducting an unknown ritual and poisoning his daughter Faith with *ûroi* (sorcery). Kaario denied this and complained that Mwîti had assaulted her.

At the hearing, Mwîti detailed Kaario's alleged offence, saying that she and Margaret had, between them, lifted up a sheep and forced Faith to walk back and forth beneath it, carrying a baby. The sheep's ear was cut and blood dripped on to the girl, staining her. These 'evil deeds' were performed in secret and, Mwîti argued, had something to do with Faith's current sickness, including fainting spells, which had begun around one and a half years earlier and which medical doctors had been unable to treat.

---

3 Except for Kîeri, all individuals in this case are referred to by pseudonyms.

Mwîti and Kaario, whose homesteads were on either side of a path, had formerly been on close terms; helping each other out in everyday life. Even after the alleged sorcery, Kaario would take Mwîti's sick daughter to local clinics and the Methodist hospital in Maûa. Mwîti spent a lot of money on treatment and eventually the girl was taken to a general hospital in Nairobi – to no avail, as the fainting spells continued throughout each day. Finally, Mwîti took Faith to a Christian pastor for prayers and, at church, she began to talk about being part of a bizarre ritual. The pastor reported this to Mwîti who, confused, began to suspect Kaario of sorcery.

Mwîti visited his neighbour and asked for an explanation. Kaario acknowledged that she had conducted a ritual, but it was simply *kîengeere* – a recognised medical treatment in the Kîmîîrû tradition which Margaret had asked her to performed for her sick baby granddaughter. The sheep's blood, she said, was not intended to harm Faith but rather treat the baby. Mwîti reported to the council that he had tried to understand Kaario's explanations but had become confused when he overheard a rumour that his neighbour was annoyed with him and planned to accuse him of libel.

Another rumour had been circulating in the neighbourhood – that, years ago, Kaario had killed her own child and was now trying to harm Faith. On 26 August, a mob of villagers gathered tyres and kerosene, planning to burn Kaario to death. She escaped by a hairsbreadth, but was intercepted by Mwîti. Local security officers and elders then intervened to save Kaario and advised her to explain the *kîengeere* publicly to make herself understood. Kaario agreed and actually went on to repeat the ritual – cutting the ear of a sheep and lifting it up with her husband, Kîeri, while Faith, carrying Margaret's baby granddaughter wrapped in a cloth, once again passed beneath.

At the council hearing, Margaret was summoned to testify about the *kîengeere*. She argued that she was not familiar with it, and gave the following testimony (which proved to be much more descriptive than Kaario's, who provided only brief answers under examination):

Appendix 217

Margaret:	Let me tell you how it was. As God is my witness, this is what happened. On that day, my daughter's baby became sick, and kept crying. I didn't know anything about *kîengeere*. But I believed there was something like that in our tradition... When the baby was crying, she (Kaario) said to me, 'Let us use a sheep (*ngeerre*) in my place. I will come with the animal this evening.' When I reached there (Kaario's homestead), she asked me whether I had brought the baby. I did not know what she was going to do. I went back home and returned with my grandchild. She said, 'Because the girl (Faith) is my neighbour and friend whom I love, there is no problem.' Then, Kaario called the girl, she came, and what they described was done. I know nothing about the ritual. The girl passed under the sheep, as Mwîti said...
Elder:	I'd like to ask you something. Now, you are a witness (*mûkûûjî*).
Margaret:	Yes, I am a witness.
Elder:	Who is the sorcerer?
Margaret:	I don't know who the sorcerer is.
Elder:	Good. You were there when the sheep was cut. So, what is sorcery? The sheep or something else?
Margaret:	I don't know... You (elders) are the ones who know.

Njûrincheke elders are indeed experts in Kîmîîrû customs and traditions. However, none of those at the hearing passed comment on the 'true' nature of *kîengeere*. Neither did they comment on Kaario's description of the ritual, nor judge whether she had performed it correctly.[4] In

---

4 On 21 September, two weeks after the hearing, I interviewed one of the elders who had listened to Kaario's testimony. He said, 'I personally recognised that the ritual

fact, the elders questioned Kaario and Margaret as though they were completely unfamiliar with *kîengeere*, before proceeding to another point of interrogation.

The secretary of the Njûrincheke council asked Kaario, 'Why and how was she (Faith) involved in *kîengeere* on that day?' Kaario replied, 'We were not treating Mwîti's daughter, but Margaret's grandchild.' The elders were apparently unsatisfied with this answer because Kaario gave no reason why Faith in particular was summoned. If she had said it was necessary for a virgin girl to carry the sick baby, and that Faith suited this purpose, her defence might have been received as reasonable and persuasive.

Mwîti, certain that Kaario was responsible for Faith's sickness, was eager for her to take an *îchiaro* oath (see Introduction for an explanation of the *îchiaro* system). Kaario, meanwhile, remained composed throughout the trial – unshakably confident in her innocence. Nevertheless, she did not have adequate evidence in her defence and, to prove herself, had no option but to take the oath. She accepted this without hesitation, in the knowledge that its administration under a false accusation could do her no harm.

The elders agreed to the administration of the oath and Mwîti enlisted Kaario's *mwîchiaro* counterpart who, although *îchiaro* to Kaario's father, did not know her well. This was significant because, if Kaario had been allowed to choose a *mwîchiaro* with whom she was familiar, he might have been partial in her favour.

It is notable that Kaario was required to swear not before her husband's *mwîchiaro, of* the Amwari clan, but her father's *mwîchiaro, of*

---

was *kîengeere*. Kaario followed the Kîmîîrû tradition. Nevertheless, the differences between the parties remained vast, and I could not persuade Mwîti to understand Kaario's behaviour. She should have informed Mwîti before performing the ritual. She failed to inform him, and that is her big mistake.' The same elder said that Kaario was known as a traditional medical expert, especially in removing a *ng'wani* (natal tooth). Most of the elders I interviewed agreed that Kaario was wrong in neglecting her responsibility to consult with Mwîti before calling Faith to perform *kîengeere* but that, this aside, her administration of the ritual satisfied Kîmîîrû tradition.

the Athimba. This further demonstrates the biological determinism described in Chapter 5, in which women retain their original *ichiaro* relationship even after marriage. It is certainly understood that wives should respect their husbands' *ichiaro* partners, but their achieved status does not replace their ascribed one.

On Saturday 10 September 2005, Mwîti brought Mpuria, Kaario's *mwîchiaro* from the Andûûne clan (see Cases 5.5 and 5.6), before whom the accused took the oath. First, a feast with abundant goat's meat was held, to both satisfy the elders and acquire a special piece of flesh – an oath fetish. Pieces of meat were distributed to nearly all present – including myself and other *nkûrûmbû* (non-initiates of the Njûrincheke council) but excluding Mwîti and Kaario.

At around 4.45 pm, the Njûrincheke elders ushered the *nkûrûmbû* out of the venue. The administration of the *îchiaro* oath is not a secret ceremony, but the elders did not wish for it to be open to the public. I am therefore unable to give precise details of the event below; presenting an outline instead.

Seated on the grass, surrounded by the Njûrincheke elders, Kaario was questioned by her *mwîchiaro*.

Mwîchiaro: Do you have powers of sorcery?

Kaario: No!

Mwîchiaro: Have you ever seen sorcery?

Kaario: No!

Mwîchiaro: [Chews a piece of goat's meat (thought to be breast meat) then gives the same piece to Kaario] If you have powers of sorcery and pretend that you don't have it, this piece of meat will kill you.

Kaario then swore that she was innocent and swallowed the piece of meat[5], thereby ingesting her *mwîchiaro's* saliva – a substance vital to the *îchiaro* oath.[6]

Immediately after the ritual, a group of elders finalised the case by cursing Mwîti, Kaario and her *mwîchiaro counterpart*. *Îchiaro* oaths are unilateral, in that only the accused – and not the accuser – is required to swear them. However, the elders recognised the need to control Mwîti's behaviour, and so cursed him too, as well as cautioning him not to repeat his assaults on Kaario and instructing him to await the outcome of the oath.

The elders told Kaario that, if she were to suffer any misfortunes in the future, she must admit her guilt and consult with them regarding a cleansing ceremony. Kaario was also cautioned not to conspire with her *mwîchiaro* to conduct a secret cleansing ceremony and nullify the revitalising oath's dangerous power. If Kaario had shared close relations with her *mwîchiaro*, it would have been difficult for him to refuse any such request.

In Kaario's case, then, a unilateral oath was reinforced by a multilateral curse. Such curses are homogenous among the Îgembe, with the attendants rubbing their palms together (*kwikitha rwîî*) while the curse words are pronounced. Concluding phrases follow, such as, 'May it be cut like this!' or, 'May he/she be cut like this!' The attendants then make a clap (*kwiita rwîî*). It is common for the whole process to be repeated two or three times.

The following is part of the curse directed by M'Anampiû, a Njûrincheke elder.

---

5   Meat may be replaced by *mîraa* if it too is chewed by the *mwîchiaro* then swallowed by the oath taker.
6   Saliva (*mata*) is used for blessings in many contexts. At the cleansing ceremony of the *îchiaro* oath, the *mwîchiaro* spits saliva at the oath taker. Later, the breast meat of a female sheep, together with honey and *kîleenchu* (Kikuyu grass), are used to heal (*kûoria*) the oath.

Appendix

Mwekûrrû ûû, mwaarî o M'Mûkiri.

This woman (the accused), the daughter of M'Mûkiri.

Îndî amwîra, nkûwatûa nî muuma, îjûû ûmbikîrie mata...

But if she (the accused) says to him (her *mwîchiaro*), 'I have been caught by *muuma*, please come and spit saliva on me [for cleansing]...'

Amwikîria, atîrîija atîachookanîîrria Îembe ûû...

Then he spits saliva on her, without coming back to [consult with] this council...

Ijîjî na nkenye, ng'ombe chiaake, ibua rîaake, mathaa yaake, tharike yaake...

His boys and girls, his cows, his blessings, his sperm, his blood...

Îrotwîîka ûû!

May it be cut like this! [*kwiita rwîî*]

References

Abel, Richard L. 1969. "Customary laws of wrongs in Kenya: An essay in research method." *The American Journal of Comparative Law* 17 (4): 573–626. doi: 10.2307/839188.

Ambler, Charles H. 1988. *Kenyan Communities in the Age of Imperialism: The central region in the late nineteenth century*. New Haven: Yale University Press.

Baba, Jun. 2020. "Ontology of photograph among the Tigania: Inquiry into the relation of Meru culture and modern technology." In *Family Dynamics and Memories in Kenyan Villages*, edited by Njûgûna Gîchere, S. A. Mûgambi Mwithimbû and Shin-ichiro Ishida, 77–99. Nairobi: National Museums of Kenya.

Baker, Bruce. 2004. "Multi-choice policing in Africa: Is the continent following the South African pattern?" *Society in Transition* 35 (2): 204–223. doi: 10.1080/21528586.2004.10419116.

Beidelman, Thomas O. 1986. *Moral Imagination in Kaguru Modes of Thought*. Bloomington: Indiana University Press.

—— 1993. "Secrecy and society: The paradox of knowing and the knowing of paradox." In *Secrecy: African Art That Conceals and Reveals*, edited by Mary H. Nooter, 41–47. New York: Museum for African Art.

Bernard, Frank Edward. 1972. *East of Mount Kenya: Meru agriculture in transition*. Vol. nr. 75, *Afrika-Studien*: Weltforum Verlag.

—— 1979. "Meru District in the Kenyan spatial economy: 1890–1950." In *The Spatial Structure of Development: A study of Kenya*, edited by Robert A. Obudho and D. R. F. Taylor, 264–290. Boulder: Westview Press.

Bernardi, Bernardo. 1959. *The Mugwe, a Failing Prophet: A study of a religious and public dignitary of the Meru of Kenya*. London: Oxford University Press.

Bohannan, Paul. 1960. "Patterns of murder and suicide." In *African Homicide and Suicide*, edited by Paul Bohannan, 230–266. Princeton: Princeton University Press.

Brown, Douglas. 1966. "The award of compensation in criminal cases in East Africa." *Journal of African Law* 10(1): 33–39.

Buruchara, R. A. 1986. "Agriculture." In *Meru District Socio-cultural Profile*, edited by Gideon S. Were. Nairobi: Republic of Kenya.

Bushe Commission. 1934. *Report of the Commission of Inquiry into the Administration of Justice in Kenya, Uganda and the Tanganyika Territory in Criminal Matters, May, 1933, and Correspondence Arising out of the Report*. London: H. M. Stationery Office.

Carrier, Neil. 2005. "'Miraa is cool': The cultural importance of miraa (khat) for Tigania and Igembe youth in Kenya." *Journal of African Cultural Studies* 17 (2): 201–218.

—— 2007. *Kenyan Khat: The social life of a stimulant*. Leiden: Brill.

Coldham, Simon. 2000. "Criminal justice policies in commonwealth Africa: Trends and prospects. " *Journal of African Law* 44(2): 218–238.

DALEO. 2001. Meru North District Annual Report, 2000.

—— 2002. Meru North District Annual Report, 2001.

—— 2003. Meru North District Annual Report, 2002.

Dinesen, Isak. 1938. *Out of Africa*. New York: Random House.

Dolan, Catherine. 2001. "The 'good wife': Struggles over resources in the Kenyan horticultural sector." *The Journal of Development Studies* 37: 39–70.

Donovan, Dolores A. and Getachew Assefa 2003. "Homicide in Ethiopia: Human rights, federalism, and legal pluralism." *The American Journal of Comparative Law* 51(3): 505–552.

Dundas, Charles. 1915. "The organization and laws of some Bantu tribes in East Africa." *The Journal of the Royal Anthropological Institute of Great Britain and Ireland* 45: 234–306. doi: 10.2307/2843478.

—— 1921. "Native laws of some Bantu tribes of East Africa." *The Journal of the Royal Anthropological Institute of Great Britain and Ireland* 51: 217–278. doi: 10.2307/2843522.

Duranti, Alessandro. 2015. *The Anthropology of Intentions: Language in a world of others*. Cambridge: Cambridge University Press.

Fadiman, Jeffrey. 1993. *When We Began There Were Witchmen: An oral history from Mount Kenya*. Berkeley: University of California Press.

Gallagher, Shaun. 2017. "The narrative sense of others." *HAU: Journal of Ethnographic Theory* 7 (2): 467–473. doi: 10.14318/hau7.2.039.

Giorgis, B. G. 1964. *A Tentative Kimeru Dictionary*. Meru: Meru Catholic Bookshop.

Goldsmith, Paul. 1995. "Symbiosis and transformation in Kenya's Meru District." Ph. D., University of Florida.

Hale, Charles R. 2006. "Activist research v. cultural critique: Indigenous land rights and the contradictions of politically engaged anthropology." *Cultural Anthropology* 21 (1): 96–120. doi: 10.1525/can.2006.21.1.96.

Hashimoto, Eri. 2018. *E Kuoth: Minami Sudan Nuer shakai niokeru yogen to junan no minzokushi* [E Kuoth: An ethnography of prophecy and suffering among the Nuer of South Sudan]. Fukuoka: Kyusyu University Press.

References

Hviding, Edvard. 1993. "Indigenous essentialism? 'Simplifying' customary land ownership in New Georgia, Solomon Islands." *Bijdragen tot de taal-, land- en volkenkunde / Journal of the Humanities and Social Sciences of Southeast Asia* 149 (4): 802–824. doi: 10.1163/22134379-90003114.

Ishida, Shin-ichiro. 2008. "Contemporary agriculture in Nyambene District." In *The Indigenous Knowledge of the Ameru of Kenya*, edited by Njûgûna Gîchere and Shin-ichiro Ishida, 121–146. Meru: Meru Museum.

——— 2010. "Legal pluralism and human rights in a Kenyan court: an analysis of dowry claim cases." In *In Search of Justice and Peace: Traditional and informal justice systems in Africa*, edited by Manfred O. Hinz and Clever Mapaure, 133–166. Windhoek: Namibia Scientific Society.

——— 2023. "Anthropology, indigenous methodology, and the restatement of African laws: Lessons from research collaborations in Kenya." Legal Pluralism and Critical Social Analysis 55(3): 321–338. doi: 10.1080/27706869.2023.2286662

Kapuściński, Ryszard. 2002. *The Shadow of the Sun*. Translated by Klara Glowczewska, *Vintage international*. New York: Vintage Books.

Kenya, Ministry of State for Provincial Administration and Internal Security. 2008. "Reforms in the police force: Concept of community policing paying dividends." *The Administrator* 1: 11–12.

Kenya, National Task Force on Community Policing. 2015. Draft Guidelines for Implementation of Community Policing -Nyumba Kumi, Usalama wa Msingi.

Kenya, Republic of. 1966. *Report of the Mission on land consolidation and registration in Kenya 1965–1966: With appendices*: s.n.

——— 1981. *Kenya Population Census, 1979*. Nairobi: Central Bureau of Statistics, Ministry of Economic, Planning and Development.

——— 1997. *Nyambene District Development Plan 1997–2001*, edited by Office of the Vice-President and Ministry of Planning and National Development. Nairobi.

——— 2001a. *The 1999 Population & Housing Census: Counting our people for development*. Nairobi: Central Bureau of Statistics.

——— 2001b. *Meru North District PRSP Consultation Report for the Period 2001–2004*. Nairobi: Ministry of Finance and Planning.

——— 2002. *Field Crops Technical Handbook* (Second Edition). Nairobi: Ministry of Agriculture and Rural Development.

——— 2010. *The 2009 Kenya Population & Housing Census: "Counting our people for the implementation of vision 2030"*. Nairobi: Kenya National Bureau of Statistics.

Kioko, Eric Mutisya. 2017. "Conflict resolution and crime surveillance in Kenya: Local peace committees and nyumba kumi." *Africa Spectrum* 52 (1): 3–32.

Kokwaro, J. O. 1979. *Classification of East African Crops*. Kenya Literature Bureau.

Komma, Toru. 1997. "'Two nations in one' as observed through two murder cases among the Kipsigis of Kenya." In *State and Ethnicity*, (in Japanese), edited by the Kanagawa University Institute for Humanities Research, 138–169. Kyoto: Keiso-shobo.

Krueger, James S. 2016. "Autonomy and morality: Legal pluralism factors impacting sustainable natural resource management among miraa farmers in Nyambene Hills, Kenya." *The Journal of Legal Pluralism and Unofficial Law* 48 (3): 415–440. doi: 10.1080/07329113.2016.1239318.

Lambert, H. E. 1956. *Kikuyu Social and Political Institutions*. London: Oxford University Press.

Lamont, Mark. 2005. "Historicity of generation: Uncertainties of Meru age-class formation in central Kenya." Ph.D., University of Edinburgh.

—— 2010. "Lip-synch gospel: Christian music and the ethnopoetics of identity in Kenya." *Africa* 80 (3): 473–496. doi: 10.3366/afr.2010.0306.

—— 2011. "Decomposing pollution? Corpses, burials, and affliction among the Meru of Central Kenya." In *Funerals in Africa: Explorations of a social phenomenon*, edited by Michael Jindra and Joël Noret, 88–108. New York: Berghahn Books.

—— 2018. "Forced male circumcision and the politics of foreskin in Kenya." *African Studies* 77 (2): 293–311. doi: 10.1080/00020184.2018.1452850.

Lienhardt, R. G. 1961. *Divinity and Experience: The religion of the Dinka*. Oxford: Clarendon Press.

Mahner, Jurg. 1975. "The outsider and the insider in Tigania Meru." *Africa: Journal of the International African Institute* 45 (4): 400–409. doi: 10.2307/1159453.

Matsuda, Motoji. 2016. "African potentials for conflict prevention: Community policing in Kenya." In *African Potentials 1: African cultures of settling conflict*, edited by Motoji Matsuda and Misa Hirano, 237–275. Kyoto: Kyoto University Press.

Matsuzono, Makio. 2020. "'I hate to see my late husband': Death and the last words among the Îgembe of Kenya " In *Family Dynamics and Memories in Kenyan Villages*, edited by Njûgûna Gîchere, S. A. Mûgambi Mwithimbû and Shin-ichiro Ishida, 21–56. Nairobi: National Museums of Kenya.

Mbiti, John S. 1969. *African Religions and Philosophy*. London: Heinemann.

Meggitt, Mervyn John. 1965. *The Lineage System of the Mae-Enga of New Guinea*. London: Oliver & Boyd.

Menkiti, Ifeanyi A. 1984. "Person and community in African traditional thought." In *African philosophy: An introduction*, 171–181. Lanham: University Press of America.

Middleton, John, and Greet Kershaw. 1965. *The Central Tribes of the North-eastern Bantu: The Kikuyu, including Embu, Meru, Mbere, Chuka, Mwimbi, Tharaka, and the Kamba of Kenya*. International African Institute.

References

Morris, H. F. 1974. "The award of blood money in East African manslaughter cases." *Journal of African Law* 18(1): 104–112.

Mushanga, Tibamanya Mwene. 2011. *Homicide and Its Social Causes*. Nairobi: Law Africa.

M'Imanyara, Alfred M. 1992. *The Restatement of Bantu Origin and Meru History*. Nairobi: Longman Kenya.

Mwithimbû, S. A. Mûgambi. 2014. "Njûriîncheke: An instrument of peace and conflict resolution." In *Culture in Peace and Conflict Resolution within Communities of Central Kenya*, edited by Njûgûna Gîchere, S. A. Mûgambi Mwithimbû and Shinichiro Ishida, 70–92. Nairobi: National Museums of Kenya.

Mwiti, Edward Steven. 2004. *1200 Kimeru Proverbs: Including idiomatic expressions and similes*. Nairobi: E. S. Mwiti.

Nakabayashi, Nobuhiro. 1991. *Living with the State: Iskha clans in Western Kenya*. (in Japanese) Yokohama: Seori-shobo.

Needham, Rodney. 1960. "The Left hand of the Mugwe: An analytical note on the structure of Meru symbolism." *Africa* 30 (1): 20–33. doi: 10.2307/1157738.

Neumann, Arthur H. 1898. *Elephant-hunting in East Equatorial Africa: Being an account of three years' ivory-hunting under Mount Kenia and among the Ndorobo savages of the Lorogi Mountains, including a trip to the north of Lake Rudolph*. London: Rowland Ward.

Nyaga, Daniel. 1997. *Customs and Traditions of the Meru*. Nairobi: East African Educational Publishers.

Okupa, Effua. 1998. *International Bibliography of African Customary Law*. Hamburg: LIT Verlag.

Ortéga y Gassét, José. 1932. *The Revolt of the Masses*. New York: W. W. Norton.

Parsons, Timothy H. 2012. "Being Kikuyu in Meru: Challenging the tribal geography of colonial Kenya." *The Journal of African History* 53: 65–86.

Peatrik, Anne-Marie. 2005. "Old system, new conflicts: Age, generation and discord among the Meru, Kenya." In *The Qualities of Time: Anthropological approaches*, edited by Wendy James and David Mills, 285–300. London: Routledge.

——— 2019. *A Complex Polity: Generations, initiation, and territory, among the old Meru of Kenya*. Nanterre: Les Publications de la Société d'ethnologie.

Rimita, David Maitai. 1988. *The Njuri-Ncheke of Meru*. Meru: Kolbe Press.

Ruteere, Mutuma, and Marie-Emmanuelle Pommerolle. 2003. "Democratizing security or decentralizing repression? The ambiguities of community policing in Kenya." *African Affairs* 102 (409): 587–604.

Searle, John. 1990. "Collective intentions and actions." In *Intentions in Communication*, edited by Philip R. Cohen, Jerry Morgan and Martha Pollack, 401–415. Cambridge: MIT Press.

Sillitoe, Paul. 2016. "The dialogue between indigenous studies and engaged anthropology: Some first impressions." In *Indigenous Studies and Engaged Anthropology*, edited by Paul Sillitoe, 1–30. London: Routledge.

Spivak, Gayatri Chakravorty. 1988. "Subaltern studies: Deconstructing historiography." In *Selected Subaltern Studies*, edited by Ranajit Guha and Gayatri Chakravorty Spivak, 3–32. New York: Oxford University Press.

Stasik, Michael, Valerie Hänsch, and Daniel Mains. 2020. "Temporalities of waiting in Africa." *Critical African Studies* 12(1): 1–9. doi: 10.1080/21681392.2020.1717361.

Steinhart, Edward I. 1989. "Hunters, poachers and gamekeepers: Towards a social history of hunting in colonial Kenya." *The Journal of African History* 30 (2): 247–264. doi: 10.1017/S0021853700024129.

—— 2006. *Black Poachers, White Hunters: A social history of hunting in colonial Kenya*. Oxford: James Currey.

Sutton, Inez. 1994. "Salt in kenya: A survey of literature." *Journal of Eastern African Research & Development* 24: 163–182.

Sylvain, Renée. 2014. "Essentialism and the indigenous politics of recognition in Southern Africa." *American Anthropologist* 116 (2): 251–264.

Thomas, Samuel P. 1995. "Shifting meanings of time, productivity and social worth in the life course in Meru, Kenya." *Journal of Cross-Cultural Gerontology* 10: 233–256.

Thuku, Mûthee. 2008. "Ameru folk plant classification and naming systems: An overview." In *The Indigenous Knowledge of the Ameru of Kenya*, edited by Njûgûna Gîchere and Shin-ichiro Ishida, 72–95. Meru: Meru Museum.

Tuomela, Raimo. 2013. *Social Ontology: Collective intentionality and group agents*. Oxford: Oxford University Press.

Turner, Victor Witter. 1957. *Schism and Continuity in an African Society: A study of Ndembu village life*. Published on behalf of the Institute for Social Research, University of Zambia by Manchester University Press.

Archival Material

Ministry of Lands and Settlement (Meru), *Land consolidation monthly report, March 1967*, Kenya National Archives, DC/MRU/2/4/19/61.

Ministry of Lands and Settlement (Nairobi), *Lawrance report on land consolidation and registration: Consequential changes in government policy* (28 June 1967), Kenya National Archives, DC/MRU/2/4/19/76.

Index

adjudication, *see* land adjudication
advisor, 70, 72, 76, 80–81, 83, 100, 104–106, 108, 112, 114, 130, 133, 139, 143, 181
age-class, 2–3, 5, 16, 20, 25, 27, 33, 35–39, 41–54, 56–58, 76, 81–82, 85–86, 89–90, 92, 95, 97–98, 102, 112, 117–119, 121, 123, 129–131, 134, 136, 142, 145, 149–151, 153, 165, 169, 172–188, 193, 199–200, 202–203, 207, 209–210, 212
age-classes among the Îgembe
 Bwantai, 5, 27, 33, 35, 37, 39, 40–45, 49, 52–53, 76, 95, 97, 118, 149–150, 165, 172, 178, 183, 185, 199, 210, 212
 Gîchûnge, 5, 43–48, 52–53, 56, 85, 90, 95, 185, 199, 209–210
 Îthaliî, 45, 48, 102, 123, 178
 Kîramunya, 5, 43–45, 47–49, 52–53, 145, 174, 179, 183, 199
 Lubetaa, 5, 35, 41–46, 48–49, 52–53, 58, 76, 81–82, 95, 97, 112, 119, 129–131, 134, 136, 142, 149–150, 172, 175, 178–179, 184, 200, 202
 Mîchûbû, 5, 20–21, 25, 35, 43–45, 47, 58, 82, 95, 97, 102, 117, 142, 149–151, 153, 181
 Mîrîti, 5, 27, 33, 35, 41–43, 45, 48–49, 52–53, 57–58, 76, 82, 86, 89, 92, 97–98, 112, 142, 150, 169, 177, 183, 186, 188, 199–200, 203, 215
 Ratanya, 5, 20, 35, 42–46, 48–49, 51, 58, 82, 97, 102, 112, 117, 119, 121, 131, 142, 150, 180, 184, 187, 202–203
agnatic clans among the Îgembe
 Akachiû, 57–58, 76, 82–83, 85–92, 97, 130–131, 154–155, 158, 164, 169, 187–188, 199, 209

Amwari, 31, 58, 82, 97, 128, 130–133, 151, 154–155, 175
Andûûne, 5, 58, 82–83, 98, 113, 115, 127, 150–151, 153–155, 163, 165, 167, 206, 219
Antûambui, 55–59, 74, 76–77, 79–83, 85–86, 88–92, 97, 154–155, 164, 199
Antûambûi, 5, 55, 96, 98, 113–114, 119, 143–148, 150–152, 154–155, 167, 200, 203, 206, 209
Athimba, 2, 4–5, 9, 31, 55, 57–58, 82, 93–100, 102, 104–107, 109, 112–113, 116–119, 123, 126–136, 138–149, 151–155, 165, 167, 177–182, 186, 199–204, 206, 209–211, 215, 219
Athîrû Gaiti, 1, 2, 6, 9, 11, 15–17, 21, 27, 29–31, 35–37, 40–41, 43–48, 50, 52, 54, 56–57, 87, 90, 93–96, 98, 100, 102, 109–110, 129, 134, 139–141, 155, 170–172, 175, 179, 182, 195, 201–202, 207, 209–210, 215

banana, 19, 21, 24, 39, 55, 99, 176, 182
biological determinism, 5, 58, 69, 152, 167, 200, 219
blessing, 8, 31, 62–63, 74, 86, 100, 104, 110, 117, 135, 180–181, 202, 206, 211, 220
bride price, 4–5, 94, 101, 118–119, 127, 189, 192

cash crop, 14, 28, 32–33, 199, 209
chief, 17, 40, 46, 50, 58–59, 62, 75, 80, 88–90, 92, 120–121, 123, 149, 183
circuit cultivation, 14–16, 20, 29, 30, 32
circumcision, 17, 33, 35, 41–47, 49–53, 97, 150, 172, 175, 192, 199

229

clan, 2–5, 8–9, 16–17, 20, 31–33, 46, 55–59, 62, 64–66, 69–107, 109–121, 123–124, 126–156, 158–159, 163–167, 169, 175–182, 184, 186–188, 195, 199–211
   affiliation, 4, 31, 69, 74, 76, 82–83, 86, 95, 152, 167, 175, 177, 195, 207
   house, 90–91, 99–100, 105–106, 109, 112, 115–116, 120, 123, 128–129, 131, 133–138, 146–148, 179, 181, 201, 211
cleansing, 31, 86, 147, 165, 202, 206, 220–221
coffee, 16, 18, 26–27, 32, 173, 199
collective immortality, 1, 171, 193–197, 200, 207
communal intention, 1, 3, 7–9, 200–201, 207, 210
community policing, 57, 88–90, 92, 199, 209
compensation, 4, 38, 40, 86, 93–95, 98–102, 104–112, 114–118, 122, 128, 130–135, 137–142, 144–149, 165, 179, 181, 189, 199, 201–202, 204–206, 209–211, 213–215
   finger, 134–135, 137, 206
   homicide, 4, 93–95, 98–102, 104–112, 114–118, 122, 128, 130–133, 138–142, 144–149, 179, 181, 199, 201–202, 205, 209–211
confession, 86, 91, 107, 148, 150, 165, 167
confidential talk, 108, 137
curse, 6, 8, 31, 55, 59, 63, 65, 67, 69–71, 74, 79, 84, 86, 91–92, 112, 144–145, 151, 154, 156–157, 159, 161–163, 165–167, 173, 177, 189, 202, 204–206, 208–209, 211

dispute, 4, 6, 31, 55, 75, 79, 86, 107–109, 139–142, 149–154, 165, 167, 175, 177, 194, 201–203, 205–208, 215

education, 28, 43, 63, 65, 73, 194
egalitarianism (egalitarian), 5, 143, 166–167, 208
election, 28, 48–49, 75, 89–90, 134, 139, 155, 203–204, 206
ewe, 55, 100, 119, 131–132, 146, 192
expert, 5, 37, 55, 98, 100, 102–103, 105, 109, 144, 166, 167, 217–218

famine, 14, 44, 52
feather, 3, 169, 200
forgiveness, 117–118, 127–128, 135
friendship, 9, 71, 95, 110, 134, 152, 171, 176, 193–194

goat, 6, 24, 25, 31, 76–77, 90–91, 100–103, 105–106, 114, 117, 119, 122, 128, 131–133, 146–148, 152, 154, 176, 179, 184–185, 192, 211, 219

honey, 26, 43, 115–116, 119, 131, 192, 220, *see also* mead
horn, 3, 37–38, 56, 77–78, 86
hospital, 28, 37, 72, 91, 122, 125, 130, 134, 140–141, 173, 178, 180, 194, 202, 205, 211, 216

îchiaro, 4–6, 8, 31, 55, 57–59, 64–71, 74, 76–92, 94, 96, 98, 113–114, 119, 121, 123–124, 127, 143–146, 148–163, 165–167, 176–178, 200–201, 203–209, 211, 218–221
Îgembe,
   see also agnatic clans among the Îgembe
   Îgembe South Division, 130, 133, 139
   Îgembe Southeast Division, 9, 15–27, 29–33, 55–58, 88, 90, 92, 94, 109, 123, 131, 139–140, 169, 178, 184
Imenti, 3, 5, 37–38, 44, 46–47, 184, 188–189, 192–194
individualism, 4, 207–208

Index

Kamba, 14
Kenyan government, 29–30, 57, 80, 88–89, 92, 139, 199
khat, 3, 13, 26, see also *mîraa*
Kîegoi, 17–18, 29–30, 80
Kîmîîrû, 4–5, 8–9, 13–14, 21, 23, 25–26, 32, 37–38, 42, 45, 55, 82, 98–100, 102, 106, 110, 126, 136, 151, 160, 169, 170–173, 175, 178–179, 188, 193–196, 207, 216–218
Kîrîmakîerû, 13, 159–162, see also White Hill
Kîthia, 98–99, 119, 134–138, 142, 145, 147, 149, 152, 177–179, 193, 203
kîthiri, 79, 130, 133–134, 144–145, 148, 177
kûchia rîîtwa, 170, 184, 193
kûringa nthenge, 6, 31, 55
kûrûmithua ndewa, 35–43, 48–54
kwiita rwîî, 66, 69–70, 72–74, 87, 104, 156, 163, 166, 220–221

land
  adjudication, 16, 20, 29–32, 37, 52, 139–141, 199, 201
  ancestral, 29, 31, 140, 202
  see also title deed
  tenure reform, 14, 29–32
leadership, 1, 56–58, 86, 88–90, 92, 138, 207

M'Lichoro, 95, 98, 102–103, 105, 117, 119–121, 123–125, 127, 142, 146–148
mask, 8, 46
mass circumcision, 17, 46, 50, 52–53
maternal relatives, 9, 174, 176, 178, 184, 186–187, 192
Maûa, 9, 17, 28, 40, 56, 91, 102, 106, 118, 121, 127, 140, 152, 169, 173, 178
Mbiti, 82–83, 98, 153–160, 162–163, 165, 167, 206
mbûrago (ancestral land), 31, 140

mead, 75, 91, 114, 192
millet, 19, 21, 72, 74–75, 115, 131
Mîori, 49, 52, 103, 142
mîraa (*Catha edulis*, or khat), 3, 13, 15–17, 20, 24, 26–29, 32–33, 40, 52, 59, 73, 75, 79, 114, 119, 122, 128, 130, 146, 148–150, 154, 182, 186–188, 192, 199, 209
  crisis, 32, 199
mîrongo îthatu, 43
mother's brother, 101, 172, 174–176, 179
Mûringene, 9, 57, 64, 83, 93–99, 129, 143–145, 149, 151–154, 165, 184–187, 201, 210, 215
Mûteethia, 98, 112–114, 117, 119–127, 136–137, 142, 147, 152, 180–181, 203–205
Mwasimba, 9, 86, 89, 169, 171, 187–189, 191–194, 209
Mwithûne, 9, 55, 57–58, 60, 64, 76–77, 79–80, 85, 90

Ngatûnyi, 98, 119–124, 126–127, 144, 146–148, 155, 167, 203–206
Njûrincheke, 5, 17, 41, 43, 47, 49, 52–53, 59, 66, 78–80, 93–94, 96, 99–100, 103–104, 108, 117, 130–133, 137–139, 142, 144, 146–147, 151, 154, 163, 166, 172–173, 175–178, 200, 202–203, 205, 207, 215, 217–220
nkilîba (confidential talk), 108, 137
ntaau (namesake), 8–9, 170–179, 183–188, 190, 193–194, 196, 200

open field, 35–36, 41, 46, 50, 53–54, 86, 88, 106, 111

personal name, 8–9, 170–171, 173, 193–196
personhood, 8, 169–171, 175, 193, 195, 197, 200–201, 207
plain, 13, 17–18, 20–22, 26, 31–32, 109,

140, 161, 184, 199

rainfall, 13, 17–18, 21–23, 176, 209
ram, 43, 55, 100–101, 105–106, 115, 117, 119, 131–132, 136, 145–147, 150, 192, 206, 211
reconciliation, 94, 117–119, 122, 124, 126–128, 141, 147, 149, 201, 206, 213
ruling elderhood, 33, 47–50, 89, 199–200
rwaanda (sparsely populated lower areas), 17, 140, 163, 184

sheep, 24, 55–56, 59, 62, 64, 66–69, 76–77, 79–81, 84–85, 108, 117, 128, 179, 215–217, 220, *see also* ewe;ram
song, 21, 28, 66–67

Thaichû, 14, 17–18, 20–21, 29, 32, 58, 90, 103, 139
Tigania, 3–5, 14, 39, 44–48, 50, 95, 97, 196
title deed, 16, 28, 30–31, 139
transfer of power, 46, 49, 51–53, 142, 200

ûtaara ngeere, 55–57, 59, 69, 74–85, 88–90, 92, 199

waiting, 1, 6, 66, 125, 202, 208, 211–212
White Hill (Kîrîmakîerû), 13, 15, 159, 161